NES

Middle Grades Mathematics

SECRETS

Study Guide

Your Key to Exam Success

DEAR FUTURE EXAM SUCCESS STORY

First of all, **THANK YOU** for purchasing Mometrix study materials!

Second, congratulations! You are one of the few determined test-takers who are committed to doing whatever it takes to excel on your exam. **You have come to the right place.** We developed these study materials with one goal in mind: to deliver you the information you need in a format that's concise and easy to use.

In addition to optimizing your guide for the content of the test, we've outlined our recommended steps for breaking down the preparation process into small, attainable goals so you can make sure you stay on track.

We've also analyzed the entire test-taking process, identifying the most common pitfalls and showing how you can overcome them and be ready for any curveball the test throws you.

Standardized testing is one of the biggest obstacles on your road to success, which only increases the importance of doing well in the high-pressure, high-stakes environment of test day. Your results on this test could have a significant impact on your future, and this guide provides the information and practical advice to help you achieve your full potential on test day.

Your success is our success

We would love to hear from you! If you would like to share the story of your exam success or if you have any questions or comments in regard to our products, please contact us at **800-673-8175** or **support@mometrix.com**.

Thanks again for your business and we wish you continued success!

Sincerely,
The Mometrix Test Preparation Team

Written and edited by the Mometrix Exam Secrets Test Prep Team
Printed in the United States of America

TABLE OF CONTENTS

Introduction

Thank you for purchasing this resource! You have made the choice to prepare yourself for a test that could have a huge impact on your future, and this guide is designed to help you be fully ready for test day. Obviously, it's important to have a solid understanding of the test material, but you also need to be prepared for the unique environment and stressors of the test, so that you can perform to the best of your abilities.

For this purpose, the first section that appears in this guide is the **Secret Keys**. We've devoted countless hours to meticulously researching what works and what doesn't, and we've boiled down our findings to the five most impactful steps you can take to improve your performance on the test. We start at the beginning with study planning and move through the preparation process, all the way to the testing strategies that will help you get the most out of what you know when you're finally sitting in front of the test.

We recommend that you start preparing for your test as far in advance as possible. However, if you've bought this guide as a last-minute study resource and only have a few days before your test, we recommend that you skip over the first two Secret Keys since they address a long-term study plan.

If you struggle with **test anxiety**, we strongly encourage you to check out our recommendations for how you can overcome it. Test anxiety is a formidable foe, but it can be beaten, and we want to make sure you have the tools you need to defeat it.

Secret Key #1 – Plan Big, Study Small

There's a lot riding on your performance. If you want to ace this test, you're going to need to keep your skills sharp and the material fresh in your mind. You need a plan that lets you review everything you need to know while still fitting in your schedule. We'll break this strategy down into three categories.

Information Organization

Start with the information you already have: the official test outline. From this, you can make a complete list of all the concepts you need to cover before the test. Organize these concepts into groups that can be studied together, and create a list of any related vocabulary you need to learn so you can brush up on any difficult terms. You'll want to keep this vocabulary list handy once you actually start studying since you may need to add to it along the way.

Time Management

Once you have your set of study concepts, decide how to spread them out over the time you have left before the test. Break your study plan into small, clear goals so you have a manageable task for each day and know exactly what you're doing. Then just focus on one small step at a time. When you manage your time this way, you don't need to spend hours at a time studying. Studying a small block of content for a short period each day helps you retain information better and avoid stressing over how much you have left to do. You can relax knowing that you have a plan to cover everything in time. In order for this strategy to be effective though, you have to start studying early and stick to your schedule. Avoid the exhaustion and futility that comes from last-minute cramming!

Study Environment

The environment you study in has a big impact on your learning. Studying in a coffee shop, while probably more enjoyable, is not likely to be as fruitful as studying in a quiet room. It's important to keep distractions to a minimum. You're only planning to study for a short block of time, so make the most of it. Don't pause to check your phone or get up to find a snack. It's also important to **avoid multitasking**. Research has consistently shown that multitasking will make your studying dramatically less effective. Your study area should also be comfortable and well-lit so you don't have the distraction of straining your eyes or sitting on an uncomfortable chair.

The time of day you study is also important. You want to be rested and alert. Don't wait until just before bedtime. Study when you'll be most likely to comprehend and remember. Even better, if you know what time of day your test will be, set that time aside for study. That way your brain will be used to working on that subject at that specific time and you'll have a better chance of recalling information.

Finally, it can be helpful to team up with others who are studying for the same test. Your actual studying should be done in as isolated an environment as possible, but the work of organizing the information and setting up the study plan can be divided up. In between study sessions, you can discuss with your teammates the concepts that you're all studying and quiz each other on the details. Just be sure that your teammates are as serious about the test as you are. If you find that your study time is being replaced with social time, you might need to find a new team.

Secret Key #2 – Make Your Studying Count

You're devoting a lot of time and effort to preparing for this test, so you want to be absolutely certain it will pay off. This means doing more than just reading the content and hoping you can remember it on test day. It's important to make every minute of study count. There are two main areas you can focus on to make your studying count:

Retention

It doesn't matter how much time you study if you can't remember the material. You need to make sure you are retaining the concepts. To check your retention of the information you're learning, try recalling it at later times with minimal prompting. Try carrying around flashcards and glance at one or two from time to time or ask a friend who's also studying for the test to quiz you.

To enhance your retention, look for ways to put the information into practice so that you can apply it rather than simply recalling it. If you're using the information in practical ways, it will be much easier to remember. Similarly, it helps to solidify a concept in your mind if you're not only reading it to yourself but also explaining it to someone else. Ask a friend to let you teach them about a concept you're a little shaky on (or speak aloud to an imaginary audience if necessary). As you try to summarize, define, give examples, and answer your friend's questions, you'll understand the concepts better and they will stay with you longer. Finally, step back for a big picture view and ask yourself how each piece of information fits with the whole subject. When you link the different concepts together and see them working together as a whole, it's easier to remember the individual components.

Finally, practice showing your work on any multi-step problems, even if you're just studying. Writing out each step you take to solve a problem will help solidify the process in your mind, and you'll be more likely to remember it during the test.

Modality

Modality simply refers to the means or method by which you study. Choosing a study modality that fits your own individual learning style is crucial. No two people learn best in exactly the same way, so it's important to know your strengths and use them to your advantage.

For example, if you learn best by visualization, focus on visualizing a concept in your mind and draw an image or a diagram. Try color-coding your notes, illustrating them, or creating symbols that will trigger your mind to recall a learned concept. If you learn best by hearing or discussing information, find a study partner who learns the same way or read aloud to yourself. Think about how to put the information in your own words. Imagine that you are giving a lecture on the topic and record yourself so you can listen to it later.

For any learning style, flashcards can be helpful. Organize the information so you can take advantage of spare moments to review. Underline key words or phrases. Use different colors for different categories. Mnemonic devices (such as creating a short list in which every item starts with the same letter) can also help with retention. Find what works best for you and use it to store the information in your mind most effectively and easily.

Secret Key #3 – Practice the Right Way

Your success on test day depends not only on how many hours you put into preparing, but also on whether you prepared the right way. It's good to check along the way to see if your studying is paying off. One of the most effective ways to do this is by taking practice tests to evaluate your progress. Practice tests are useful because they show exactly where you need to improve. Every time you take a practice test, pay special attention to these three groups of questions:

- The questions you got wrong
- The questions you had to guess on, even if you guessed right
- The questions you found difficult or slow to work through

This will show you exactly what your weak areas are, and where you need to devote more study time. Ask yourself why each of these questions gave you trouble. Was it because you didn't understand the material? Was it because you didn't remember the vocabulary? Do you need more repetitions on this type of question to build speed and confidence? Dig into those questions and figure out how you can strengthen your weak areas as you go back to review the material.

Additionally, many practice tests have a section explaining the answer choices. It can be tempting to read the explanation and think that you now have a good understanding of the concept. However, an explanation likely only covers part of the question's broader context. Even if the explanation makes sense, **go back and investigate** every concept related to the question until you're positive you have a thorough understanding.

As you go along, keep in mind that the practice test is just that: practice. Memorizing these questions and answers will not be very helpful on the actual test because it is unlikely to have any of the same exact questions. If you only know the right answers to the sample questions, you won't be prepared for the real thing. **Study the concepts** until you understand them fully, and then you'll be able to answer any question that shows up on the test.

It's important to wait on the practice tests until you're ready. If you take a test on your first day of study, you may be overwhelmed by the amount of material covered and how much you need to learn. Work up to it gradually.

On test day, you'll need to be prepared for answering questions, managing your time, and using the test-taking strategies you've learned. It's a lot to balance, like a mental marathon that will have a big impact on your future. Like training for a marathon, you'll need to start slowly and work your way up. When test day arrives, you'll be ready.

Start with the strategies you've read in the first two Secret Keys—plan your course and study in the way that works best for you. If you have time, consider using multiple study resources to get different approaches to the same concepts. It can be helpful to see difficult concepts from more than one angle. Then find a good source for practice tests. Many times, the test website will suggest potential study resources or provide sample tests.

Practice Test Strategy

If you're able to find at least three practice tests, we recommend this strategy:

UNTIMED AND OPEN-BOOK PRACTICE

Take the first test with no time constraints and with your notes and study guide handy. Take your time and focus on applying the strategies you've learned.

TIMED AND OPEN-BOOK PRACTICE

Take the second practice test open-book as well, but set a timer and practice pacing yourself to finish in time.

TIMED AND CLOSED-BOOK PRACTICE

Take any other practice tests as if it were test day. Set a timer and put away your study materials. Sit at a table or desk in a quiet room, imagine yourself at the testing center, and answer questions as quickly and accurately as possible.

Keep repeating timed and closed-book tests on a regular basis until you run out of practice tests or it's time for the actual test. Your mind will be ready for the schedule and stress of test day, and you'll be able to focus on recalling the material you've learned.

Secret Key #4 – Pace Yourself

Once you're fully prepared for the material on the test, your biggest challenge on test day will be managing your time. Just knowing that the clock is ticking can make you panic even if you have plenty of time left. Work on pacing yourself so you can build confidence against the time constraints of the exam. Pacing is a difficult skill to master, especially in a high-pressure environment, so **practice is vital**.

Set time expectations for your pace based on how much time is available. For example, if a section has 60 questions and the time limit is 30 minutes, you know you have to average 30 seconds or less per question in order to answer them all. Although 30 seconds is the hard limit, set 25 seconds per question as your goal, so you reserve extra time to spend on harder questions. When you budget extra time for the harder questions, you no longer have any reason to stress when those questions take longer to answer.

Don't let this time expectation distract you from working through the test at a calm, steady pace, but keep it in mind so you don't spend too much time on any one question. Recognize that taking extra time on one question you don't understand may keep you from answering two that you do understand later in the test. If your time limit for a question is up and you're still not sure of the answer, mark it and move on, and come back to it later if the time and the test format allow. If the testing format doesn't allow you to return to earlier questions, just make an educated guess; then put it out of your mind and move on.

On the easier questions, be careful not to rush. It may seem wise to hurry through them so you have more time for the challenging ones, but it's not worth missing one if you know the concept and just didn't take the time to read the question fully. Work efficiently but make sure you understand the question and have looked at all of the answer choices, since more than one may seem right at first.

Even if you're paying attention to the time, you may find yourself a little behind at some point. You should speed up to get back on track, but do so wisely. Don't panic; just take a few seconds less on each question until you're caught up. Don't guess without thinking, but do look through the answer choices and eliminate any you know are wrong. If you can get down to two choices, it is often worthwhile to guess from those. Once you've chosen an answer, move on and don't dwell on any that you skipped or had to hurry through. If a question was taking too long, chances are it was one of the harder ones, so you weren't as likely to get it right anyway.

On the other hand, if you find yourself getting ahead of schedule, it may be beneficial to slow down a little. The more quickly you work, the more likely you are to make a careless mistake that will affect your score. You've budgeted time for each question, so don't be afraid to spend that time. Practice an efficient but careful pace to get the most out of the time you have.

Secret Key #5 – Have a Plan for Guessing

When you're taking the test, you may find yourself stuck on a question. Some of the answer choices seem better than others, but you don't see the one answer choice that is obviously correct. What do you do?

The scenario described above is very common, yet most test takers have not effectively prepared for it. Developing and practicing a plan for guessing may be one of the single most effective uses of your time as you get ready for the exam.

In developing your plan for guessing, there are three questions to address:

- When should you start the guessing process?
- How should you narrow down the choices?
- Which answer should you choose?

When to Start the Guessing Process

Unless your plan for guessing is to select C every time (which, despite its merits, is not what we recommend), you need to leave yourself enough time to apply your answer elimination strategies. Since you have a limited amount of time for each question, that means that if you're going to give yourself the best shot at guessing correctly, you have to decide quickly whether or not you will guess.

Of course, the best-case scenario is that you don't have to guess at all, so first, see if you can answer the question based on your knowledge of the subject and basic reasoning skills. Focus on the key words in the question and try to jog your memory of related topics. Give yourself a chance to bring the knowledge to mind, but once you realize that you don't have (or you can't access) the knowledge you need to answer the question, it's time to start the guessing process.

It's almost always better to start the guessing process too early than too late. It only takes a few seconds to remember something and answer the question from knowledge. Carefully eliminating wrong answer choices takes longer. Plus, going through the process of eliminating answer choices can actually help jog your memory.

Summary: Start the guessing process as soon as you decide that you can't answer the question based on your knowledge.

How to Narrow Down the Choices

The next chapter in this book (**Test-Taking Strategies**) includes a wide range of strategies for how to approach questions and how to look for answer choices to eliminate. You will definitely want to read those carefully, practice them, and figure out which ones work best for you. Here though, we're going to address a mindset rather than a particular strategy.

Your chances of guessing an answer correctly depend on how many options you are choosing from.

How many choices you have	How likely you are to guess correctly
5	20%
4	25%
3	33%
2	50%
1	100%

You can see from this chart just how valuable it is to be able to eliminate incorrect answers and make an educated guess, but there are two things that many test takers do that cause them to miss out on the benefits of guessing:

- Accidentally eliminating the correct answer
- Selecting an answer based on an impression

We'll look at the first one here, and the second one in the next section.

To avoid accidentally eliminating the correct answer, we recommend a thought exercise called **the $5 challenge**. In this challenge, you only eliminate an answer choice from contention if you are willing to bet $5 on it being wrong. Why $5? Five dollars is a small but not insignificant amount of money. It's an amount you could afford to lose but wouldn't want to throw away. And while losing $5 once might not hurt too much, doing it twenty times will set you back $100. In the same way, each small decision you make—eliminating a choice here, guessing on a question there—won't by itself impact your score very much, but when you put them all together, they can make a big difference. By holding each answer choice elimination decision to a higher standard, you can reduce the risk of accidentally eliminating the correct answer.

The $5 challenge can also be applied in a positive sense: If you are willing to bet $5 that an answer choice *is* correct, go ahead and mark it as correct.

Summary: Only eliminate an answer choice if you are willing to bet $5 that it is wrong.

Which Answer to Choose

You're taking the test. You've run into a hard question and decided you'll have to guess. You've eliminated all the answer choices you're willing to bet $5 on. Now you have to pick an answer. Why do we even need to talk about this? Why can't you just pick whichever one you feel like when the time comes?

The answer to these questions is that if you don't come into the test with a plan, you'll rely on your impression to select an answer choice, and if you do that, you risk falling into a trap. The test writers know that everyone who takes their test will be guessing on some of the questions, so they intentionally write wrong answer choices to seem plausible. You still have to pick an answer though, and if the wrong answer choices are designed to look right, how can you ever be sure that you're not falling for their trap? The best solution we've found to this dilemma is to take the decision out of your hands entirely. Here is the process we recommend:

Once you've eliminated any choices that you are confident (willing to bet $5) are wrong, select the first remaining choice as your answer.

Whether you choose to select the first remaining choice, the second, or the last, the important thing is that you use some preselected standard. Using this approach guarantees that you will not be enticed into selecting an answer choice that looks right, because you are not basing your decision on how the answer choices look.

This is not meant to make you question your knowledge. Instead, it is to help you recognize the difference between your knowledge and your impressions. There's a huge difference between thinking an answer is right because of what you know, and thinking an answer is right because it looks or sounds like it should be right.

Summary: To ensure that your selection is appropriately random, make a predetermined selection from among all answer choices you have not eliminated.

Test-Taking Strategies

This section contains a list of test-taking strategies that you may find helpful as you work through the test. By taking what you know and applying logical thought, you can maximize your chances of answering any question correctly!

It is very important to realize that every question is different and every person is different: no single strategy will work on every question, and no single strategy will work for every person. That's why we've included all of them here, so you can try them out and determine which ones work best for different types of questions and which ones work best for you.

Question Strategies

Read Carefully

Read the question and answer choices carefully. Don't miss the question because you misread the terms. You have plenty of time to read each question thoroughly and make sure you understand what is being asked. Yet a happy medium must be attained, so don't waste too much time. You must read carefully, but efficiently.

Contextual Clues

Look for contextual clues. If the question includes a word you are not familiar with, look at the immediate context for some indication of what the word might mean. Contextual clues can often give you all the information you need to decipher the meaning of an unfamiliar word. Even if you can't determine the meaning, you may be able to narrow down the possibilities enough to make a solid guess at the answer to the question.

Prefixes

If you're having trouble with a word in the question or answer choices, try dissecting it. Take advantage of every clue that the word might include. Prefixes and suffixes can be a huge help. Usually they allow you to determine a basic meaning. Pre- means before, post- means after, pro - is positive, de- is negative. From prefixes and suffixes, you can get an idea of the general meaning of the word and try to put it into context.

Hedge Words

Watch out for critical hedge words, such as *likely, may, can, sometimes, often, almost, mostly, usually, generally, rarely*, and *sometimes.* Question writers insert these hedge phrases to cover every possibility. Often an answer choice will be wrong simply because it leaves no room for exception. Be on guard for answer choices that have definitive words such as *exactly* and *always.*

Switchback Words

Stay alert for *switchbacks.* These are the words and phrases frequently used to alert you to shifts in thought. The most common switchback words are *but, although*, and *however.* Others include *nevertheless, on the other hand, even though, while, in spite of, despite, regardless of.* Switchback words are important to catch because they can change the direction of the question or an answer choice.

Face Value

When in doubt, use common sense. Accept the situation in the problem at face value. Don't read too much into it. These problems will not require you to make wild assumptions. If you have to go beyond creativity and warp time or space in order to have an answer choice fit the question, then you should move on and consider the other answer choices. These are normal problems rooted in reality. The applicable relationship or explanation may not be readily apparent, but it is there for you to figure out. Use your common sense to interpret anything that isn't clear.

Answer Choice Strategies

ANSWER SELECTION

The most thorough way to pick an answer choice is to identify and eliminate wrong answers until only one is left, then confirm it is the correct answer. Sometimes an answer choice may immediately seem right, but be careful. The test writers will usually put more than one reasonable answer choice on each question, so take a second to read all of them and make sure that the other choices are not equally obvious. As long as you have time left, it is better to read every answer choice than to pick the first one that looks right without checking the others.

ANSWER CHOICE FAMILIES

An answer choice family consists of two (in rare cases, three) answer choices that are very similar in construction and cannot all be true at the same time. If you see two answer choices that are direct opposites or parallels, one of them is usually the correct answer. For instance, if one answer choice says that quantity *x* increases and another either says that quantity *x* decreases (opposite) or says that quantity *y* increases (parallel), then those answer choices would fall into the same family. An answer choice that doesn't match the construction of the answer choice family is more likely to be incorrect. Most questions will not have answer choice families, but when they do appear, you should be prepared to recognize them.

ELIMINATE ANSWERS

Eliminate answer choices as soon as you realize they are wrong, but make sure you consider all possibilities. If you are eliminating answer choices and realize that the last one you are left with is also wrong, don't panic. Start over and consider each choice again. There may be something you missed the first time that you will realize on the second pass.

AVOID FACT TRAPS

Don't be distracted by an answer choice that is factually true but doesn't answer the question. You are looking for the choice that answers the question. Stay focused on what the question is asking for so you don't accidentally pick an answer that is true but incorrect. Always go back to the question and make sure the answer choice you've selected actually answers the question and is not merely a true statement.

EXTREME STATEMENTS

In general, you should avoid answers that put forth extreme actions as standard practice or proclaim controversial ideas as established fact. An answer choice that states the "process should be used in certain situations, if..." is much more likely to be correct than one that states the "process should be discontinued completely." The first is a calm rational statement and doesn't even make a definitive, uncompromising stance, using a hedge word *if* to provide wiggle room, whereas the second choice is a radical idea and far more extreme.

BENCHMARK

As you read through the answer choices and you come across one that seems to answer the question well, mentally select that answer choice. This is not your final answer, but it's the one that will help you evaluate the other answer choices. The one that you selected is your benchmark or standard for judging each of the other answer choices. Every other answer choice must be compared to your benchmark. That choice is correct until proven otherwise by another answer choice beating it. If you find a better answer, then that one becomes your new benchmark. Once you've decided that no other choice answers the question as well as your benchmark, you have your final answer.

PREDICT THE ANSWER

Before you even start looking at the answer choices, it is often best to try to predict the answer. When you come up with the answer on your own, it is easier to avoid distractions and traps because you will know exactly what to look for. The right answer choice is unlikely to be word-for-word what you came up with, but it should be a close match. Even if you are confident that you have the right answer, you should still take the time to read each option before moving on.

General Strategies

TOUGH QUESTIONS

If you are stumped on a problem or it appears too hard or too difficult, don't waste time. Move on! Remember though, if you can quickly check for obviously incorrect answer choices, your chances of guessing correctly are greatly improved. Before you completely give up, at least try to knock out a couple of possible answers. Eliminate what you can and then guess at the remaining answer choices before moving on.

CHECK YOUR WORK

Since you will probably not know every term listed and the answer to every question, it is important that you get credit for the ones that you do know. Don't miss any questions through careless mistakes. If at all possible, try to take a second to look back over your answer selection and make sure you've selected the correct answer choice and haven't made a costly careless mistake (such as marking an answer choice that you didn't mean to mark). This quick double check should more than pay for itself in caught mistakes for the time it costs.

PACE YOURSELF

It's easy to be overwhelmed when you're looking at a page full of questions; your mind is confused and full of random thoughts, and the clock is ticking down faster than you would like. Calm down and maintain the pace that you have set for yourself. Especially as you get down to the last few minutes of the test, don't let the small numbers on the clock make you panic. As long as you are on track by monitoring your pace, you are guaranteed to have time for each question.

DON'T RUSH

It is very easy to make errors when you are in a hurry. Maintaining a fast pace in answering questions is pointless if it makes you miss questions that you would have gotten right otherwise. Test writers like to include distracting information and wrong answers that seem right. Taking a little extra time to avoid careless mistakes can make all the difference in your test score. Find a pace that allows you to be confident in the answers that you select.

KEEP MOVING

Panicking will not help you pass the test, so do your best to stay calm and keep moving. Taking deep breaths and going through the answer elimination steps you practiced can help to break through a stress barrier and keep your pace.

Final Notes

The combination of a solid foundation of content knowledge and the confidence that comes from practicing your plan for applying that knowledge is the key to maximizing your performance on test day.

As your foundation of content knowledge is built up and strengthened, you'll find that the strategies included in this chapter become more and more effective in helping you quickly sift through the distractions and traps of the test to isolate the correct answer.

Now it's time to move on to the test content chapters of this book, but be sure to keep your goal in mind. As you read, think about how you will be able to apply this information on the test. If you've already seen sample questions for the test and you have an idea of the question format and style, try to come up with questions of your own that you can answer based on what you're reading. This will give you valuable practice applying your knowledge in the same ways you can expect to on test day.

Good luck and good studying!

Number Sense and Operations

Numbers

Classifications of Numbers

Numbers are the basic building blocks of mathematics. Specific features of numbers are identified by the following terms:

Integer – any positive or negative whole number, including zero. Integers do not include fractions $\left(\frac{1}{3}\right)$, decimals (0.56), or mixed numbers $\left(7\frac{3}{4}\right)$.

Prime number – any whole number greater than 1 that has only two factors, itself and 1; that is, a number that can be divided evenly only by 1 and itself.

Composite number – any whole number greater than 1 that has more than two different factors; in other words, any whole number that is not a prime number. For example: The composite number 8 has the factors of 1, 2, 4, and 8.

Even number – any integer that can be divided by 2 without leaving a remainder. For example: 2, 4, 6, 8, and so on.

Odd number – any integer that cannot be divided evenly by 2. For example: 3, 5, 7, 9, and so on.

Decimal number – any number that uses a decimal point to show the part of the number that is less than one. Example: 1.234.

Decimal point – a symbol used to separate the ones place from the tenths place in decimals or dollars from cents in currency.

Decimal place – the position of a number to the right of the decimal point. In the decimal 0.123, the 1 is in the first place to the right of the decimal point, indicating tenths; the 2 is in the second place, indicating hundredths; and the 3 is in the third place, indicating thousandths.

The **decimal**, or base 10, system is a number system that uses ten different digits (0, 1, 2, 3, 4, 5, 6, 7, 8, 9). An example of a number system that uses something other than ten digits is the **binary**, or base 2, number system, used by computers, which uses only the numbers 0 and 1. It is thought that the decimal system originated because people had only their 10 fingers for counting.

Rational numbers include all integers, decimals, and fractions. Any terminating or repeating decimal number is a rational number.

Irrational numbers cannot be written as fractions or decimals because the number of decimal places is infinite and there is no recurring pattern of digits within the number. For example, pi (π) begins with 3.141592 and continues without terminating or repeating, so pi is an irrational number.

Real numbers are the set of all rational and irrational numbers.

Review Video: Numbers and Their Classifications
Visit mometrix.com/academy and enter code: 461071

Review Video: Rational and Irrational Numbers
Visit mometrix.com/academy and enter code: 280645

THE NUMBER LINE

A number line is a graph to see the distance between numbers. Basically, this graph shows the relationship between numbers. So, a number line may have a point for zero and may show negative numbers on the left side of the line. Also, any positive numbers are placed on the right side of the line. For example, consider the points labeled on the following number line:

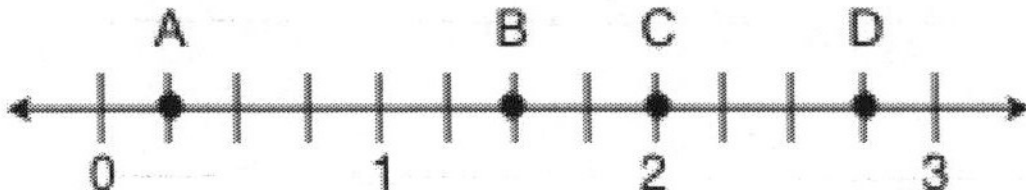

We can use the dashed lines on the number line to identify each point. Each dashed line between two whole numbers is $\frac{1}{4}$. The line halfway between two numbers is $\frac{1}{2}$.

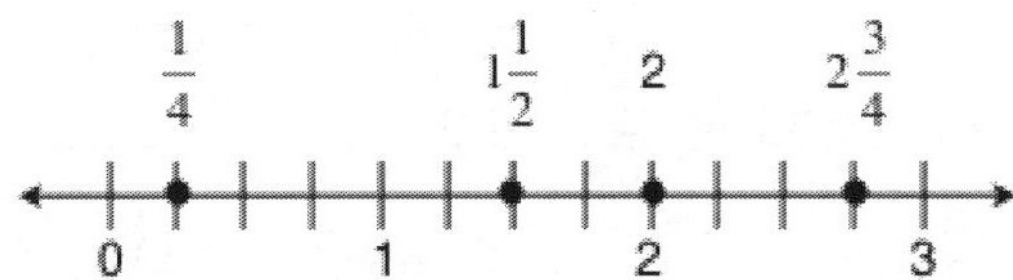

Review Video: Negative and Positive Number Line
Visit mometrix.com/academy and enter code: 816439

NUMBERS IN WORD FORM AND PLACE VALUE

When writing numbers out in word form or translating word form to numbers, it is essential to understand how a place value system works. In the decimal or base-10 system, each digit of a number represents how many of the corresponding place value – a specific factor of 10 – are contained in the number being represented. To make reading numbers easier, every three digits to the left of the decimal place is preceded by a comma. The following table demonstrates some of the place values:

Power of 10	10^3	10^2	10^1	10^0	10^{-1}	10^{-2}	10^{-3}
Value	1,000	100	10	1	0.1	0.01	0.001
Place	thousands	hundreds	tens	ones	tenths	hundredths	thousandths

For example, consider the number 4,546.09, which can be separated into each place value like this:

4: thousands
5: hundreds
4: tens
6: ones
0: tenths
9: hundredths

This number in word form would be *four thousand five hundred forty-six and nine hundredths.*

Review Video: Number Place Value
Visit mometrix.com/academy and enter code: 205433

ABSOLUTE VALUE

A precursor to working with negative numbers is understanding what **absolute values** are. A number's absolute value is simply the distance away from zero a number is on the number line. The absolute value of a number is always positive and is written $|x|$. For example, the absolute value of 3, written as $|3|$, is 3 because the distance between 0 and 3 on a number line is three units. Likewise, the absolute value of -3, written as $|-3|$, is 3 because the distance between 0 and -3 on a number line is three units. So, $|3| = |-3|$.

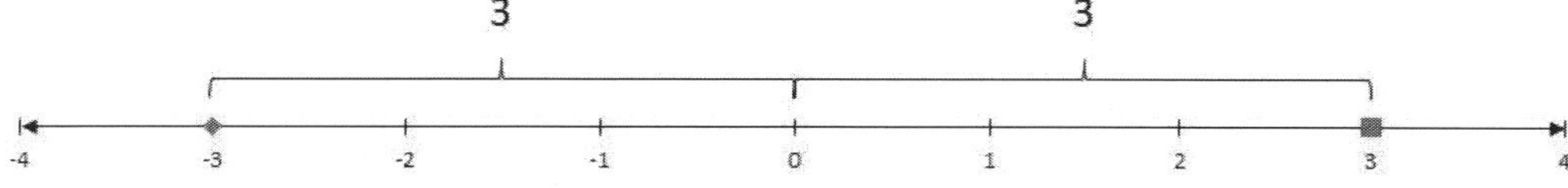

Review Video: Absolute Value
Visit mometrix.com/academy and enter code: 314669

Operations

OPERATIONS

An **operation** is simply a mathematical process that takes some value(s) as input(s) and produces an output. Elementary operations are often written in the following form: *value operation value*. For instance, in the expression $1 + 2$ the values are 1 and 2 and the operation is addition. Performing the operation gives the output of 3. In this way we can say that $1 + 2$ and 3 are equal, or $1 + 2 = 3$.

ADDITION

Addition increases the value of one quantity by the value of another quantity (both called **addends**). For example, $2 + 4 = 6; 8 + 9 = 17$. The result is called the **sum**. With addition, the order does not matter, $4 + 2 = 2 + 4$.

When adding signed numbers, if the signs are the same simply add the absolute values of the addends and apply the original sign to the sum. For example, $(+4) + (+8) = +12$ and $(-4) + (-8) = -12$. When the original signs are different, take the absolute values of the addends and subtract the smaller value from the larger value, then apply the original sign of the larger value to the difference. For instance, $(+4) + (-8) = -4$ and $(-4) + (+8) = +4$.

SUBTRACTION

Subtraction is the opposite operation to addition; it decreases the value of one quantity (the **minuend**) by the value of another quantity (the **subtrahend**). For example, $6 - 4 = 2; 17 - 8 = 9$. The result is called the **difference**. Note that with subtraction, the order does matter, $6 - 4 \neq 4 - 6$.

For subtracting signed numbers, change the sign of the subtrahend and then follow the same rules used for addition. For example, $(+4) - (+8) = (+4) + (-8) = -4$.

Review Video: Addition and Subtraction
Visit mometrix.com/academy and enter code: 521157

MULTIPLICATION

Multiplication can be thought of as repeated addition. One number (the **multiplier**) indicates how many times to add the other number (the **multiplicand**) to itself. For example, 3×2 (three times two) $= 2 + 2 + 2 = 6$. With multiplication, the order does not matter: $2 \times 3 = 3 \times 2$ or $3 + 3 = 2 + 2 + 2$, either way the result (the **product**) is the same.

If the signs are the same the product is positive when multiplying signed numbers. For example, $(+4) \times (+8) = +32$ and $(-4) \times (-8) = +32$. If the signs are opposite, the product is negative. For example, $(+4) \times (-8) = -32$ and $(-4) \times (+8) = -32$. When more than two factors are multiplied together, the sign of the product is determined by how many negative factors are present. If there are an odd number of negative factors then the product is negative, whereas an even number of negative factors indicates a positive product. For instance, $(+4) \times (-8) \times (-2) = +64$ and $(-4) \times (-8) \times (-2) = -64$.

DIVISION

Division is the opposite operation to multiplication; one number (the **divisor**) tells us how many parts to divide the other number (the **dividend**) into. The result of division is called the **quotient**. For example, $20 \div 4 = 5$; if 20 is split into 4 equal parts, each part is 5. With division, the order of the numbers does matter, $20 \div 4 \neq 4 \div 20$.

The rules for dividing signed numbers are similar to multiplying signed numbers. If the dividend and divisor have the same sign, the quotient is positive. If the dividend and divisor have opposite signs, the quotient is negative. For example, $(-4) \div (+8) = -0.5$.

Review Video: Multiplication and Division
Visit mometrix.com/academy and enter code: 643326

PARENTHESES

Parentheses are used to designate which operations should be done first when there are multiple operations. Example: $4 - (2 + 1) = 1$; the parentheses tell us that we must add 2 and 1, and then subtract the sum from 4, rather than subtracting 2 from 4 and then adding 1 (this would give us an answer of 3).

Review Video: Mathematical Parentheses
Visit mometrix.com/academy and enter code: 978600

EXPONENTS

An **exponent** is a superscript number placed next to another number at the top right. It indicates how many times the base number is to be multiplied by itself. Exponents provide a shorthand way to write what would be a longer mathematical expression, for example: $2^4 = 2 \times 2 \times 2 \times 2$. A number with an exponent of 2 is said to be "squared," while a number with an exponent of 3 is said to be "cubed." The value of a number raised to an exponent is called its power. So, 8^4 is read as "8 to the 4th power," or "8 raised to the power of 4."

The properties of exponents are as follows:

Property	Description
$a^1 = a$	Any number to the power of 1 is equal to itself
$1^n = 1$	The number 1 raised to any power is equal to 1
$a^0 = 1$	Any number raised to the power of 0 is equal to 1
$a^n \times a^m = a^{n+m}$	Add exponents to multiply powers of the same base number
$a^n \div a^m = a^{n-m}$	Subtract exponents to divide powers of the same base number
$(a^n)^m = a^{n \times m}$	When a power is raised to a power, the exponents are multiplied

Property	Description
$(a \times b)^n = a^n \times b^n$ $(a \div b)^n = a^n \div b^n$	Multiplication and division operations inside parentheses can be raised to a power. This is the same as each term being raised to that power.
$a^{-n} = \frac{1}{a^n}$	A negative exponent is the same as the reciprocal of a positive exponent

Note that exponents do not have to be integers. Fractional or decimal exponents follow all the rules above as well. Example: $5^{\frac{1}{4}} \times 5^{\frac{3}{4}} = 5^{\frac{1}{4}+\frac{3}{4}} = 5^1 = 5$.

Review Video: Exponents
Visit mometrix.com/academy and enter code: 600998

Review Video: Laws of Exponents
Visit mometrix.com/academy and enter code: 532558

Roots

A **root**, such as a square root, is another way of writing a fractional exponent. Instead of using a superscript, roots use the radical symbol ($\sqrt{\ }$) to indicate the operation. A radical will have a number underneath the bar, and may sometimes have a number in the upper left: $\sqrt[n]{a}$, read as "the nth root of a." The relationship between radical notation and exponent notation can be described by this equation: $\sqrt[n]{a} = a^{\frac{1}{n}}$. The two special cases of $n = 2$ and $n = 3$ are called square roots and cube roots. If there is no number to the upper left, it is understood to be a square root ($n = 2$). Nearly all of the roots you encounter will be square roots. A square root is the same as a number raised to the one-half power. When we say that a is the square root of b ($a = \sqrt{b}$), we mean that a multiplied by itself equals b: ($a \times a = b$).

A **perfect square** is a number that has an integer for its square root. There are 10 perfect squares from 1 to 100: 1, 4, 9, 16, 25, 36, 49, 64, 81, 100 (the squares of integers 1 through 10).

Review Video: Roots
Visit mometrix.com/academy and enter code: 795655

Review Video: Square Root and Perfect Square
Visit mometrix.com/academy and enter code: 648063

Order of Operations

Order of operations is a set of rules that dictates the order in which we must perform each operation in an expression so that we will evaluate it accurately. If we have an expression that includes multiple different operations, order of operations tells us which operations to do first. The most common mnemonic for order of operations is **PEMDAS**, or "Please Excuse My Dear Aunt Sally." PEMDAS stands for parentheses, exponents, multiplication, division, addition, and subtraction. It is important to understand that multiplication and division have equal precedence, as do addition and subtraction, so those pairs of operations are simply worked from left to right in order.

For example, evaluating the expression $5 + 20 \div 4 \times (2 + 3) - 6$ using the correct order of operations would be done like this:

- **P:** Perform the operations inside the parentheses: $(2 + 3) = 5$
- **E:** Simplify the exponents.
  - The equation now looks like this: $5 + 20 \div 4 \times 5 - 6$
- **MD:** Perform multiplication and division from left to right: $20 \div 4 = 5$; then $5 \times 5 = 25$

- The equation now looks like this: $5 + 25 - 6$
- **AS:** Perform addition and subtraction from left to right: $5 + 25 = 30$; then $30 - 6 = 24$

Review Video: Order of Operations
Visit mometrix.com/academy and enter code: 259675

Subtraction with Regrouping

A great way to make use of some of the features built into the decimal system would be regrouping when attempting longform subtraction operations. When subtracting within a place value, sometimes the minuend is smaller than the subtrahend, **regrouping** enables you to 'borrow' a unit from a place value to the left in order to get a positive difference. For example, consider subtracting 189 from 525 with regrouping.

First, set up the subtraction problem in vertical form:

$$\begin{array}{r} 525 \\ -\ 189 \\ \hline \end{array}$$

Notice that the numbers in the ones and tens columns of 525 are smaller than the numbers in the ones and tens columns of 189. This means you will need to use regrouping to perform subtraction:

$$\begin{array}{rccc} & 5 & 2 & 5 \\ - & 1 & 8 & 9 \\ \hline \end{array}$$

To subtract 9 from 5 in the ones column you will need to borrow from the 2 in the tens columns:

$$\begin{array}{rccc} & 5 & 1 & 15 \\ - & 1 & 8 & 9 \\ \hline & & & 6 \end{array}$$

Next, to subtract 8 from 1 in the tens column you will need to borrow from the 5 in the hundreds column:

$$\begin{array}{rccc} & 4 & 11 & 15 \\ - & 1 & 8 & 9 \\ \hline & & 3 & 6 \end{array}$$

Last, subtract the 1 from the 4 in the hundreds column:

$$\begin{array}{rccc} & 4 & 11 & 15 \\ - & 1 & 8 & 9 \\ \hline & 3 & 3 & 6 \end{array}$$

Factoring

Factors and Greatest Common Factor

Factors are numbers that are multiplied together to obtain a **product**. For example, in the equation $2 \times 3 = 6$, the numbers 2 and 3 are factors. A **prime number** has only two factors (1 and itself), but other numbers can have many factors.

A **common factor** is a number that divides exactly into two or more other numbers. For example, the factors of 12 are 1, 2, 3, 4, 6, and 12, while the factors of 15 are 1, 3, 5, and 15. The common factors of 12 and 15 are 1 and 3.

A **prime factor** is also a prime number. Therefore, the prime factors of 12 are 2 and 3. For 15, the prime factors are 3 and 5.

The **greatest common factor** (GCF) is the largest number that is a factor of two or more numbers. For example, the factors of 15 are 1, 3, 5, and 15; the factors of 35 are 1, 5, 7, and 35. Therefore, the greatest common factor of 15 and 35 is 5.

Review Video: Factors
Visit mometrix.com/academy and enter code: 920086

Review Video: Greatest Common Factor (GCF)
Visit mometrix.com/academy and enter code: 838699

MULTIPLES AND LEAST COMMON MULTIPLE

Often listed out in multiplication tables, **multiples** are integer increments of a given factor. In other words, dividing a multiple by the factor number will result in an integer. For example, the multiples of 7 include: $1 \times 7 = 7,\ 2 \times 7 = 14,\ 3 \times 7 = 21,\ 4 \times 7 = 28,\ 5 \times 7 = 35$. Dividing 7, 14, 21, 28, or 35 by 7 will result in the integers 1, 2, 3, 4, and 5, respectively.

The least common multiple (**LCM**) is the smallest number that is a multiple of two or more numbers. For example, the multiples of 3 include 3, 6, 9, 12, 15, etc.; the multiples of 5 include 5, 10, 15, 20, etc. Therefore, the least common multiple of 3 and 5 is 15.

Review Video: Multiples
Visit mometrix.com/academy and enter code: 626738

Review Video: Multiples and Least Common Multiple (LCM)
Visit mometrix.com/academy and enter code: 520269

Rational Numbers

FRACTIONS

A **fraction** is a number that is expressed as one integer written above another integer, with a dividing line between them $\left(\frac{x}{y}\right)$. It represents the **quotient** of the two numbers "x divided by y." It can also be thought of as x out of y equal parts.

The top number of a fraction is called the **numerator**, and it represents the number of parts under consideration. The 1 in $\frac{1}{4}$ means that 1 part out of the whole is being considered in the calculation. The bottom number of a fraction is called the **denominator**, and it represents the total number of equal parts. The 4 in $\frac{1}{4}$ means that the whole consists of 4 equal parts. A fraction cannot have a denominator of zero; this is referred to as "*undefined*."

Fractions can be manipulated, without changing the value of the fraction, by multiplying or dividing (but not adding or subtracting) both the numerator and denominator by the same number. If you divide both numbers by a common factor, you are **reducing** or simplifying the fraction. Two fractions that have the same value but are expressed differently are known as **equivalent fractions**. For example, $\frac{2}{10}, \frac{3}{15}, \frac{4}{20}$, and $\frac{5}{25}$ are all equivalent fractions. They can also all be reduced or simplified to $\frac{1}{5}$.

When two fractions are manipulated so that they have the same denominator, this is known as finding a **common denominator**. The number chosen to be that common denominator should be the least common multiple of the two original denominators. Example: $\frac{3}{4}$ and $\frac{5}{6}$; the least common multiple of 4 and 6 is 12. Manipulating to achieve the common denominator: $\frac{3}{4} = \frac{9}{12}$; $\frac{5}{6} = \frac{10}{12}$.

Proper Fractions and Mixed Numbers

A fraction whose denominator is greater than its numerator is known as a **proper fraction**, while a fraction whose numerator is greater than its denominator is known as an **improper fraction**. Proper fractions have values *less than one* and improper fractions have values *greater than one.*

A **mixed number** is a number that contains both an integer and a fraction. Any improper fraction can be rewritten as a mixed number. Example: $\frac{8}{3} = \frac{6}{3} + \frac{2}{3} = 2 + \frac{2}{3} = 2\frac{2}{3}$. Similarly, any mixed number can be rewritten as an improper fraction. Example: $1\frac{3}{5} = 1 + \frac{3}{5} = \frac{5}{5} + \frac{3}{5} = \frac{8}{5}$.

Review Video: Proper and Improper Fractions and Mixed Numbers
Visit mometrix.com/academy and enter code: 211077

Review Video: Fractions
Visit mometrix.com/academy and enter code: 262335

Adding and Subtracting Fractions

If two fractions have a common denominator, they can be added or subtracted simply by adding or subtracting the two numerators and retaining the same denominator. If the two fractions do not already have the same denominator, one or both of them must be manipulated to achieve a common denominator before they can be added or subtracted. Example: $\frac{1}{2} + \frac{1}{4} = \frac{2}{4} + \frac{1}{4} = \frac{3}{4}$.

Review Video: Adding and Subtracting Fractions
Visit mometrix.com/academy and enter code: 378080

Multiplying Fractions

Two fractions can be multiplied by multiplying the two numerators to find the new numerator and the two denominators to find the new denominator. Example: $\frac{1}{3} \times \frac{2}{3} = \frac{1 \times 2}{3 \times 3} = \frac{2}{9}$.

Review Video: Multiplying Fractions
Visit mometrix.com/academy and enter code: 638849

Dividing Fractions

Two fractions can be divided by flipping the numerator and denominator of the second fraction and then proceeding as though it were a multiplication. Example: $\frac{2}{3} \div \frac{3}{4} = \frac{2}{3} \times \frac{4}{3} = \frac{8}{9}$.

Review Video: Dividing Fractions
Visit mometrix.com/academy and enter code: 300874

Multiplying a Mixed Number by a Whole Number or a Decimal

When multiplying a mixed number by something, it is usually best to convert it to an improper fraction first. Additionally, if the multiplicand is a decimal, it is most often simplest to convert it to a fraction. For instance, to multiply $4\frac{3}{8}$ by 3.5, begin by rewriting each quantity as a whole number plus a proper fraction. Remember, a mixed number is a fraction added to a whole number and a decimal is a representation of the sum of fractions, specifically tenths, hundredths, thousandths, and so on:

$$4\frac{3}{8} \times 3.5 = \left(4 + \frac{3}{8}\right) \times \left(3 + \frac{1}{2}\right)$$

Next, the quantities being added need to be expressed with the same denominator. This is achieved by multiplying and dividing the whole number by the denominator of the fraction. Recall that a whole number is equivalent to that number divided by 1:

$$= \left(\frac{4}{1} \times \frac{8}{8} + \frac{3}{8}\right) \times \left(\frac{3}{1} \times \frac{2}{2} + \frac{1}{2}\right)$$

When multiplying fractions, remember to multiply the numerators and denominators separately:

$$= \left(\frac{4 \times 8}{1 \times 8} + \frac{3}{8}\right) \times \left(\frac{3 \times 2}{1 \times 2} + \frac{1}{2}\right)$$
$$= \left(\frac{32}{8} + \frac{3}{8}\right) \times \left(\frac{6}{2} + \frac{1}{2}\right)$$

Now that the fractions have the same denominators, they can be added:

$$= \frac{35}{8} \times \frac{7}{2}$$

Finally, perform the last multiplication and then simplify:

$$= \frac{35 \times 7}{8 \times 2} = \frac{245}{16} = \frac{240}{16} + \frac{5}{16} = 15\frac{5}{16}$$

DECIMALS

Decimals are one way to represent parts of a whole. Using the place value system, each digit to the right of a decimal point denotes the number of units of a corresponding *negative* power of ten. For example, consider the decimal 0.24. We can use a model to represent the decimal. Since a dime is worth one-tenth of a dollar and a penny is worth one-hundredth of a dollar, one possible model to represent this fraction is to have 2 dimes representing the 2 in the tenths place and 4 pennies representing the 4 in the hundredths place:

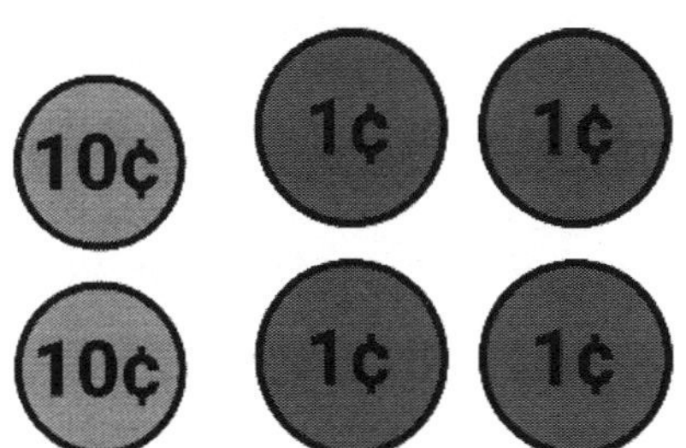

To write the decimal as a fraction, put the decimal in the numerator with 1 in the denominator. Multiply the numerator and denominator by tens until there are no more decimal places. Then simplify the fraction to lowest terms. For example, converting 0.24 to a fraction:

$$0.24 = \frac{0.24}{1} = \frac{0.24 \times 100}{1 \times 100} = \frac{24}{100} = \frac{6}{25}$$

Review Video: Decimals
Visit mometrix.com/academy and enter code: 837268

Operations with Decimals

Adding and Subtracting Decimals

When adding and subtracting decimals, the decimal points must always be aligned. Adding decimals is just like adding regular whole numbers. Example: $4.5 + 2 = 6.5$.

If the problem-solver does not properly align the decimal points, an incorrect answer of 4.7 may result. An easy way to add decimals is to align all of the decimal points in a vertical column visually. This will allow one to see exactly where the decimal should be placed in the final answer. Begin adding from right to left. Add each column in turn, making sure to carry the number to the left if a column adds up to more than 9. The same rules apply to the subtraction of decimals.

Review Video: Adding and Subtracting Decimals
Visit mometrix.com/academy and enter code: 381101

Multiplying Decimals

A simple multiplication problem has two components: a **multiplicand** and a **multiplier**. When multiplying decimals, work as though the numbers were whole rather than decimals. Once the final product is calculated, count the number of places to the right of the decimal in both the multiplicand and the multiplier. Then, count that number of places from the right of the product and place the decimal in that position.

For example, 12.3×2.56 has a total of three places to the right of the respective decimals. Multiply 123×256 to get 31488. Now, beginning on the right, count three places to the left and insert the decimal. The final product will be 31.488.

Review Video: Multiplying Decimals
Visit mometrix.com/academy and enter code: 731574

Dividing Decimals

Every division problem has a **divisor** and a **dividend**. The dividend is the number that is being divided. In the problem $14 \div 7$, 14 is the dividend and 7 is the divisor. In a division problem with decimals, the divisor must be converted into a whole number. Begin by moving the decimal in the divisor to the right until a whole number is created. Next, move the decimal in the dividend the same number of spaces to the right. For example, 4.9 into 24.5 would become 49 into 245. The decimal was moved one space to the right to create a whole number in the divisor, and then the same was done for the dividend. Once the whole numbers are created, the problem is carried out normally: $245 \div 49 = 5$.

Review Video: Dividing Decimals
Visit mometrix.com/academy and enter code: 560690

PERCENTAGES

Percentages can be thought of as fractions that are based on a whole of 100; that is, one whole is equal to 100%. The word **percent** means "per hundred." Percentage problems are often presented in three main ways:

- Find what percentage of some number another number is.
  - Example: What percentage of 40 is 8?
- Find what number is some percentage of a given number.
  - Example: What number is 20% of 40?
- Find what number another number is a given percentage of.
  - Example: What number is 8 20% of?

There are three components in each of these cases: a **whole** (W), a **part** (P), and a **percentage** (%). These are related by the equation: $P = W \times \%$. This can easily be rearranged into other forms that may suit different questions better: $\% = \frac{P}{W}$ and $W = \frac{P}{\%}$. Percentage problems are often also word problems. As such, a large part of solving them is figuring out which quantities are what. For example, consider the following word problem:

In a school cafeteria, 7 students choose pizza, 9 choose hamburgers, and 4 choose tacos. What percentage of student choose tacos?

To find the whole, you must first add all of the parts: $7 + 9 + 4 = 20$. The percentage can then be found by dividing the part by the whole ($\% = \frac{P}{W}$): $\frac{4}{20} = \frac{20}{100} = 20\%$.

Review Video: Percentages
Visit mometrix.com/academy and enter code: 141911

Review Video: Finding Percentage of Number Given Whole
Visit mometrix.com/academy and enter code: 932623

CONVERTING BETWEEN PERCENTAGES, FRACTIONS, AND DECIMALS

Converting decimals to percentages and percentages to decimals is as simple as moving the decimal point. To *convert from a decimal to a percentage*, move the decimal point **two places to the right**. To *convert from a percentage to a decimal*, move it **two places to the left**. It may be helpful to remember that the percentage number will always be larger than the equivalent decimal number. For example:

$$0.23 = 23\% \quad 5.34 = 534\% \quad 0.007 = 0.7\%$$
$$700\% = 7.00 \quad 86\% = 0.86 \quad 0.15\% = 0.0015$$

To convert a fraction to a decimal, simply divide the numerator by the denominator in the fraction. To convert a decimal to a fraction, put the decimal in the numerator with 1 in the denominator. Multiply the numerator and denominator by tens until there are no more decimal places. Then simplify the fraction to lowest terms. For example, converting 0.24 to a fraction:

$$0.24 = \frac{0.24}{1} = \frac{0.24 \times 100}{1 \times 100} = \frac{24}{100} = \frac{6}{25}$$

Fractions can be converted to a percentage by finding equivalent fractions with a denominator of 100. For example,

$$\frac{7}{10} = \frac{70}{100} = 70\% \quad \frac{1}{4} = \frac{25}{100} = 25\%$$

To convert a percentage to a fraction, divide the percentage number by 100 and reduce the fraction to its simplest possible terms. For example,

$$60\% = \frac{60}{100} = \frac{3}{5} \quad 96\% = \frac{96}{100} = \frac{24}{25}$$

Review Video: Converting Decimals to Fractions and Percentages
Visit mometrix.com/academy and enter code: 986765

Review Video: Converting Fractions to Percentages and Decimals
Visit mometrix.com/academy and enter code: 306233

Review Video: Converting Percentages to Decimals and Fractions
Visit mometrix.com/academy and enter code: 287297

Rational Numbers

The term **rational** means that the number can be expressed as a ratio or fraction. That is, a number, r, is rational if and only if it can be represented by a fraction $\frac{a}{b}$ where a and b are integers and b does not equal 0. The set of rational numbers includes integers and decimals. If there is no finite way to represent a value with a fraction of integers, then the number is **irrational**. Common examples of irrational numbers include: $\sqrt{5}$, $(1 + \sqrt{2})$, and π.

Review Video: Rational Numbers
Visit mometrix.com/academy and enter code: 280645

Algebra and Functions

Proportions and Ratios

Proportions

A proportion is a relationship between two quantities that dictates how one changes when the other changes. A **direct proportion** describes a relationship in which a quantity increases by a set amount for every increase in the other quantity, or decreases by that same amount for every decrease in the other quantity. Example: Assuming a constant driving speed, the time required for a car trip increases as the distance of the trip increases. The distance to be traveled and the time required to travel are directly proportional.

Inverse proportion is a relationship in which an increase in one quantity is accompanied by a decrease in the other, or vice versa. Example: the time required for a car trip decreases as the speed increases, and increases as the speed decreases, so the time required is inversely proportional to the speed of the car.

Ratios

A **ratio** is a comparison of two quantities in a particular order. Example: If there are 14 computers in a lab, and the class has 20 students, there is a student to computer ratio of 20 to 14, commonly written as 20:14. Ratios are normally reduced to their smallest whole number representation, so 20:14 would be reduced to 10:7 by dividing both sides by 2.

Constant of Proportionality

When two quantities have a proportional relationship, there exists a **constant of proportionality** between the quantities; the product of this constant and one of the quantities is equal to the other quantity. For example, if one lemon costs $0.25, two lemons cost $0.50, and three lemons cost $0.75, there is a proportional relationship between the total cost of lemons and the number of lemons purchased. The constant of proportionality is the **unit price**, namely $0.25/lemon. Notice that the total price of lemons, t, can be found by multiplying the unit price of lemons, p, and the number of lemons, n: $t = pn$.

Work/Unit Rate

Unit rate expresses a quantity of one thing in terms of one unit of another. For example, if you travel 30 miles every two hours, a unit rate expresses this comparison in terms of one hour: in one hour you travel 15 miles, so your unit rate is 15 miles per hour. Other examples are how much one ounce of food costs (price per ounce) or figuring out how much one egg costs out of the dozen (price per 1 egg, instead of price per 12 eggs). The denominator of a unit rate is always 1. Unit rates are used to compare different situations to solve problems. For example, to make sure you get the best deal when deciding which kind of soda to buy, you can find the unit rate of each. If soda #1 costs $1.50 for a 1-liter bottle, and soda #2 costs $2.75 for a 2-liter bottle, it would be a better deal to buy soda #2, because its unit rate is only $1.375 per 1-liter, which is cheaper than soda #1. Unit rates can also help determine the length of time a given event will take. For example, if you can paint 2 rooms in 4.5 hours, you can determine how long it will take you to paint 5 rooms by solving for the unit rate per room and then multiplying that by 5.

Review Video: Rates and Unit Rates
Visit mometrix.com/academy and enter code: 185363

SLOPE

On a graph with two points, (x_1, y_1) and (x_2, y_2), the **slope** is found with the formula $m = \frac{y_2 - y_1}{x_2 - x_1}$; where $x_1 \neq x_2$ and m stands for slope. If the value of the slope is **positive**, the line has an *upward direction* from left to right. If the value of the slope is **negative**, the line has a *downward direction* from left to right. Consider the following example:

A new book goes on sale in bookstores and online stores. In the first month, 5,000 copies of the book are sold. Over time, the book continues to grow in popularity. The data for the number of copies sold is in the table below.

# of Months on Sale	1	2	3	4	5
# of Copies Sold (In Thousands)	5	10	15	20	25

So, the number of copies that are sold and the time that the book is on sale is a proportional relationship. In this example, an equation can be used to show the data: $y = 5x$, where x is the number of months that the book is on sale. Also, y is the number of copies sold. So, the slope of the corresponding line is $\frac{\text{rise}}{\text{run}} = \frac{5}{1} = 5$.

Review Video: Finding the Slope of a Line
Visit mometrix.com/academy and enter code: 766664

FINDING AN UNKNOWN IN EQUIVALENT EXPRESSIONS

It is often necessary to apply information given about a rate or proportion to a new scenario. For example, if you know that Jedha can run a marathon (26 miles) in 3 hours, how long would it take her to run 10 miles at the same pace? Start by setting up equivalent expressions:

$$\frac{26\text{ mi}}{3\text{ hr}} = \frac{10\text{ mi}}{x\text{ hr}}$$

Now, cross multiply and, solve for x:

$$26x = 30$$
$$x = \frac{30}{26} = \frac{15}{13}$$
$$x \cong 1.15\text{ hrs } or \text{ 1 hr 9 min}$$

So, at this pace, Jedha could run 10 miles in about 1.15 hours or about 1 hour and 9 minutes.

Expressions

TERMS AND COEFFICIENTS

Mathematical expressions consist of a combination of one or more values arranged in terms that are added together. As such, an expression could be just a single number, including zero. A **variable term** is the product of a real number, also called a **coefficient**, and one or more variables, each of which may be raised to an exponent. Expressions may also include numbers without a variable, called **constants** or

constant terms. The expression $6s^2$, for example, is a single term where the coefficient is the real number 6 and the variable is s^2. Note that if a term is written as simply a variable to some exponent, like t^2, then the coefficient is 1, because $t^2 = 1t^2$.

LINEAR EXPRESSIONS

A **single variable linear expression** is the sum of a single variable term, where the variable has no exponent, and a constant, which may be zero. For instance, the expression $2w + 7$ has $2w$ as the variable term and 7 as the constant term. It is important to realize that terms are separated by addition or subtraction. Since an expression is a sum of terms, expressions such as $5x - 3$ can be written as $5x + (-3)$ to emphasize that the constant term is negative. A real-world example of a single variable linear expression is the perimeter of a square, four times the side length, often expressed: $4s$.

In general, a **linear expression** is the sum of any number of variable terms so long as none of the variables have an exponent. For example, $3m + 8n - \frac{1}{4}p + 5.5q - 1$ is a linear expression, but $3y^3$ is not. In the same way, the expression for the perimeter of a general triangle, the sum of the side lengths: $a + b + c$, is considered to be linear, but the expression for the area of square, the side length squared: s^2, is not.

Equations

LINEAR EQUATIONS

Equations that can be written as $ax + b = 0$, where $a \neq 0$, are referred to as **one variable linear equations**. A solution to such an equation is called a **root**. In the case where we have the equation $5x + 10 = 0$, if we solve for x we get a solution of $x = -2$. In other words, the root of the equation is -2. This is found by first subtracting 10 from both sides, which gives $5x = -10$. Next, simply divide both sides by the coefficient of the variable, in this case 5, to get $x = -2$. This can be checked by plugging -2 back into the original equation $(5)(-2) + 10 = -10 + 10 = 0$.

The **solution set** is the set of all solutions of an equation. In our example, the solution set would simply be -2. If there were more solutions (there usually are in multivariable equations) then they would also be included in the solution set. When an equation has no true solutions, this is referred to as an **empty set**. Equations with identical solution sets are **equivalent equations**. An **identity** is a term whose value or determinant is equal to 1.

Linear equations can be written many ways. Below is a list of some forms linear equations can take:

- **Standard Form**: $Ax + By = C$; the slope is $\frac{-A}{B}$ and the y-intercept is $\frac{C}{B}$
- **Slope Intercept Form**: $y = mx + b$, where m is the slope and b is the y-intercept
- **Point-Slope Form**: $y - y_1 = m(x - x_1)$, where m is the slope and (x_1, y_1) is a point on the line
- **Two-Point Form**: $\frac{y-y_1}{x-x_1} = \frac{y_2-y_1}{x_2-x_1}$, where (x_1, y_1) and (x_2, y_2) are two points on the given line
- **Intercept Form**: $\frac{x}{x_1} + \frac{y}{y_1} = 1$, where $(x_1, 0)$ is the point at which a line intersects the x-axis, and $(0, y_1)$ is the point at which the same line intersects the y-axis

Review Video: Slope-Intercept and Point-Slope Forms
Visit mometrix.com/academy and enter code: 113216

Solving One-Variable Linear Equations

Multiply all terms by the lowest common denominator to eliminate any fractions. Look for addition or subtraction to undo so you can isolate the variable on one side of the equal sign. Divide both sides by the coefficient of the variable. When you have a value for the variable, substitute this value into the original equation to make sure you have a true equation. Consider the following example:

Kim's savings are represented by the table below. Represent her savings, using an equation.

X (Months)	Y (Total Savings)
2	\$1300
5	\$2050
9	\$3050
11	\$3550
16	\$4800

The table shows a function with a constant rate of change, or slope, of 250. Given the points on the table, the slopes can be calculated as $(2050 - 1300)/(5 - 2)$, $(3050 - 2050)/(9 - 5)$, $(3550 - 3050)/(11 - 9)$, and $(4800 - 3550)/(16 - 11)$, each of which equals 250. Thus, the table shows a constant rate of change, indicating a linear function. The slope-intercept form of a linear equation is written as $y = mx + b$, where m represents the slope and b represents the y-intercept. Substituting the slope into this form gives $y = 250x + b$. Substituting corresponding x- and y-values from any point into this equation will give the y-intercept, or b. Using the point, (2, 1300), gives $1300 = 250(2) + b$, which simplifies as b = 800. Thus, her savings may be represented by the equation, $y = 250x + 800$.

Rules for Manipulating Equations

Like Terms

Like terms are terms in an equation that have the same variable, regardless of whether or not they also have the same coefficient. This includes terms that *lack* a variable; all constants (i.e. numbers without variables) are considered like terms. If the equation involves terms with a variable raised to different powers, the like terms are those that have the variable raised to the same power.

For example, consider the equation $x^2 + 3x + 2 = 2x^2 + x - 7 + 2x$. In this equation, 2 and -7 are like terms; they are both constants. $3x$, x, and $2x$ are like terms: they all include the variable x raised to the first power. x^2 and $2x^2$ are like terms; they both include the variable x, raised to the second power. $2x$ and $2x^2$ are not like terms; although they both involve the variable x, the variable is not raised to the same power in both terms. The fact that they have the same coefficient, 2, is not relevant.

Carrying Out the Same Operation on Both Sides of an Equation

When solving an equation, the general procedure is to carry out a series of operations on both sides of an equation, choosing operations that will tend to simplify the equation when doing so. The reason why the same operation must be carried out on both sides of the equation is because that leaves the meaning of the equation unchanged, and yields a result that is equivalent to the original equation. This would not be the case if we carried out an operation on one side of an equation and not the other. Consider what an equation means: it is a statement that two values or expressions are equal. If we carry out the same operation on both sides of the equation—add 3 to both sides, for example—then the two sides of the equation are changed in the same way, and so remain equal. If we do that to only one side of the equation—add 3 to one side but not the other—then that wouldn't be true; if we change one side of the equation but not the other then the two sides are no longer equal.

Advantage of Combining Like Terms

Combining like terms refers to adding or subtracting like terms—terms with the same variable—and therefore reducing sets of like terms to a single term. The main advantage of doing this is that it simplifies the equation. Often combining like terms can be done as the first step in solving an equation, though it can also be done later, such as after distributing terms in a product.

For example, consider the equation $2(x + 3) + 3(2 + x + 3) = -4$. The 2 and the 3 in the second set of parentheses are like terms, and we can combine them, yielding $2(x + 3) + 3(x + 5) = -4$. Now we can carry out the multiplications implied by the parentheses, distributing outer 2 and 3 accordingly: $2x + 6 + 3x + 15 = -4$. The $2x$ and the $3x$ are like terms, and we can add them together: $5x + 6 + 15 = -4$. Now, the constants 6, 15, and -4 are also like terms, and we can combine them as well: subtracting 6 and 15 from both sides of the equation, we get $5x = -4 - 6 - 15$, or $5x = -25$, which simplifies further to $x = -5$.

Canceling Terms on Opposite Sides of an Equation

Two terms on opposite sides of an equation can be canceled if and only if they *exactly* match each other. They must have the same variable raised to the same power and the same coefficient. For example, in the equation $3x + 2x^2 + 6 = 2x^2 - 6$, $2x^2$ appears on both sides of the equation, and can be canceled, leaving $3x + 6 = -6$. The 6 on each side of the equation can*not* be canceled, because it is added on one side of the equation and subtracted on the other. While they cannot be canceled, however, the 6 and -6 are like terms and can be combined, yielding $3x = -12$, which simplifies further to $x = -4$.

It's also important to note that the terms to be canceled must be independent terms and cannot be part of a larger term. For example, consider the equation $2(x + 6) = 3(x + 4) + 1$. We cannot cancel the xs, because even though they match each other they are part of the larger terms $2(x + 6)$ and $3(x + 4)$. We must first distribute the 2 and 3, yielding $2x + 12 = 3x + 12 + 1$. Now we see that the terms with the x's do not match, but the 12's do, and can be canceled, leaving $2x = 3x + 1$, which simplifies to $x = -1$.

Process for Manipulating Equations

Isolating Variables

To **isolate a variable** means to manipulate the equation so that the variable appears by itself on one side of the equation, and does not appear at all on the other side. Generally, an equation or inequality is considered to be solved once the variable is isolated and the other side of the equation or inequality is simplified as much as possible. In the case of a two-variable equation or inequality, only one variable need be isolated; it will not usually be possible to simultaneously isolate both variables.

For a linear equation—an equation in which the variable only appears raised to the first power—isolating a variable can be done by first moving all the terms with the variable to one side of the equation and all other terms to the other side. (*Moving* a term really means adding the inverse of the term to both sides; when a term is *moved* to the other side of the equation its sign is flipped.) Then combine like terms on each side. Finally, divide both sides by the coefficient of the variable, if applicable. The steps need not necessarily be done in this order, but this order will always work.

Equations with More Than One Solution

Some types of non-linear equation, such as equations involving squares of variables, may have more than one solution. For example, the equation $x^2 = 4$ has two solutions: 2 and -2. Equations with absolute values can also have multiple solutions: $|x| = 1$ has the solutions $x = 1$ and $x = -1$.

It is also possible for a linear equation to have more than one solution, but only if the equation is true regardless of the value of the variable. In this case, the equation is considered to have infinitely many solutions, because any possible value of the variable is a solution. We know a linear equation has infinitely many solutions if when we combine like terms the variables cancel, leaving a true statement.

For example, consider the equation $2(3x + 5) = x + 5(x + 2)$. Distributing, we get $6x + 10 = x + 5x + 10$; combining like terms gives $6x + 10 = 6x + 10$, and the $6x$ terms cancel to leave $10 = 10$. This is clearly true, so the original equation is true for any value of x. We could also have canceled the 10s leaving $0 = 0$, but again this is clearly true—in general if both sides of the equation match exactly, it has infinitely many solutions.

Equations with No Solution

Some types of non-linear equations, such as equations involving squares of variables, may have no solution. For example, the equation $x^2 = -2$ has no solutions in the real numbers, because the square of any real number must be positive. Similarly, $|x| = -1$ has no solution, because the absolute value of a number is always positive.

It is also possible for an equation to have no solution even if does not involve any powers greater than one or absolute values or other special functions. For example, the equation $2(x + 3) + x = 3x$ has no solution. We can see that if we try to solve it: first we distribute, leaving $2x + 6 + x = 3x$. But now if we try to combine all the terms with the variable, we find that they cancel: we have $3x$ on the left and $3x$ on the right, canceling to leave us with $6 = 0$. This is clearly false. In general, whenever the variable terms in an equation cancel leaving different constants on both sides, it means that the equation has no solution. (If we are left with the *same* constant on both sides, the equation has infinitely many solutions instead.)

Features of Equations That Require Special Treatment

Linear Equations

A linear equation is an equation in which variables only appear by themselves: not multiplied together, not with exponents other than one, and not inside absolute value signs or any other functions. For example, the equation $x + 1 - 3x = 5 - x$ is a linear equation: while x appears multiple times, it never appears with an exponent other than one, or inside any function. The two-variable equation $2x - 3y = 5 + 2x$ is also a linear equation. In contrast, the equation $x^2 - 5 = 3x$ is *not* a linear equation, because it involves the term x^2. $\sqrt{x} = 5$ is not a linear equation, because it involves a square root. $(x - 1)^2 = 4$ is not a linear equation because even though there's no exponent on the x directly, it appears as part of an expression that is squared. The two-variable equation $x + xy - y = 5$ is not a linear equation because it includes the term xy, where two variables are multiplied together.

Linear equations can always be solved (or shown to have no solution) by combining like terms and performing simple operations on both sides of the equation. Some non-linear equations can also be solved by similar methods, but others may require more advanced methods of solution, if they can be solved analytically at all.

Solving Equations Involving Roots

In an equation involving roots, the first step is to isolate the term with the root, if possible, and then raise both sides of the equation to the appropriate power to eliminate it. Consider an example equation, $2\sqrt{x + 1} - 1 = 3$. In this case, begin by adding 1 to both sides, yielding $2\sqrt{x + 1} = 4$, and then dividing both sides by 2, yielding $\sqrt{x + 1} = 2$. Now square both sides, yielding $x + 1 = 4$. Finally, subtracting 1 from both sides yields $x = 3$.

Squaring both sides of an equation may, however, yield a spurious solution—a solution to the squared equation that is *not* a solution of the original equation. It's therefore necessary to plug the solution back into the original equation to make sure it works. In this case, it does: $2\sqrt{3 + 1} - 1 = 2\sqrt{4} - 1 = 2(2) - 1 = 4 - 1 = 3$.

The same procedure applies for roots other than square roots. For example, given the equation $3 + \sqrt[3]{2x} = 5$, we can first subtract 3 from both sides, yielding $\sqrt[3]{2x} = 2$ and isolating the root. Raising both sides to the third power yields $2x = 2^3$, i.e. $2x = 8$. We can now divide both sides by 2 to get $x = 4$.

Solving Equations with Exponents

To solve an equation involving an exponent, the first step is to isolate the variable with the exponent. We can then take the appropriate root of both sides to eliminate the exponent. For instance, for the equation $2x^3 + 17 = 5x^3 - 7$, we can subtract $5x^3$ from both sides to get $-3x^3 + 17 = -7$, and then subtract 17 from both sides to get $-3x^3 = -24$. Finally, we can divide both sides by -3 to get $x^3 = 8$. Finally, we can take the cube root of both sides to get $x = \sqrt[3]{8} = 2$.

One important but often overlooked point is that equations with an exponent greater than 1 may have more than one answer. The solution to $x^2 = 9$ isn't simply $x = 3$; it's $x = \pm 3$: that is, $x = 3$ or $x = -3$. For a slightly more complicated example, consider the equation $(x - 1)^2 - 1 = 3$. Adding one to both sides yields $(x - 1)^2 = 4$; taking the square root of both sides yields $x - 1 = 2$. We can then add 1 to both sides to get $x = 3$. However, there's a second solution: we also have the possibility that $x - 1 = -2$, in which case $x = -1$. Both $x = 3$ and $x = -1$ are valid solutions, as can be verified by substituting them both into the original equation.

Solving Equations with Absolute Values

When solving an equation with an absolute value, the first step is to isolate the absolute value term. We then consider the two possibilities: when the expression inside the absolute value is positive or when it is negative. In the former case, the expression in the absolute value equals the expression on the other side of the equation; in the latter, it equals the additive inverse of that expression—the expression times negative one. We consider each case separately, and finally check for spurious solutions.

For instance, consider solving $|2x - 1| + x = 5$ for x. We can first isolate the absolute value by moving the x to the other side: $|2x - 1| = -x + 5$. Now, we have two possibilities. First, that $2x - 1$ is positive, and hence $2x - 1 = -x + 5$. Rearranging and combining like terms yields $3x = 6$, and hence $x = 2$. The other possibility is that $2x - 1$ is negative, and hence $2x - 1 = -(-x + 5) = x - 5$. In this case, rearranging and combining like terms yields $x = -4$. Substituting $x = 2$ and $x = -4$ back into the original equation, we see that they are both valid solutions.

Note that the absolute value of a sum or difference applies to the sum or difference as a whole, not to the individual terms: in general, $|2x - 1|$ is not equal to $|2x + 1|$ or to $|2x| - 1$.

Review Video: Solving Absolute Value Inequalities
Visit mometrix.com/academy and enter code: 997008

Spurious Solutions

A **spurious solution** may arise when we square both sides of an equation as a step in solving it, or under certain other operations on the equation. It is a solution to the squared or otherwise modified equation that is *not* a solution of the original equation. To identify a spurious solution, it's useful when you solve an equation involving roots or absolute values to plug the solution back into the original equation to make sure it's valid.

Choosing Which Variable to Isolate in Two-Variable Equations

Similar to methods for a one-variable equation, solving a two-variable equation involves isolating a variable: manipulating the equation so that a variable appears by itself on one side of the equation, and not at all on the other side. However, in a two-variable equation, you will usually only be able to isolate one of the variables; the other variable may appear on the other side along with constant terms, or with exponents or other functions.

Often one variable will be much more easily isolated than the other, and therefore that's the variable you should choose. If one variable appears with various exponents, and the other only raised it to the first power, the latter variable is the one to isolate: given the equation $a^2 + 2b = a^3 + b + 3$, the b only appears to the first power, whereas a appears squared and cubed, so b is the variable that can be solved for: combining like terms and isolating the b on the left side of the equation, we get $b = a^3 - a^2 + 3$. If both variables are equally easy to isolate, then it's best to isolate the independent variable, if one is defined; if the two variables are x and y, the convention is that y is the independent variable.

Practice

P1. Seeing the equation $2x + 4 = 4x + 7$, a student divides the first terms on each side by 2, yielding $x + 4 = 2x + 7$, and then combines like terms to get $x = -3$. However, this is incorrect, as can be seen by substituting -3 into the original equation. Explain what is wrong with the student's reasoning.

P2. Describe the steps necessary to solve the equation $2x + 1 - x = 4 + 3x + 7$.

P3. Describe the steps necessary to solve the equation $2(x + 5) = 7(4 - x)$.

P4. Find all real solutions to the equation $1 - \sqrt{x} = 2$.

P5. Find all real solutions to the equation $|x + 1| = 2x + 5$.

P6. Solve for x: $-x + 2\sqrt{x+5} + 1 = 3$.

P7. Ray earns $10 an hour at his job. Write an equation for his earnings as a function of time spent working. Determine how long Ray has to work in order to earn $360.

P8. Simplify the following: $3x + 2 + 2y = 5y - 7 + |2x - 1|$

Practice Solutions

P1. As stated, it's easy to verify that the student's solution is incorrect: $2(-3) + 4 = -2$ and $4(-3) + 7 = -5$; clearly $-2 \neq -5$. The mistake was in the first step, which illustrates a common type of error in solving equations. The student tried to simplify the two variable terms by dividing them by 2. However, it's not valid to multiply or divide only one term on each side of an equation by a number; when multiplying or dividing, the operation must be applied to *every* term in the equation. So, dividing by 2 would yield not $x + 4 = 2x + 7$, but $x + 2 = 2x + \frac{7}{2}$. While this is now valid, that fraction is inconvenient to work with, so this may not be the best first step in solving the equation. Rather, it may have been better to first combine like terms: subtracting $4x$ from both sides yields $-2x + 4 = 7$; subtracting 4 from both sides yields $-2x = 3$; and *now* we can divide both sides by -2 to get $x = -\frac{3}{2}$.

P2. Our ultimate goal is to isolate the variable, x. To that end we first move all the terms containing x to the left side of the equation, and all the constant terms to the right side. Note that when we move a term to the other side of the equation its sign changes. We are therefore now left with $2x - x - 3x = 4 + 7 - 1$.

Next, we combine the like terms on each side of the equation, adding and subtracting the terms as appropriate. This leaves us with $-2x = 10$.

At this point, we're almost done; all that remains is to divide both sides by -2 to leave the x by itself. We now have our solution, $x = -5$. We can verify that this is a correct solution by substituting it back into the original equation.

P3. Generally, in equations that have a sum or difference of terms multiplied by another value or expression, the first step is to multiply those terms, distributing as necessary: $2(x + 5) = 2(x) + 2(5) =$

$2x + 10$, and $7(4 - x) = 7(4) - 7(x) = 28 - 7x$. So, the equation becomes $2x + 10 = 28 - 7x$. We can now add $7x$ to both sides to eliminate the variable from the right-hand side: $9x + 10 = 28$. Similarly, we can subtract 10 from both sides to move all the constants to the right: $9x = 18$. Finally, we can divide both sides by 9, yielding the final answer, $x = 2$.

P4. It's not hard to isolate the root: subtract one from both sides, yielding $-\sqrt{x} = 1$. Finally, multiply both sides by –1, yielding $\sqrt{x} = -1$. Squaring both sides of the equation yields $x = 1$. However, if we plug this back into the original equation, we get $1 - \sqrt{1} = 2$, which is false. Therefore $x = 1$ is a spurious solution, and the equation has no real solutions.

P5. This equation has two possibilities: $x + 1 = 2x + 5$, which simplifies to $x = -4$; or $x + 1 = -(2x + 5) = -2x - 5$, which simplifies to $x = -2$. However, if we try substituting both values back into the original equation, we see that only $x = -2$ yields a true statement. $x = -4$ is a spurious solution; $x = -2$ is the only valid solution to the equation.

P6. Start by isolating the term with the root. We can do that by moving the $-x$ and the 1 to the other side, yielding $2\sqrt{x + 5} = 3 + x - 1$, or $2\sqrt{x + 5} = x + 2$. Dividing both sides of the equation by 2 would give us a fractional term that could be messy to deal with, so we won't do that for now. Instead, we square both sides of the equation; note that on the left-hand side the 2 is outside the square root sign, so we have to square it. As a result, we get $4(x + 5) = (x + 2)^2$. Expanding both sides gives us $4x + 20 = x^2 + 4x + 4$. In this case, we see that we have $4x$ on both sides, so we can cancel the $4x$ (which is what allows us to solve this equation despite the different powers of x). We now have $20 = x^2 + 4$, or $x^2 = 16$. Since the variable is raised to an even power, we need to take the positive and negative roots, so $x = \pm 4$: that is, $x = 4$ or $x = -4$. Substituting both values into the original equation, we see that $x = 4$ satisfies the equation but $x = -4$ does not; hence $x = -4$ is a spurious solution, and the only solution to the equation is $x = 4$.

P7. The number of dollars that Ray earns is dependent on the number of hours he works, so earnings will be represented by the dependent variable y and hours worked will be represented by the independent variable x. He earns 10 dollars per hour worked, so his earnings can be calculated as $y = 10x$. To calculate the number of hours Ray must work in order to earn \$360, plug in 360 for y and solve for x:

$$360 = 10x$$
$$x = \frac{360}{10} = 36$$

P8. To simplify this equation, we must isolate one of its variables on one side of the equation. In this case, the x appears under an absolute value sign, which makes it difficult to isolate. The y, on the other hand, only appears without an exponent—the equation is linear in y. We will therefore choose to isolate the y. The first step, then, is to move all the terms with y to the left side of the equation, which we can do by subtracting $5y$ from both sides:

$$3x + 2 - 3y = -7 + |2x - 1|$$

We can then move all the terms that do *not* include y to the right side of the equation, by subtracting $3x$ and 2 from both sides of the equation:

$$-3y = -3x - 9 + |2x - 1|$$

Finally, we can isolate the y by dividing both sides by –3.

$$y = x + 3 - \frac{1}{3}|2x - 1|$$

This is as far as we can simplify the equation; we cannot combine the terms inside and outside the absolute value sign. We can therefore consider the equation to be solved.

Inequalities

Working with Inequalities

Commonly in algebra and other upper-level fields of math you find yourself working with mathematical expressions that do not equal each other. The statement comparing such expressions with symbols such as < (less than) or > (greater than) is called an *inequality*. An example of an inequality is $7x > 5$. To solve for x, simply divide both sides by 7 and the solution is shown to be $x > \frac{5}{7}$. Graphs of the solution set of inequalities are represented on a number line. Open circles are used to show that an expression approaches a number but is never quite equal to that number.

Review Video: Inequalities
Visit mometrix.com/academy and enter code: 347842

Conditional inequalities are those with certain values for the variable that will make the condition true and other values for the variable where the condition will be false. **Absolute inequalities** can have any real number as the value for the variable to make the condition true, while there is no real number value for the variable that will make the condition false. Solving inequalities is done by following the same rules as for solving equations with the exception that when multiplying or dividing by a negative number the direction of the inequality sign must be flipped or reversed. **Double inequalities** are situations where two inequality statements apply to the same variable expression. An example of this is $-c < ax + b < c$.

Determining Solutions to Inequalities

To determine whether a coordinate is a solution of an inequality, you can substitute the values of the coordinate into the inequality, simplify, and check whether the resulting statement holds true. For instance, to determine whether $(-2, 4)$ is a solution of the inequality $y \geq -2x + 3$, substitute the values into the inequality, $4 \geq -2(-2) + 3$. Simplify the right side of the inequality and the result is $4 \geq 7$, which is a false statement. Therefore, the coordinate is not a solution of the inequality. You can also use this method to determine which part of the graph of an inequality is shaded. The graph of $y \geq -2x + 3$ includes the solid line $y = -2x + 3$ and, since it excludes the point $(-2, 4)$ to the left of the line, it is shaded to the right of the line.

Flipping Inequality Signs

When given an inequality, we can always turn the entire inequality around, swapping the two sides of the inequality and changing the inequality sign. For instance, $x + 2 > 2x - 3$ is equivalent to $2x - 3 < x + 2$. Aside from that, normally the inequality does not change if we carry out the same operation on both sides of the inequality. There is, however, one principal exception: if we *multiply* or *divide* both sides of the inequality by a *negative number*, the inequality is flipped. For example, if we take the inequality $-2x < 6$ and divide both sides by -2, the inequality flips and we are left with $x > -3$. This *only* applies to multiplication and division, and only with negative numbers. Multiplying or dividing both sides by a positive number, or adding or subtracting any number regardless of sign, does not flip the inequality.

Compound Inequalities

A **compound inequality** is an equality that consists of two inequalities combined with *and* or *or*. The two components of a proper compound inequality must be of opposite type: that is, one must be greater than (or greater than or equal to), the other less than (or less than or equal to). For instance, "$x + 1 < 2$ or $x + 1 > 3$" is a compound inequality, as is "$2x \geq 4$ and $2x \leq 6$." An *and* inequality can be written more compactly by having one inequality on each side of the common part: "$2x \geq 1$ and $2x \leq 6$," can also be written as $1 \leq 2x \leq 6$.

In order for the compound inequality to be meaningful, the two parts of an *and* inequality must overlap; otherwise no numbers satisfy the inequality. On the other hand, if the two parts of an *or* inequality overlap, then *all* numbers satisfy the inequality and as such is usually not meaningful.

Solving a compound inequality requires solving each part separately. For example, given the compound inequality "$x + 1 < 2$ or $x + 1 > 3$," the first inequality, $x + 1 < 2$, reduces to $x < 1$, and the second part, $x + 1 > 3$, reduces to $x > 2$, so the whole compound inequality can be written as "$x < 1$ or $x > 2$." Similarly, $1 \leq 2x \leq 6$ can be solved by dividing each term by 2, yielding $\frac{1}{2} \leq x \leq 3$.

Solving Inequalities Involving Absolute Values

To solve an inequality involving an absolute value, first isolate the term with the absolute value. Then proceed to treat the two cases separately as with an absolute value equation, but flipping the inequality in the case where the expression in the absolute value is negative (since that essentially involves multiplying both sides by -1.) The two cases are then combined into a compound inequality; if the absolute value is on the greater side of the inequality, then it is an *or* compound inequality, if on the lesser side, then it's an *and*.

Consider the inequality $2 + |x - 1| \geq 3$. We can isolate the absolute value term by subtracting 2 from both sides: $|x - 1| \geq 1$. Now, we're left with the two cases $x - 1 \geq 1$ or $x - 1 \leq -1$: note that in the latter, negative case, the inequality is flipped. $x - 1 \geq 1$ reduces to $x \geq 2$, and $x - 1 \leq -1$ reduces to $x \leq 0$. Since in the inequality $|x - 1| \geq 1$ the absolute value is on the greater side, the two cases combine into an *or* compound inequality, so the final, solved inequality is "$x \leq 0$ or $x \geq 2$."

Solving Inequalities Involving Square Roots

Solving an inequality with a square root involves two parts. First, we solve the inequality as if it were an equation, isolating the square root and then squaring both sides of the equation. Second, we restrict the solution to the set of values of x for which the value inside the square root sign is non-negative.

For example, in the inequality, $\sqrt{x - 2} + 1 < 5$, we can isolate the square root by subtracting 1 from both sides, yielding $\sqrt{x - 2} < 4$. Squaring both sides of the inequality yields $x - 2 < 16$, so $x < 18$. Since we can't take the square root of a negative number, we also require the part inside the square root to be non-negative. In this case, that means $x - 2 \geq 0$. Adding 2 to both sides of the inequality yields $x \geq 2$. Our final answer is a compound inequality combining the two simple inequalities: $x \geq 2$ and $x < 18$, or $2 \leq x < 18$.

Note that we only get a compound inequality if the two simple inequalities are in opposite directions; otherwise we take the one that is more restrictive.

The same technique can be used for other even roots, such as fourth roots. It is *not*, however, used for cube roots or other odd roots—negative numbers *do* have cube roots, so the condition that the quantity inside the root sign cannot be negative does not apply.

Special Circumstances

Sometimes an inequality involving an absolute value or an even exponent is true for all values of x, and we don't need to do any further work to solve it. This is true if the inequality, once the absolute value or exponent term is isolated, says that term is greater than a negative number (or greater than or equal to zero). Since an absolute value or a number raised to an even exponent is *always* non-negative, this inequality is always true.

GRAPHICAL SOLUTIONS TO EQUATIONS AND INEQUALITIES

When equations are shown graphically, they are usually shown on a **Cartesian coordinate plane**. The Cartesian coordinate plane consists of two number lines placed perpendicular to each other, and intersecting at the zero point, also known as the origin. The horizontal number line is known as the x-axis, with positive values to the right of the origin, and negative values to the left of the origin. The vertical number line is known as the y-axis, with positive values above the origin, and negative values below the origin. Any point on the plane can be identified by an ordered pair in the form (x, y), called coordinates. The x-value of the coordinate is called the abscissa, and the y-value of the coordinate is called the ordinate. The two number lines divide the plane into **four quadrants**: I, II, III, and IV.

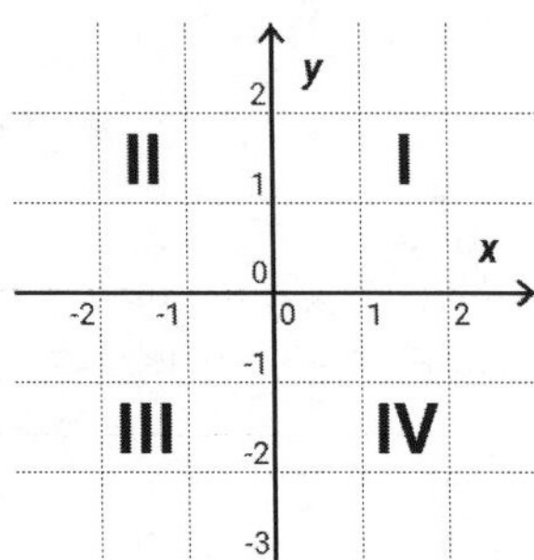

Note that in quadrant I $x > 0$ and $y > 0$, in quadrant II $x < 0$ and $y > 0$, in quadrant III $x < 0$ and $y < 0$, and in quadrant IV $x > 0$ and $y < 0$.

Recall that if the value of the slope of a line is positive, the line slopes upward from left to right. If the value of the slope is negative, the line slopes downward from left to right. If the y-coordinates are the same for two points on a line, the slope is 0 and the line is a **horizontal line**. If the x-coordinates are the same for two points on a line, there is no slope and the line is a **vertical line**. Two or more lines that have equivalent slopes are **parallel lines. Perpendicular lines** have slopes that are negative reciprocals of each other, such as $\frac{a}{b}$ and $\frac{-b}{a}$.

GRAPHING SIMPLE INEQUALITIES

To graph a simple inequality, we first mark on the number line the value that signifies the end point of the inequality. If the inequality is strict (involves a less than or greater than), we use a hollow circle; if it is not strict (less than or equal to or greater than or equal to), we use a solid circle. We then fill in the part of the number line that satisfies the inequality: to the left of the marked point for less than (or less than or equal to), to the right for greater than (or greater than or equal to).

For example, we would graph the inequality $x < 5$ by putting a hollow circle at 5 and filling in the part of the line to the left:

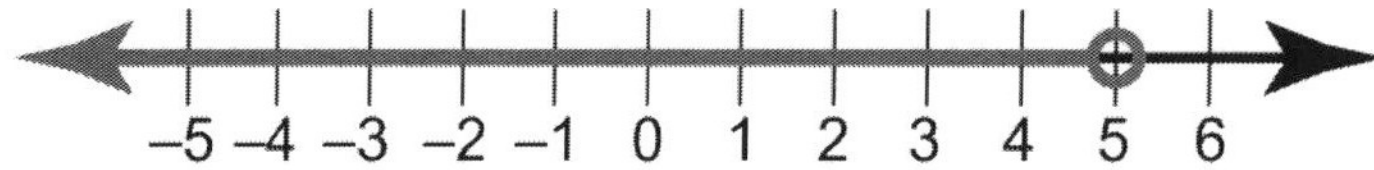

GRAPHING COMPOUND INEQUALITIES

To graph a compound inequality, we fill in both parts of the inequality for an *or* inequality, or the overlap between them for an *and* inequality. More specifically, we start by plotting the endpoints of each inequality on the number line. For an *or* inequality, we then fill in the appropriate side of the line for each inequality. Typically, the two component inequalities do not overlap, that means the shaded part is *outside* the two points. For an *and* inequality, we instead fill in the part of the line that meets both inequalities.

For the inequality "$x \leq -3$ or $x > 4$," we first put a solid circle at -3 and a hollow circle at 4. We then fill the parts of the line *outside* these circles:

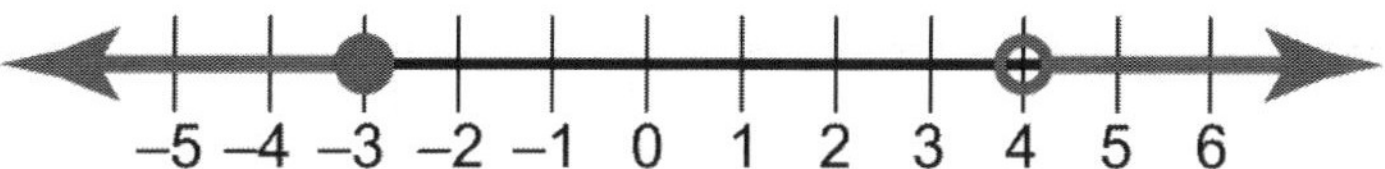

Graphing Inequalities Including Absolute Values

An inequality with an absolute value can be converted to a compound inequality. To graph the inequality, first convert it to a compound inequality, and then graph that normally. If the absolute value is on the greater side of the inequality, we end up with an *or* inequality; we plot the endpoints of the inequality on the number line and fill in the part of the line *outside* those points. If the absolute value is on the smaller side of the inequality, we end up with an *and* inequality; we plot the endpoints of the inequality on the number line and fill in the part of the line *between* those points.

For example, the inequality $|x + 1| \geq 4$ can be rewritten as $x \geq 3$ or $x \leq -5$. We place solid circles at the points 3 and -5 and fill in the part of the line *outside* them:

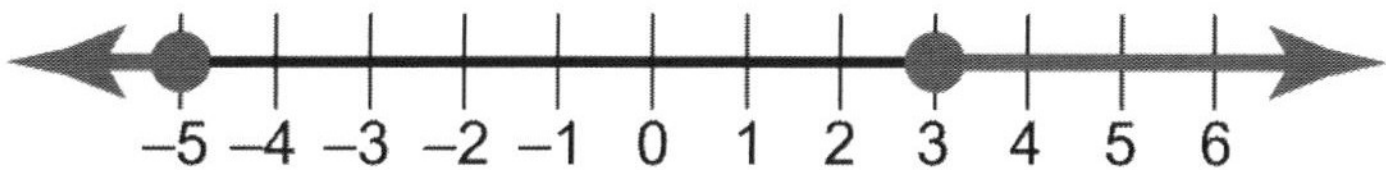

Graphing Equations in Two Variables

One way of graphing an equation in two variables is to plot enough points to get an idea for its shape, and then draw the appropriate curve through those points. A point can be plotted by substituting in a value for one variable and solving for the other. If the equation is linear, we only need two points, and can then draw a straight line between them.

For example, consider the equation $y = 2x - 1$. This is a linear equation—both variables only appear raised to the first power—so we only need two points. When $x = 0$, $y = 2(0) - 1 = -1$. When $x = 2$, $y = 2(2) - 1 = 3$. We can therefore choose the points $(0, -1)$ and $(2, 3)$, and draw a line between them:

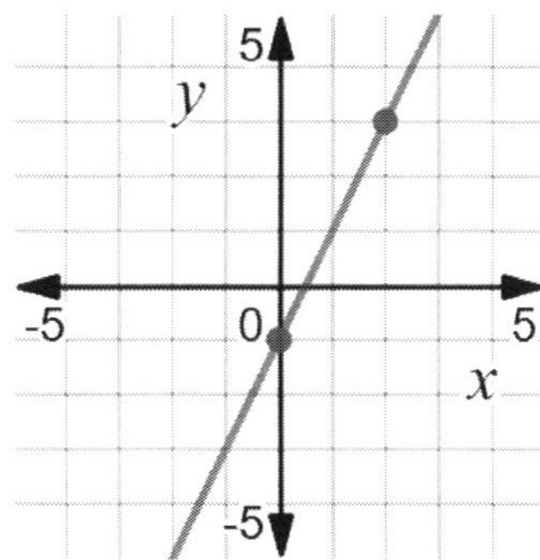

Graphing Inequalities in Two Variables

To graph an inequality in two variables, we first graph the border of the inequality. This means graphing the equation that we get if we replace the inequality sign with an equals sign. If the inequality is strict (> or <), we graph the border with a dashed or dotted line; if it is not strict (≥ or ≤), we use a solid line. We can then test any point not on the border to see if it satisfies the inequality. If it does, we shade in that side of the border; if not, we shade in the other side. As an example, consider $y > 2x + 2$. To graph this inequality, we first graph the border, $y = 2x + 2$. Since it is a strict inequality, we use a dashed line. Then, we choose a test point. This can be any point not on the border; in this case, we will choose the origin, $(0, 0)$. (This makes the calculation easy and is generally a good choice unless the border passes through the origin.) Putting this into the original inequality, we get $0 > 2(0) + 2$, i.e. $0 > 2$. This is *not* true, so we shade in the side of the border that does *not* include the point $(0, 0)$:

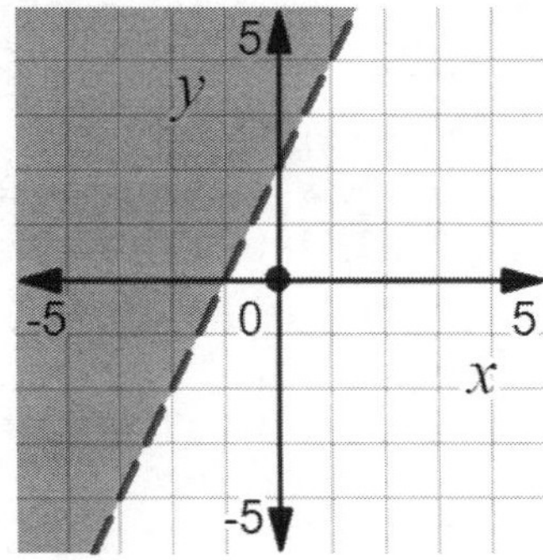

Graphing Compound Inequalities in Two Variables

One way to graph a compound inequality in two variables is to first graph each of the component inequalities. For an *and* inequality, we then shade in only the parts where the two graphs overlap; for an *or* inequality, we shade in any region that pertains to either of the individual inequalities.

Consider the graph of "$y \geq x - 1$ *and* $y \leq -x$":

We first shade in the individual inequalities:

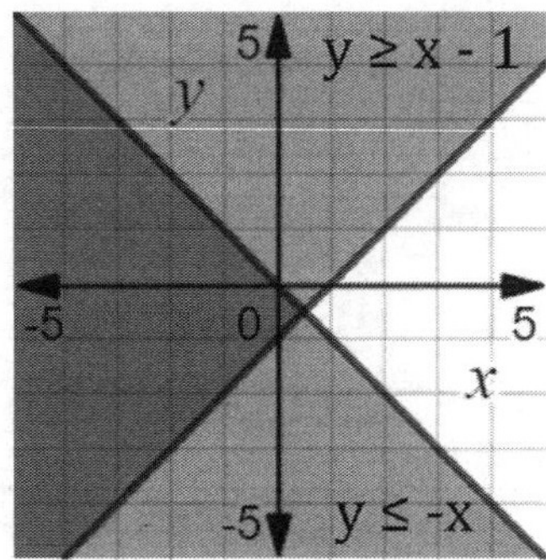

Now, since the compound inequality has an *and*, we only leave shaded the overlap—the part that pertains to *both* inequalities:

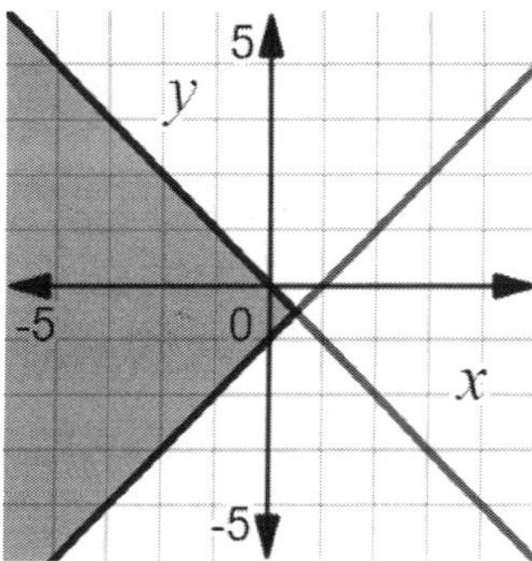

If instead the inequality had been "$y \geq x - 1$ *or* $y \leq -x$," our final graph would involve the *total* shaded area:

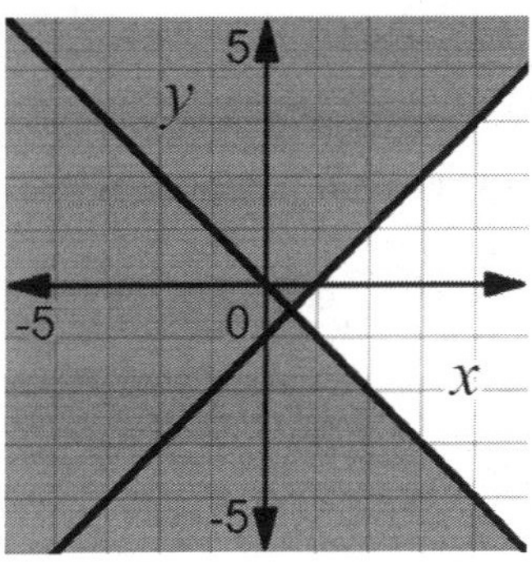

Practice

P1. Analyze the following inequalities:

(a) $2 - |x + 1| < 3$
(b) $2(x - 1)^2 + 7 \leq 1$

P2. Graph the following on a number line:

(a) $x \geq 3$
(b) $-2 \leq x \leq 6$
(c) $|x| < 2$

Practice Solutions

P1. (a) Subtracting 2 from both sides yields $-|x + 1| < 1$; multiplying by -1—and flipping the inequality, since we're multiplying by a negative number—yields $|x + 1| > -1$. But since the absolute value cannot be negative, it's *always* greater than -1, so this inequality is true for all values of x.

(b) Subtracting 7 from both sides yields $2(x - 1)^2 \leq -6$; dividing by 2 yields $(x - 1)^2 \leq -3$. But $(x - 1)^2$ must be nonnegative, and hence cannot be less than or equal to -3; this inequality has no solution.

P2. (a) We would graph the inequality $x \geq 3$ by putting a solid circle at 3 and filling in the part of the line to the right:

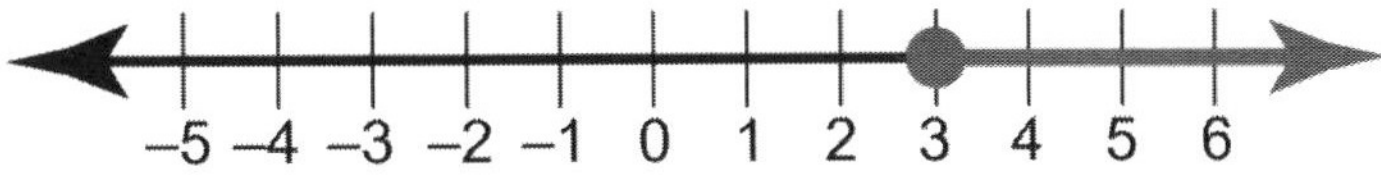

(b) The inequality $-2 \leq x \leq 6$ is equivalent to "$x \geq -2$ and $x \leq 6$." To plot this compound inequality, we first put solid circles at -2 and 6, and then fill in the part of the line *between* these circles:

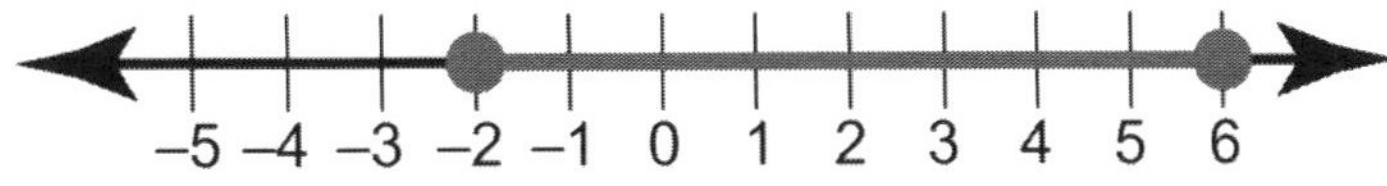

(c) The inequality $|x| < 2$ can be rewritten as "$x > -2$ and $x < 2$." We place hollow circles at the points –2 and 2 and fill in the part of the line between them:

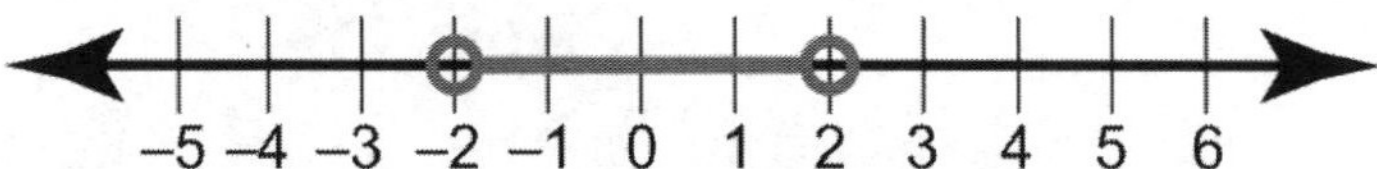

Systems of Equations

Solving Systems of Equations

Systems of equations are a set of simultaneous equations that all use the same variables. A solution to a system of equations must be true for each equation in the system. **Consistent systems** are those with at least one solution. **Inconsistent systems** are systems of equations that have no solution.

Review Video: Systems of Equations
Visit mometrix.com/academy and enter code: 658153

Substitution

To solve a system of linear equations by **substitution**, start with the easier equation and solve for one of the variables. Express this variable in terms of the other variable. Substitute this expression in the other equation, and solve for the other variable. The solution should be expressed in the form (x, y). Substitute the values into both of the original equations to check your answer. Consider the following system of equations:

$$x + 6y = 15$$
$$3x - 12y = 18$$

Solving the first equation for x: $x = 15 - 6y$

Substitute this value in place of x in the second equation, and solve for y:

$$\begin{aligned} 3(15 - 6y) - 12y &= 18 \\ 45 - 18y - 12y &= 18 \\ 30y &= 27 \\ y &= \frac{27}{30} = \frac{9}{10} = 0.9 \end{aligned}$$

Plug this value for y back into the first equation to solve for x:

$$x = 15 - 6(0.9) = 15 - 5.4 = 9.6$$

Check both equations if you have time:

$$\begin{aligned} 9.6 + 6(0.9) &= 15 \\ 9.6 + 5.4 &= 15 \\ 15 &= 15 \end{aligned} \qquad \begin{aligned} 3(9.6) - 12(0.9) &= 18 \\ 28.8 - 10.8 &= 18 \\ 18 &= 18 \end{aligned}$$

Therefore, the solution is (9.6, 0.9).

Elimination

To solve a system of equations using **elimination**, begin by rewriting both equations in standard form $Ax + By = C$. Check to see if the coefficients of one pair of like variables add to zero. If not, multiply one or both of the equations by a non-zero number to make one set of like variables add to zero. Add the two equations to solve for one of the variables. Substitute this value into one of the original equations to solve for the other variable. Check your work by substituting into the other equation. Now, let's look at solving the following system using the elimination method:

$$\begin{aligned} 5x + 6y &= 4 \\ x + 2y &= 4 \end{aligned}$$

If we multiply the second equation by -3, we can eliminate the y terms:

$$\begin{aligned} 5x + 6y &= 4 \\ -3x - 6y &= -12 \end{aligned}$$

Add the equations together and solve for x:

$$\begin{aligned} 2x &= -8 \\ x &= \frac{-8}{2} = -4 \end{aligned}$$

Plug the value for x back in to either of the original equations and solve for y:

$$\begin{aligned} -4 + 2y &= 4 \\ y &= \frac{4+4}{2} = 4 \end{aligned}$$

Check both equations if you have time:

$$\begin{aligned} 5(-4) + 6(4) &= 4 \\ -20 + 24 &= 4 \\ 4 &= 4 \end{aligned} \qquad \begin{aligned} -4 + 2(4) &= 4 \\ -4 + 8 &= 4 \\ 4 &= 4 \end{aligned}$$

Therefore, the solution is (-4, 4).

Review Video: Substitution and Elimination for Solving Linear Systems
Visit mometrix.com/academy and enter code: 958611

GRAPHICALLY

To solve a system of linear equations **graphically**, plot both equations on the same graph. The solution of the equations is the point where both lines cross. If the lines do not cross (are parallel), then there is **no solution**.

For example, consider the following system of equations:

$$\begin{aligned} y &= 2x + 7 \\ y &= -x + 1 \end{aligned}$$

Since these equations are given in slope-intercept form, they are easy to graph; the y intercepts of the lines are $(0, 7)$ and $(0, 1)$. The respective slopes are 2 and –1, thus the graphs look like this:

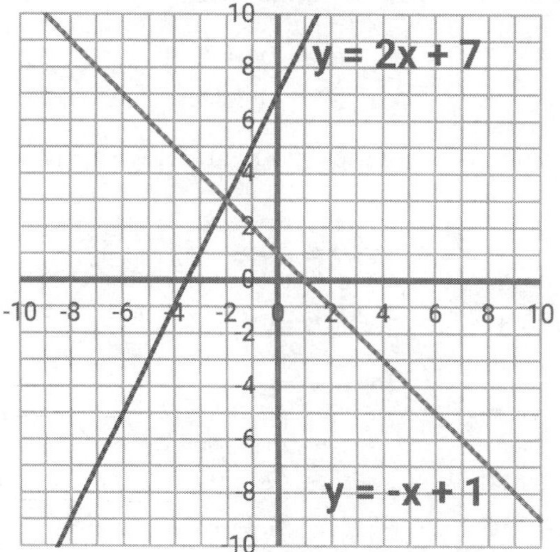

The two lines intersect at the point $(-2, 3)$, thus this is the solution to the system of equations.

Solving a system graphically is generally only practical if both coordinates of the solution are integers; otherwise the intersection will lie between gridlines on the graph and the coordinates will be difficult or impossible to determine exactly. It also helps if, as in this example, the equations are in slope-intercept form or some other form that makes them easy to graph. Otherwise, another method of solution (by substitution or elimination) is likely to be more useful.

Solving Systems of Equations Using the Trace Feature

Using the **trace feature** on a calculator requires that you rewrite each equation, isolating the y-variable on one side of the equal sign. Enter both equations in the graphing calculator and plot the graphs simultaneously. Use the trace cursor to find where the two lines cross. Use the zoom feature if necessary to obtain more accurate results. Always check your answer by substituting into the original equations. The trace method is likely to be less accurate than other methods due to the resolution of graphing calculators, but is a useful tool to provide an approximate answer.

Calculations Using Points

Sometimes you need to perform calculations using only points on a graph as input data. Using points, you can determine what the **midpoint** and **distance** are. If you know the equation for a line you can calculate the distance between the line and the point.

To find the **midpoint** of two points (x_1, y_1) and (x_2, y_2), average the x-coordinates to get the x-coordinate of the midpoint, and average the y-coordinates to get the y-coordinate of the midpoint. The formula is: $\left(\frac{x_1+x_2}{2}, \frac{y_1+y_2}{2}\right)$.

The **distance** between two points is the same as the length of the hypotenuse of a right triangle with the two given points as endpoints, and the two sides of the right triangle parallel to the x-axis and y-axis, respectively. The length of the segment parallel to the x-axis is the difference between the x-coordinates of the two points. The length of the segment parallel to the y-axis is the difference between the y-coordinates of the two points. Use the Pythagorean theorem $a^2 + b^2 = c^2$ or $c = \sqrt{a^2 + b^2}$ to find the distance. The formula is $\text{d} = \sqrt{(x_2 - x_1)^2 + (y_2 - y_1)^2}$.

When a line is in the format $Ax + By + C = 0$, where A, B, and C are coefficients, you can use a point (x_1, y_1) not on the line and apply the formula $d = \frac{|Ax_1+By_1+C|}{\sqrt{A^2+B^2}}$ to find the distance between the line and the point (x_1, y_1).

PRACTICE

P1. Solve the following systems of equations:

(a) $$\begin{aligned} 3x + 4y &= 9 \\ -12x + 7y &= 10 \end{aligned}$$

(b) $$\begin{aligned} -3x + 2y &= -1 \\ 4x - 5y &= 6 \end{aligned}$$

P2. Find the distance and midpoint between points (2, 4) and (8,6).

PRACTICE SOLUTIONS

P1. (a) If we multiply the first equation by 4, we can eliminate the x terms:

$$\begin{aligned} 12x + 16y &= 36 \\ -12x + 7y &= 10 \end{aligned}$$

Add the equations together and solve for y:

$$\begin{aligned} 23y &= 46 \\ y &= 2 \end{aligned}$$

Plug the value for y back in to either of the original equations and solve for x:

$$\begin{aligned} 3x + 4(2) &= 9 \\ x &= \frac{9-8}{3} = \frac{1}{3} \end{aligned}$$

The solution is $\left(\frac{1}{3}, 2\right)$

(b) Solving the first equation for y:

$$\begin{aligned} -3x + 2y &= -1 \\ 2y &= 3x - 1 \\ y &= \frac{3x-1}{2} \end{aligned}$$

Substitute this expression in place of y in the second equation, and solve for x:

$$\begin{aligned} 4x - 5\left(\frac{3x-1}{2}\right) &= 6 \\ 4x - \frac{15x}{2} + \frac{5}{2} &= 6 \\ 8x - 15x + 5 &= 12 \\ -7x &= 7 \\ x &= -1 \end{aligned}$$

Plug the value for x back in to either of the original equations and solve for y:

$$-3(-1) + 2y = -1$$
$$3 + 2y = -1$$
$$2y = -4$$
$$y = -2$$

The solution is $(-1, -2)$

P2. Use the formulas for distance and midpoint:

$$\text{Distance} = \sqrt{(x_2 - x_1)^2 + (y_2 - y_1)^2}$$
$$= \sqrt{(8-2)^2 + (6-4)^2}$$
$$= \sqrt{(6)^2 + (2)^2}$$
$$= \sqrt{36 + 4}$$
$$= \sqrt{40} \text{ or } 2\sqrt{10}$$

$$\text{Midpoint} = \left(\frac{x_1 + x_2}{2}, \frac{y_1 + y_2}{2}\right)$$
$$= \left(\frac{2+8}{2}, \frac{4+6}{2}\right)$$
$$= \left(\frac{10}{2}, \frac{10}{2}\right)$$
$$= (5,5)$$

Polynomial Algebra

POLYNOMIALS

Polynomials are made up of monomials and polynomials. A **monomial** is a single variable or product of constants and variables, such as x, $2x$, or $\frac{2}{x}$. There will never be addition or subtraction symbols in a monomial. Like monomials have like variables, but they may have different coefficients. **Polynomials** are algebraic expressions which use addition and subtraction to combine two or more monomials. Two terms make a **binomial**, three terms make a **trinomial**, etc. The **degree of a monomial** is the sum of the exponents of the variables. The **degree of a polynomial** is the highest degree of any individual term.

Review Video: Polynomials
Visit mometrix.com/academy and enter code: 305005

SIMPLIFYING POLYNOMIALS

Simplifying polynomials requires combining like terms. The like terms in a polynomial expression are those that have the same variable raised to the same power. It is often helpful to connect the like terms with arrows or lines in order to separate them from the other monomials. Once you have determined the like terms, you can rearrange the polynomial by placing them together. Remember to include the sign that is in front of each term. Once the like terms are placed together, you can apply each operation and simplify. When adding and subtracting polynomials, only add and subtract the **coefficient**, or the number part; the variable and exponent stay the same.

THE FOIL METHOD

In general, multiplying polynomials is done by multiplying each term in one polynomial by each term in the other and adding the results. In the specific case for multiplying binomials, there is useful acronym, FOIL, that can help you make sure to cover each combination of terms. The **FOIL method** for $(Ax + By)(Cx + Dy)$ would be:

F	Multiply the *first* terms of each binomial	$(\overbrace{Ax}^{first} + By)(\overbrace{Cx}^{first} + Dy)$	ACx^2

O	Multiply the *outer* terms	$(\overset{outer}{\widehat{Ax}} + By)(Cx + \overset{outer}{\widehat{Dy}})$	$ADxy$
I	Multiply the *inner* terms	$(Ax + \overset{inner}{\widehat{By}})(\overset{inner}{\widehat{Cx}} + Dy)$	$BCxy$
L	Multiply the *last* terms of each binomial	$(Ax + \overset{last}{\widehat{By}})(Cx + \overset{last}{\widehat{Dy}})$	BDy^2

Then add up the result of each and combine like terms: $ACx^2 + (AD + BC)xy + BDy^2$.

For example, using the FOIL method on binomials $(x + 2)$ and $(x - 3)$:

$$\begin{aligned} &\text{First:} && (\boxed{x} + 2)(\boxed{x} + (-3)) && \rightarrow && (x)(x) &&= x^2 \\ &\text{Outer:} && (\boxed{x} + 2)(x + \boxed{(-3)}) && \rightarrow && (x)(-3) &&= -3x \\ &\text{Inner:} && (x + \boxed{2})(\boxed{x} + (-3)) && \rightarrow && (2)(x) &&= 2x \\ &\text{Last:} && (x + \boxed{2})(x + \boxed{(-3)}) && \rightarrow && (2)(-3) &&= -6 \end{aligned}$$

This results in: $(x^2) + (-3x) + (2x) + (-6)$

Combine like terms: $x^2 + (-3 + 2)x + (-6) = x^2 - x - 6$

Review Video: Multiplying Terms Using the FOIL Method
Visit mometrix.com/academy and enter code: 854792

Dividing Polynomials

To divide polynomials, set up a long division problem, dividing a polynomial by either a monomial or another polynomial of equal or lesser degree.

When **dividing by a monomial**, divide each term of the polynomial by the monomial.

When **dividing by a polynomial**, begin by arranging the terms of each polynomial in order of one variable. You may arrange in ascending or descending order, but be consistent with both polynomials. To get the first term of the quotient, divide the first term of the dividend by the first term of the divisor. Multiply the first term of the quotient by the entire divisor and subtract that product from the dividend. Repeat for the second and successive terms until you either get a remainder of zero or a remainder whose degree is less than the degree of the divisor. If the quotient has a remainder, write the answer as a mixed expression in the form:

$$\text{quotient} + \frac{\text{remainder}}{\text{divisor}}$$

For example, we can evaluate the following expression in the same way as long division:

$$\frac{x^3 - 3x^2 - 2x + 5}{x - 5}$$

$$\begin{array}{r|l} & x^2 \quad + 2x \quad + 8 \\ x - 5 & x^3 - 3x^2 - 2x + 5 \\ & \underline{x^3 - 5x^2} \\ & \quad 2x^2 - 2x \\ & \quad \underline{2x^2 - 10x} \\ & \qquad 8x + 5 \\ & \qquad \underline{8x + 40} \\ & \qquad\quad 45 \end{array}$$

$$\frac{x^3 - 3x^2 - 2x + 5}{x - 5} = x^2 + 2x + 8 + \frac{45}{x - 5}$$

When **factoring** a polynomial, first check for a common monomial factor, that is look to see if each coefficient has a common factor or if each term has an x in it. If the factor is a trinomial but not a perfect trinomial square, look for a factorable form, such as one of these:

$$x^2 + (a + b)x + ab = (x + a)(x + b)$$
$$(ac)x^2 + (ad + bc)x + bd = (ax + b)(cx + d)$$

For factors with four terms, look for groups to factor. Once you have found the factors, write the original polynomial as the product of all the factors. Make sure all of the polynomial factors are prime. Monomial factors may be *prime* or *composite*. Check your work by multiplying the factors to make sure you get the original polynomial.

Below are patterns of some special products to remember to help make factoring easier:

- Perfect trinomial squares: $x^2 + 2xy + y^2 = (x + y)^2$ or $x^2 - 2xy + y^2 = (x - y)^2$
- Difference between two squares: $x^2 - y^2 = (x + y)(x - y)$
- Sum of two cubes: $x^3 + y^3 = (x + y)(x^2 - xy + y^2)$
  - Note: the second factor is *not* the same as a perfect trinomial square, so do not try to factor it further.
- Difference between two cubes: $x^3 - y^3 = (x - y)(x^2 + xy + y^2)$
  - Again, the second factor is *not* the same as a perfect trinomial square.
- Perfect cubes: $x^3 + 3x^2y + 3xy^2 + y^3 = (x + y)^3$ and $x^3 - 3x^2y + 3xy^2 - y^3 = (x - y)^3$

RATIONAL EXPRESSIONS

Rational expressions are fractions with polynomials in both the numerator and the denominator; the value of the polynomial in the denominator cannot be equal to zero. Be sure to keep track of values that make the denominator of the original expression zero as the final result inherits the same restrictions. For example, a denominator of $x - 3$ indicates that the expression is not defined when $x = 3$ and as such, regardless of any operations done to the expression, it remains undefined there.

To **add or subtract** rational expressions, first find the common denominator, then rewrite each fraction as an equivalent fraction with the common denominator. Finally, add or subtract the numerators to get the numerator of the answer, and keep the common denominator as the denominator of the answer.

When **multiplying** rational expressions factor each polynomial and cancel like factors (a factor which appears in both the numerator and the denominator). Then, multiply all remaining factors in the numerator to get the numerator of the product, and multiply the remaining factors in the denominator to get the denominator of the product. Remember: cancel entire factors, not individual terms.

To **divide** rational expressions, take the reciprocal of the divisor (the rational expression you are dividing by) and multiply by the dividend.

Review Video: Rational Expressions
Visit mometrix.com/academy and enter code: 415183

SIMPLIFYING RATIONAL EXPRESSIONS

To simplify a rational expression, factor the numerator and denominator completely. Factors that are the same and appear in the numerator and denominator have a ratio of 1. For example, look at the following expression:

$$\frac{x-1}{1-x^2}$$

The denominator, $(1-x^2)$, is a difference of squares. It can be factored as $(1-x)(1+x)$. The factor $1-x$ and the numerator $x-1$ are opposites and have a ratio of -1. Rewrite the numerator as $-1(1-x)$. So, the rational expression can be simplified as follows:

$$\frac{x-1}{1-x^2}=\frac{-1(1-x)}{(1-x)(1+x)}=\frac{-1}{1+x}$$

Note that since the original expression is only defined for $x \neq \{-1,1\}$, the simplified expression has the same restrictions.

Review Video: Reducing Rational Expressions
Visit mometrix.com/academy and enter code: 788868

PRACTICE

P1. Expand the following polynomials:

(a) $(x+3)(x-7)(2x)$

(b) $(x+2)^2(x-2)^2$

(c) $(x^2+5x+5)(3x-1)$

P2. Evaluate the following rational expressions:

(a) $\frac{x^3-2x^2-5x+6}{3x+6}$

(b) $\frac{x^2+4x+4}{4-x^2}$

PRACTICE SOLUTIONS

P1. (a) Apply the FOIL method and the distributive property of multiplication:

$$\begin{aligned}(x+3)(x-7)(2x) &= (x^2-7x+3x-21)(2x)\\ &= (x^2-4x-21)(2x)\\ &= 2x^3-8x^2-42x\end{aligned}$$

(b) Note the difference of squares form:

$$\begin{aligned}(x+2)^2(x-2)^2 &= (x+2)(x+2)(x-2)(x-2)\\ &= [(x+2)(x-2)][(x+2)(x-2)]\\ &= (x^2-4)(x^2-4)\\ &= x^4-8x^2+16\end{aligned}$$

(c) Multiply each pair of monomials and combine like terms:

$$\begin{aligned}(x^2 + 5x + 5)(3x - 1) &= 3x^3 + 15x^2 + 15x - x^2 - 5x - 5 \\ &= 3x^3 + 14x^2 + 10x - 5\end{aligned}$$

P2. (a) Rather than trying to factor the fourth-degree polynomial, we can use long division:

$$\frac{x^3 - 2x^2 - 5x + 6}{3x + 6} = \frac{x^3 - 2x^2 - 5x + 6}{3(x + 2)}$$

$$\begin{array}{r|rrrr} & x^2 & -4x & +3 & \\ \hline x+2 & x^3 & -2x^2 & -5x & +6 \\ & x^3 & +2x^2 & & \\ \hline & & -4x^2 & -5x & \\ & & -4x^2 & -8x & \\ \hline & & & 3x & +6 \\ & & & 3x & +6 \\ \hline & & & & 0 \end{array}$$

$$\frac{x^3 - 2x^2 - 5x + 6}{3(x + 2)} = \frac{x^2 - 4x + 3}{3}$$

Note that since the original expression is only defined for $x \neq \{-2\}$, the simplified expression has the same restrictions.

(b) The denominator, $(4 - x^2)$, is a difference of squares. It can be factored as $(2 - x)(2 + x)$. The numerator, $(x^2 + 4x + 4)$, is a perfect square. It can be factored as $(x + 2)(x + 2)$. So, the rational expression can be simplified as follows:

$$\frac{x^2 + 4x + 4}{4 - x^2} = \frac{(x + 2)(x + 2)}{(2 - x)(2 + x)} = \frac{(x + 2)}{(2 - x)}$$

Note that since the original expression is only defined for $x \neq \{-2,2\}$, the simplified expression has the same restrictions.

Quadratics

Solving Quadratic Equations

Quadratic equations are a special set of trinomials of the form $y = ax^2 + bx + c$ that occur commonly in math and real world applications. The **roots** of a quadratic equation are the solutions that satisfy the equation when $y = 0$; in other words, where the graph touches the x-axis. There are several ways to determine these solutions including using the quadratic formula, factoring, completing the square, and graphing the function.

Review Video: Finding the Missing Roots
Visit mometrix.com/academy and enter code: 198376

Review Video: Changing Constants in Graphs of Functions: Quadratic Equations
Visit mometrix.com/academy and enter code: 476276

Quadratic Formula

The **quadratic formula** is used to solve quadratic equations when other methods are more difficult. To use the quadratic formula to solve a quadratic equation, begin by rewriting the equation in standard form $ax^2 + bx + c = 0$, where a, b, and c are coefficients. Once you have identified the values of the coefficients, substitute those values into the quadratic formula

$$x = \frac{-b \pm \sqrt{b^2 - 4ac}}{2a}$$

Evaluate the equation and simplify the expression. Again, check each root by substituting into the original equation. In the quadratic formula, the portion of the formula under the radical $(b^2 - 4ac)$ is called the **discriminant**. If the discriminant is zero, there is only one root: $-\frac{b}{2a}$. If the discriminant is positive, there are two different real roots. If the discriminant is negative, there are no real roots, you will instead find complex roots. Often these solutions don't make sense in context and are ignored.

Review Video: Using the Quadratic Formula
Visit mometrix.com/academy and enter code: 163102

Factoring

To solve a quadratic equation by factoring, begin by rewriting the equation in standard form, $x^2 + bx + c = 0$. Remember that the goal of factoring is to find numbers f and g such that $(x + f)(x + g) = x^2 + (f + g)x + fg$, in other words $(f + g) = b$ and $fg = c$ or . This can be a really useful method when b and c are integers. Determine the factors of c and look for pairs that could sum to b.

For example, consider finding the roots of $x^2 + 6x - 16 = 0$. The factors of -16 include, -4 and 4, -8 and 2, -2 and 8, -1 and 16, and 1 and -16. The factors that sum to 6 are -2 and 8. Write these factors as the product of two binomials, $0 = (x - 2)(x + 8)$. Finally, since these binomials multiply together to equal zero, set them each equal to zero and solve each for x. This results in $x - 2 = 0$, which simplifies to $x = 2$ and $x + 8 = 0$, which simplifies to $x = -8$. Therefore, the roots of the equation are 2 and -8.

Review Video: Factoring Quadratic Equations
Visit mometrix.com/academy and enter code: 336566

Completing the Square

One way to find the roots of a quadratic equation is to find a way to manipulate it such that it follows the form of a perfect square $(x^2 + 2px + p^2)$ by adding and subtracting a constant. This process is called **completing the square**. In other words, if you are given a quadratic that is not a perfect square, $x^2 + bx + c = 0$, you can find a constant d that could be added in to make it a perfect square:

$$x^2 + bx + c + (d - d) = 0; \ \{\text{Let } b = 2p \text{ and } c + d = p^2\}$$
$$\text{then: } x^2 + 2px + p^2 - d = 0 \text{ and } d = \frac{b^2}{4} - c$$

Once you have completed the square you can find the roots of the resulting equation:

$$x^2 + 2px + p^2 - d = 0$$
$$(x + p)^2 = d$$
$$x + p = \pm\sqrt{d}$$
$$x = -p \pm \sqrt{d}$$

It is worth noting that substituting the original expressions into this solution gives the same result as the quadratic formula where $a = 1$:

$$x = -p \pm \sqrt{d} = -\frac{b}{2} \pm \sqrt{\frac{b^2}{4} - c} = -\frac{b}{2} \pm \frac{\sqrt{b^2 - 4c}}{2} = \frac{-b \pm \sqrt{b^2 - 4c}}{2}$$

Completing the square can be seen as arranging block representations of each of the terms to be as close to a square as possible and then filling in the gaps. For example, consider the quadratic expression $x^2 + 6x + 2$:

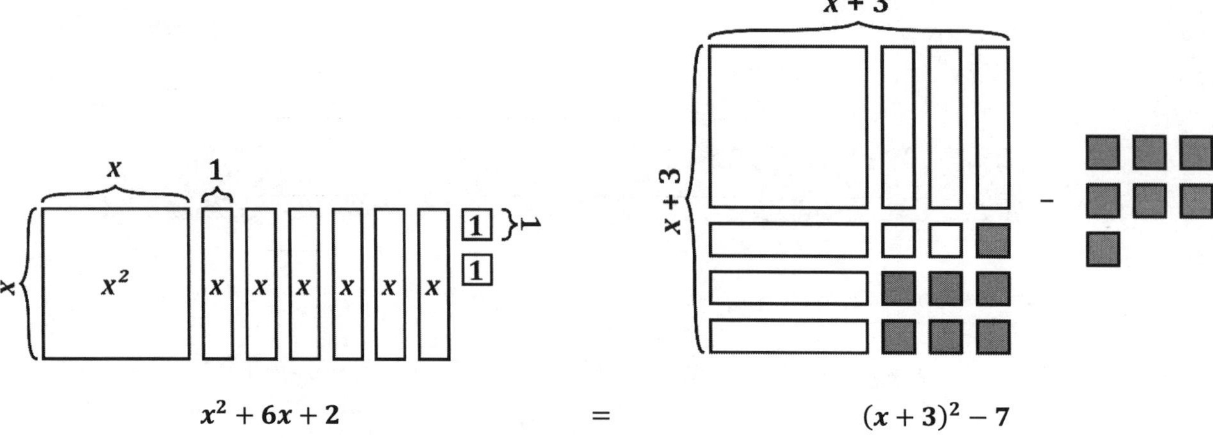

Using Given Roots to Find Quadratic Equation

One way to find the roots of a quadratic equation is to factor the equation and use the **zero product property**, setting each factor of the equation equal to zero to find the corresponding root. We can use this technique in reverse to find an equation given its roots. Each root corresponds to a linear equation which in turn corresponds to a factor of the quadratic equation.

For example, we can find a quadratic equation whose roots are $x = 2$ and $x = -1$. The root $x = 2$ corresponds to the equation $x - 2 = 0$, and the root $x = -1$ corresponds to the equation $x + 1 = 0$.

These two equations correspond to the factors $(x - 2)$ and $(x + 1)$, from which we can derive the equation $(x - 2)(x + 1) = 0$, or $x^2 - x - 2 = 0$.

Any integer multiple of this entire equation will also yield the same roots, as the integer will simply cancel out when the equation is factored. For example, $2x^2 - 2x - 4 = 0$ factors as $2(x - 2)(x + 1) = 0$.

Solving a System of Equations Consisting of a Linear Equation and a Quadratic Equation

Algebraically

Generally, the simplest way to solve a system of equations consisting of a linear equation and a quadratic equation algebraically is through the method of substitution. One possible strategy is to solve the linear equation for *y* and then substitute that expression into the quadratic equation. After expansion and combining like terms, this will result in a new quadratic equation for *x* which, like all quadratic equations, may have zero, one, or two solutions. Plugging each solution for *x* back into one of the original equations will then produce the corresponding value of *y*.

For example, consider the following system of equations:

$$x + y = 1$$
$$y = (x + 3)^2 - 2$$

We can solve the linear equation for y to yield $y = -x + 1$. Substituting this expression into the quadratic equation produces $-x + 1 = (x + 3)^2 - 2$. We can simplify this equation:

$$-x + 1 = (x + 3)^2 - 2$$
$$-x + 1 = x^2 + 6x + 9 - 2$$
$$-x + 1 = x^2 + 6x + 7$$
$$0 = x^2 + 7x + 6$$

This quadratic equation can be factored as $(x + 1)(x + 6) = 0$. It therefore has two solutions: $x_1 = -1$ and $x_2 = -6$. Plugging each of these back into the original linear equation yields $y_1 = -x_1 + 1 = -(-1) + 1 = 2$ and $y_2 = -x_2 + 1 = -(-6) + 1 = 7$. Thus, this system of equations has two solutions, $(-1, 2)$ and $(-6, 7)$.

It may help to check your work by putting each x and y value back into the original equations and verifying that they do provide a solution.

Graphically

To solve a system of equations consisting of a linear equation and a quadratic equation graphically, plot both equations on the same graph. The linear equation will of course produce a straight line, while the quadratic equation will produce a parabola. These two graphs will intersect at zero, one, or two points; each point of intersection is a solution of the system.

For example, consider the following system of equations:

$$y = -2x + 2$$
$$y = -2x^2 + 4x + 2$$

The linear equation describes a line with a y-intercept of $(0, 2)$ and a slope of -2.

To graph the quadratic equation, we can first find the vertex of the parabola: the x-coordinate of the vertex is $h = -\frac{b}{2a} = -\frac{4}{2(-2)} = 1$, and the y coordinate is $k = -2(1)^2 + 4(1) + 2 = 4$. Thus, the vertex lies at $(1, 4)$. To get a feel for the rest of the parabola, we can plug in a few more values of x to find more points; by putting in $x = 2$ and $x = 3$ in the quadratic equation, we find that the points $(2, 2)$ and $(3, -4)$ lie on the parabola; by symmetry thus do $(0, 2)$ and $(-1, -4)$. We can now plot both equations:

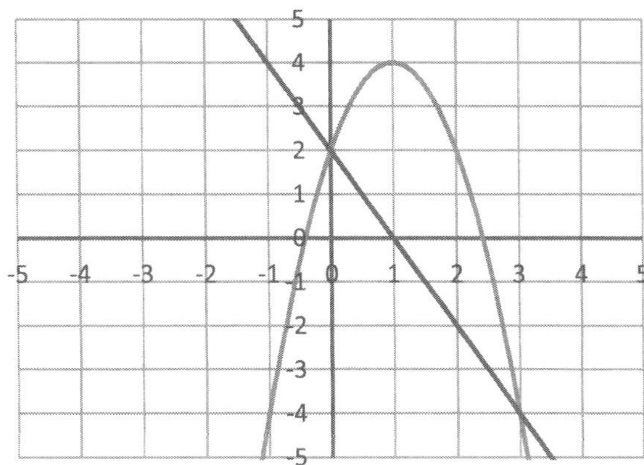

These two curves intersect at the points $(0, 2)$ and $(3, -4)$, thus these are the solutions of the equation.

PRACTICE

P1. Find the roots of $y = 2x^2 + 8x + 4$.

P2. Find a quadratic equation with roots $x = 4$ and $x = -6$.

PRACTICE SOLUTIONS

P1. First, substitute 0 in for y in the quadratic equation: $0 = 2x^2 + 8x + 4$

Next, try to factor the quadratic equation. Since $a \neq 1$, list the factors of ac, or 8:

$$(1, 8), (-1, -8), (2, 4), (-2, -4)$$

Look for the factors of ac that add up to b, or 8. Since none do, the equation cannot be factored with whole numbers. Substitute the values of a, b, and c into the quadratic formula, $x = \frac{-b \pm \sqrt{b^2 - 4ac}}{2a}$:

$$x = \frac{-8 \pm \sqrt{8^2 - 4(2)(4)}}{2(2)}$$

Use the order of operations to simplify:

$$x = \frac{-8 \pm \sqrt{64 - 32}}{4}$$
$$x = \frac{-8 \pm \sqrt{32}}{4}$$

Reduce and simplify:

$$x = \frac{-8 \pm \sqrt{(16)(2)}}{4}$$
$$x = \frac{-8 \pm 4\sqrt{2}}{4}$$
$$x = -2 \pm \sqrt{2}$$
$$x = \left(-2 + \sqrt{2}\right) \text{ and } \left(-2 - \sqrt{2}\right)$$

P2. The root $x = 4$ corresponds to the equation $x - 4 = 0$, and the root $x = -6$ corresponds to the equation $x + 6 = 0$. These two equations correspond to the factors $(x - 4)$ and $(x + 6)$, from which we can derive the equation $(x - 4)(x + 6) = 0$, or $x^2 + 2x - 24 = 0$.

Basic Functions

FUNCTION AND RELATION

When expressing functional relationships, the **variables** x and y are typically used. These values are often written as the **coordinates** (x, y). The x-value is the independent variable and the y-value is the dependent variable. A **relation** is a set of data in which there is not a unique y-value for each x-value in the dataset. This means that there can be two of the same x-values assigned to different y-values. A relation is simply a relationship between the x and y-values in each coordinate but does not apply to the relationship between the values of x and y in the data set. A **function** is a relation where one quantity depends on the other. For example, the amount of money that you make depends on the number of hours that you work. In a function, each x-value in the data set has one unique y-value because the y-value depends on the x-value.

Review Video: Definition of a Function
Visit mometrix.com/academy and enter code: 784611

Functions

A function has exactly one value of **output variable** (dependent variable) for each value of the **input variable** (independent variable). The set of all values for the input variable (here assumed to be x) is the domain of the function, and the set of all corresponding values of output variable (here assumed to be y) is the range of the function. When looking at a graph of an equation, the easiest way to determine if the equation is a function or not is to conduct the vertical line test. If a vertical line drawn through any value of x crosses the graph in more than one place, the equation is not a function.

Finding the Domain and Range of a Function

The **domain** of a function $f(x)$ is the set of all input values for which the function is defined. The **range** of a function $f(x)$ is the set of all possible output values of the function—that is, of every possible value of $f(x)$, for any value of x in the function's domain. For a function expressed in a table, every input-output pair—is given explicitly. To find the domain, we just list all the x values and to find the range, we just list all the values of $f(x)$. Consider the following example:

x	-1	4	2	1	0	3	8	6
$f(x)$	3	0	3	−1	−1	2	4	6

In this case, the domain would be {-1, 4, 2, 1, 0, 3, 8, 6}, or, putting them in ascending order, {-1, 0, 1, 2, 3, 4, 6, 8}. (Putting the values in ascending order isn't strictly necessary, but generally makes the set easier to read.) The range would be {3, 0, 3, −1, −1, 2, 4, 6}. Note that some of these values appear more than once. This is entirely permissible for a function; while each value of x must be matched to a unique value of $f(x)$, the converse is not true. We don't need to list each value more than once, so eliminating duplicates, the range is {3, 0, −1, 2, 4, 6}, or, putting them in ascending order, {−1, 0, 2, 3, 4, 6}.

Note that by definition of a function, no input value can be matched to more than one output value. It is good to double check to make sure that the data given follows this and is therefore actually a function.

Determining a Function

You can determine whether an equation is a **function** by substituting different values into the equation for x. These values are called input values. All possible input values are referred to as the **domain.** The result of substituting these values into the equation is called the output, or **range.** You can display and organize these numbers in a data table. A **data table** contains the values for x and y, which you can also list as coordinates. In order for a function to exist, the table cannot contain any repeating x-values that correspond with different y-values. If each x-coordinate has a unique y-coordinate, the table contains a function. However, there can be repeating y-values that correspond with different x-values. An example of this is when the function contains an exponent. For example, if $x^2 = y$, $2^2 = 4$, and $(-2)^2 = 4$.

Review Video: Basics of Functions
Visit mometrix.com/academy and enter code: 822500

Writing a Function Rule Using a Table

If given a set of data, place the corresponding x and y-values into a table and analyze the relationship between them. Consider what you can do to each x-value to obtain the corresponding y-value. Try adding or subtracting different numbers to and from x and then try multiplying or dividing different numbers to and from x. If none of these **operations** give you the y-value, try combining the operations.

Once you find a rule that works for one pair, make sure to try it with each additional set of ordered pairs in the table. If the same operation or combination of operations satisfies each set of coordinates, then the table contains a function. The rule is then used to write the equation of the function in "$y =$" form.

Direct and Inverse Variations of Variables

Variables that vary directly are those that either both increase at the same rate or both decrease at the same rate. For example, in the functions $y = kx$ or $y = kx^n$, where *k* and *n* are positive, the value of *y* increases as the value of *x* increases and decreases as the value of *x* decreases.

Variables that vary inversely are those where one increases while the other decreases. For example, in the functions $y = \frac{k}{x}$ or $y = \frac{k}{x^n}$ where *k* and *n* are positive, the value of *y* increases as the value of *x* decreases, and decreases as the value of *x* increases.

In both cases, *k* is the constant of variation.

Properties of Functions

There are many different ways to classify functions based on their structure or behavior. Important features of functions include:

- **End behavior**: the behavior of the function at extreme values ($f(x)$ as $x \to \pm\infty$)
- ***y*-intercept**: the value of function at $f(0)$
- **Roots**: the values of *x* where the function equals zero ($f(x) = 0$)
- **Extrema**: minimum or maximum values of the function or where the function changes direction ($f(x) \geq k$ or $f(x) \leq k$)

Classification of Functions

An **invertible function** is defined as a function, $f(x)$, for which there is another function, $f^{-1}(x)$, such that $f^{-1}(f(x)) = x$. For example, if $f(x) = 3x - 2$ the inverse function, $f^{-1}(x)$, can be found:

$$x = 3(f^{-1}(x)) - 2$$
$$\frac{x+2}{3} = f^{-1}(x)$$

$$\begin{aligned} f^{-1}(f(x)) &= \frac{3x - 2 + 2}{3} \\ &= \frac{3x}{3} \\ &= x \end{aligned}$$

Note that $f^{-1}(x)$ is a valid function over all values of *x*.

In a **one-to-one function**, each value of *x* has exactly one value for *y* on the coordinate plane (this is the definition of a function) and each value of *y* has exactly one value for *x*. While the vertical line test will determine if a graph is that of a function, the horizontal line test will determine if a function is a one-to-one function. If a horizontal line drawn at any value of *y* intersects the graph in more than one place, the graph is not that of a one-to-one function. Do not make the mistake of using the horizontal line test exclusively in determining if a graph is that of a one-to-one function. A one-to-one function must pass both the vertical line test and the horizontal line test. As such, one-to-one functions are invertible functions.

A **many-to-one function** is a function whereby the relation is a function, but the inverse of the function is not a function. In other words, each element in the domain is mapped to one and only one element in the range. However, one or more elements in the range may be mapped to the same element in the domain. A graph of a many-to-one function would pass the vertical line test, but not the horizontal line test. One result of this is the fact that many-to-one functions are not invertible.

A **monotone function** is a function whose graph either constantly increases or constantly decreases. Examples include the functions $f(x) = x$, $f(x) = -x$, or $f(x) = x^3$.

An **even function** has a graph that is symmetric with respect to the y-axis and satisfies the equation $f(x) = f(-x)$. Examples include the functions $f(x) = x^2$ and $f(x) = ax^n$, where a is any real number and n is a positive even integer.

An **odd function** has a graph that is symmetric with respect to the origin and satisfies the equation $f(x) = -f(-x)$. Examples include the functions $f(x) = x^3$ and $f(x) = ax^n$, where a is any real number and n is a positive odd integer.

Constant functions are given by the equation $f(x) = b$, where b is a real number. There is no independent variable present in the equation, so the function has a constant value for all x. The graph of a constant function is a horizontal line of slope 0 that is positioned b units from the x-axis. If b is positive, the line is above the x-axis; if b is negative, the line is below the x-axis.

Identity functions are identified by the equation $f(x) = x$, where every value of the function is equal to its corresponding value of x. The only zero is the point $(0, 0)$. The graph is a line with slope of 1.

In **linear functions**, the value of the function changes in direct proportion to x. The rate of change,represented by the slope on its graph, is constant throughout. The standard form of a linear equation is $ax + cy = d$, where a, c, and d are real numbers. As a function, this equation is commonly in the form $y = mx + b$ or $f(x) = mx + b$ where $m = -\frac{a}{c}$ and $b = \frac{d}{c}$. This is known as the slope-intercept form, because the coefficients give the slope of the graphed function (m) and its y-intercept (b). Solve the equation $mx + b = 0$ for x to get $x = -\frac{b}{m}$, which is the only zero of the function. The domain and range are both the set of all real numbers.

Algebraic functions are those that exclusively use polynomials and roots. These would include polynomial functions, rational functions, square root functions, and all combinations of these functions, such as polynomials as the radicand. These combinations may be joined by addition, subtraction, multiplication, or division, but may not include variables as exponents.

ABSOLUTE VALUE FUNCTIONS

An **absolute value function** is in the format $f(x) = |ax + b|$. Like other functions, the domain is the set of all real numbers. However, because absolute value indicates positive numbers, the range is limited to positive real numbers. To find the zero of an absolute value function, set the portion inside the absolute value sign equal to zero and solve for x. An absolute value function is also known as a piecewise function because it must be solved in pieces – one for if the value inside the absolute value sign is positive, and one for if the value is negative. The function can be expressed as

$$f(x) = \begin{cases} ax + b \text{ if } ax + b \geq 0 \\ -(ax + b) \text{ if } ax + b < 0 \end{cases}$$

This will allow for an accurate statement of the range. The graph of an example absolute value function, $f(x) = |2x - 1|$, is below:

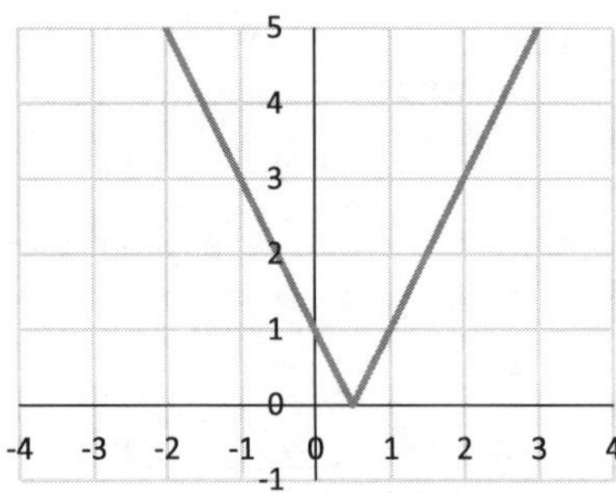

Piecewise Functions

A **piecewise function** is a function that has different definitions on two or more different intervals. The following, for instance, is one example of a piecewise-defined function:

$$f(x) = \begin{cases} x^2, & x < 0 \\ x, & 0 \le x \le 2 \\ (x-2)^2, & x > 2 \end{cases}$$

To graph this function, we'd simply graph each part separately in the appropriate domain. The final graph would look like this:

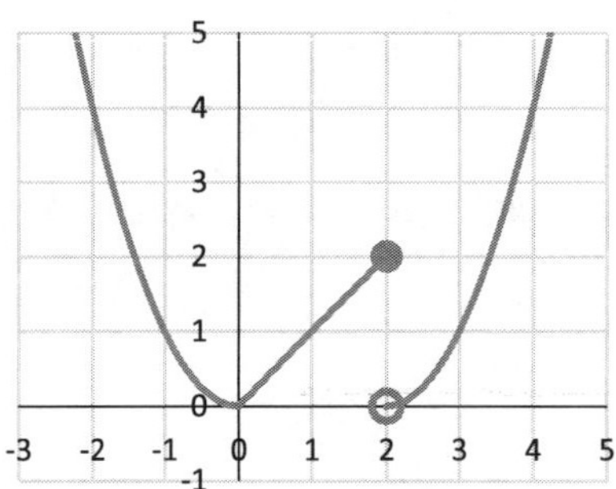

Note the filled and hollow dots at the discontinuity at $x = 2$. This is important to show which side of the graph that point corresponds to. Because $f(x) = x$ on the closed interval $0 \le x \le 2$, $f(2) = 2$. The point (2,2) is therefore marked with a filled circle, and the point (2,0), which is the endpoint of the rightmost $(x - 2)^2$ part of the graph but *not actually part of the function*, is marked with a hollow dot to indicate this.

Quadratic Functions

A **quadratic function** is a function in the form $y = ax^2 + bx + c$, where a does not equal 0. While a linear function forms a line, a quadratic function forms a **parabola**, which is a u-shaped figure that either opens upward or downward. A parabola that opens upward is said to be a **positive quadratic function** and a parabola that opens downward is said to be a **negative quadratic function**. The shape of a parabola can differ, depending on the values of *a, b,* and *c*. All parabolas contain a **vertex**, which is the highest possible point, the **maximum**, or the lowest possible point, the **minimum**. This is the point where the graph begins moving in the opposite direction. A quadratic function can have zero, one, or two solutions, and therefore, zero, one, or two x-intercepts. Recall that the x-intercepts are referred to as the zeros, or roots, of a function. A quadratic function will have only one y-intercept. Understanding the basic components of a quadratic function can give you an idea of the shape of its graph.

Example graph of a positive quadratic function, $x^2 + 2x - 3$:

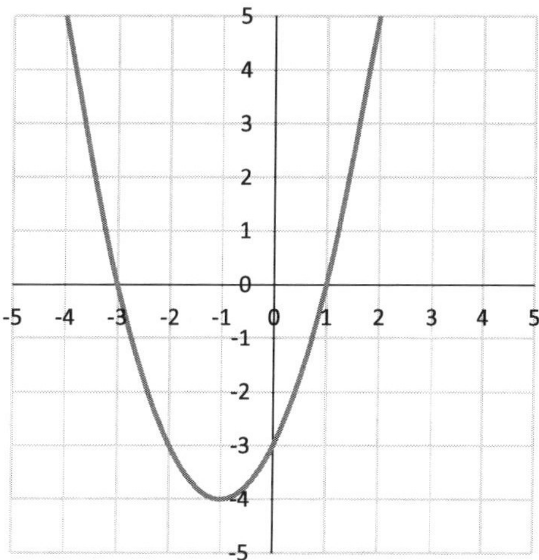

POLYNOMIAL FUNCTIONS

A **polynomial function** is a function with multiple terms and multiple powers of *x*, such as:

$$f(x) = a_n x^n + a_{n-1} x^{n-1} + a_{n-2} x^{n-2} + \cdots + a_1 x + a_0$$

where *n* is a non-negative integer that is the highest exponent in the polynomial, and $a_n \neq 0$. The domain of a polynomial function is the set of all real numbers. If the greatest exponent in the polynomial is even, the polynomial is said to be of even degree and the range is the set of real numbers that satisfy the function. If the greatest exponent in the polynomial is odd, the polynomial is said to be odd and the range, like the domain, is the set of all real numbers.

Review Video: Simplifying Rational Polynomial Functions
Visit mometrix.com/academy and enter code: 351038

RATIONAL FUNCTIONS

A **rational function** is a function that can be constructed as a ratio of two polynomial expressions: $f(x) = \frac{p(x)}{q(x)}$, where $p(x)$ and $q(x)$ are both polynomial expressions and $q(x) \neq 0$. The domain is the set of all real numbers, except any values for which $q(x) = 0$. The range is the set of real numbers that satisfies the function when the domain is applied. When you graph a rational function, you will have vertical asymptotes wherever $q(x) = 0$. If the polynomial in the numerator is of lesser degree than the polynomial in the denominator, the *x*-axis will also be a horizontal asymptote. If the numerator and denominator have equal degrees, there will be a horizontal asymptote not on the *x*-axis. If the degree of the numerator is exactly one greater than the degree of the denominator, the graph will have an oblique, or diagonal, asymptote. The asymptote will be along the line $y = \frac{p_n}{q_{n-1}} x + \frac{p_{n-1}}{q_{n-1}}$, where p_n and q_{n-1} are the coefficients of the highest degree terms in their respective polynomials.

SQUARE ROOT FUNCTIONS

A **square root function** is a function that contains a radical and is in the format $f(x) = \sqrt{ax + b}$. The domain is the set of all real numbers that yields a positive radicand or a radicand equal to zero. Because square root values are assumed to be positive unless otherwise identified, the range is all real numbers from zero to infinity. To find the zero of a square root function, set the radicand equal to zero and solve for *x*. The graph of a square root function is always to the right of the zero and always above the *x*-axis.

Example graph of a square root function, $f(x) = \sqrt{2x+1}$:

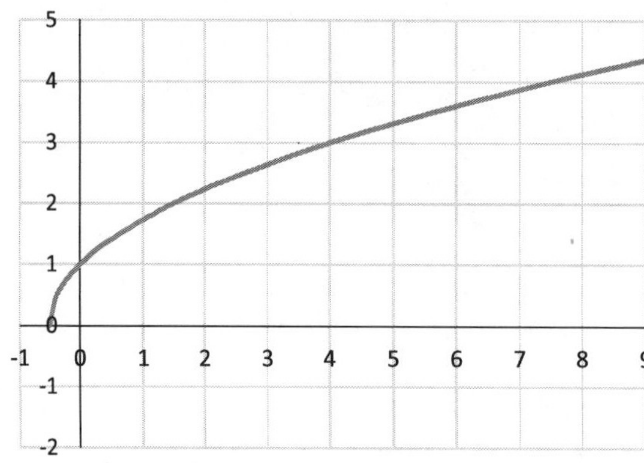

PRACTICE

P1. Martin needs a 20% medicine solution. The pharmacy has a 5% solution and a 30% solution. He needs 50 mL of the solution. If the pharmacist must mix the two solutions, how many milliliters of 5% solution and 30% solution should be used?

P2. Describe two different strategies for solving the following problem:

> Kevin can mow the yard in 4 hours. Mandy can mow the same yard in 5 hours. If they work together, how long will it take them to mow the yard?

P3. A car, traveling at 65 miles per hour, leaves Flagstaff and heads east on I-40. Another car, traveling at 75 miles per hour, leaves Flagstaff 2 hours later, from the same starting point and also heads east on I-40. Determine how many hours it will take the second car to catch the first car by:

> **(a)** Using a table.
>
> **(b)** Using algebra.

PRACTICE SOLUTIONS

P1. To solve this problem, a table may be created to represent the variables, percentages, and total amount of solution. Such a table is shown below:

	mL solution	**% medicine**	**Total mL medicine**
5% solution	x	0.05	$0.05x$
30% solution	y	0.30	$0.30y$
Mixture	$x + y = 50$	0.20	$(0.20)(50) = 10$

The variable, x, may be rewritten as $50 - y$, so the equation, $0.05(50 - y) + 0.30y = 10$, may be written and solved for y. Doing so gives $y = 30$. So, 30 mL of 30% solution are needed. Evaluating the expression, $50 - y$ for an x-value of 20, shows that 20 mL of 5% solution are needed.

P2. Two possible strategies both involve the use of rational equations to solve. The first strategy involves representing the fractional part of the yard mowed by each person in one hour and setting this sum equal to the ratio of 1 to the total time needed. The appropriate equation is $1/4 + 1/5 = 1/t$, which simplifies as $9/20 = 1/t$, and finally as $t = 20/9$. So, the time it will take them to mow the yard, when working together, is a little more than 2.2 hours.

A second strategy involves representing the time needed for each person as two fractions and setting the sum equal to 1 (representing 1 yard). The appropriate equation is $t/4 + t/5 = 1$, which simplifies as

$9t/20 = 1$, and finally as $t = 20/9$. This strategy also shows the total time to be a little more than 2.2 hours.

P3. (a) One strategy might involve creating a table of values for the number of hours and distances for each car. The table may be examined to find the same distance traveled and the corresponding number of hours taken. Such a table is shown below:

Car A		Car B	
x (hours)	y (distance)	x (hours)	y (distance)
0	0	0	
1	65	1	
2	130	2	0
3	195	3	75
4	260	4	150
5	325	5	225
6	390	6	300
7	455	7	375
8	520	8	450
9	585	9	525
10	650	10	600
11	715	11	675
12	780	12	750
13	845	13	825
14	910	14	900
15	975	15	975

The table shows that after 15 hours, the distance traveled is the same. Thus, the second car catches up with the first car after a distance of 975 miles and 15 hours.

(b) A second strategy might involve setting up and solving an algebraic equation. This situation may be modeled as $65x = 75(x - 2)$. This equation sets the distances traveled by each car equal to one another. Solving for x gives $x = 15$. Thus, once again, the second car will catch up with the first car after 15 hours.

Advanced Functions

Step Functions

The double brackets indicate a step function. For a step function, the value inside the double brackets is rounded down to the nearest integer. The graph of the function $f_0(x) = [\![x]\!]$ appears as shown on the left below. In comparison $f(x) = 2\left[\!\left[\frac{1}{3}(x - 1)\right]\!\right]$ is on the right below. The coefficient of 2 shows that it's stretched vertically by a factor of 2 (so there's a vertical distance of 2 units between successive "steps").

The coefficient of $\frac{1}{3}$ in front of the x shows that it's stretched horizontally by a factor of 3 (so each "step" is three units long), and the $x - 1$ shows that it's displaced one unit to the right.

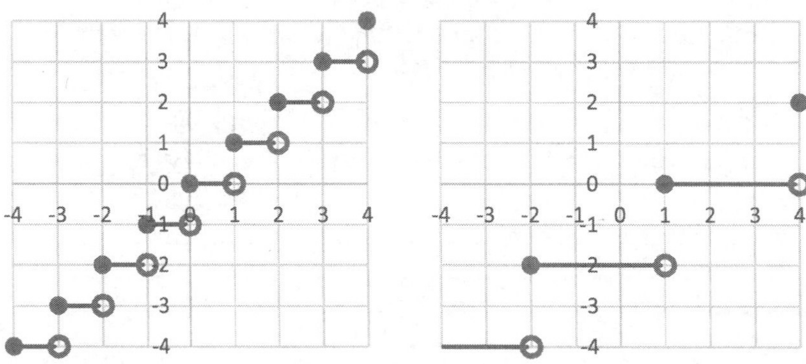

TRANSCENDENTAL FUNCTIONS

Transcendental functions are all functions that are non-algebraic. Any function that includes logarithms, trigonometric functions, variables as exponents, or any combination that includes any of these is not algebraic in nature, even if the function includes polynomials or roots.

EXPONENTIAL FUNCTIONS

Exponential functions are equations that have the format $y = b^x$, where base $b > 0$ and $b \neq 1$. The exponential function can also be written $f(x) = b^x$. Recall the properties of exponents, like the product of terms with the same base is equal to the base raised to the sum of the exponents: $a^x \times a^y = a^{x+y}$ and a term with an exponent that is raised to an exponent is equal to the base of the original term raised to the product of the exponents: $(a^x)^y = a^{xy}$. The graph of an example exponential function, $f(x) = 2^x$, is below:

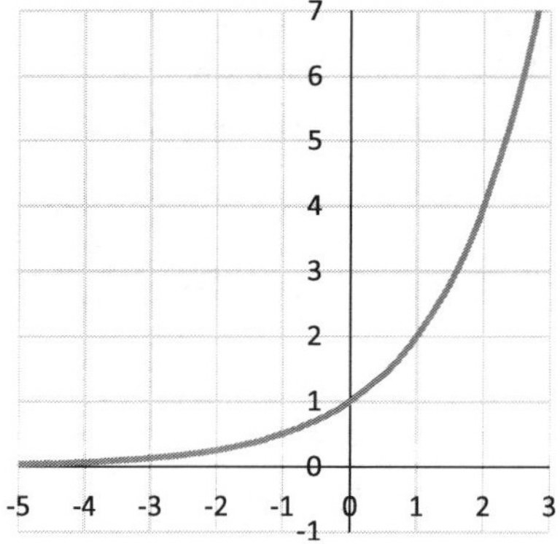

Note in the graph that the y value approaches zero to the left and infinity to the right. One of the key features of an exponential function is that there will be one end that goes off to infinity and another that asymptotically approaches a lower bound. Common forms of exponential functions include:

Geometric sequences: $a_n = a_1 \times r^{n-1}$, where a_n is the value of the nth term, a_1 is the initial value, r is the common ratio, and n is the number of terms. Note that $a_1 \times r^{1-1} = a_1 \times r^0 = a_1 \times 1 = a_1$.

Population growth: $f(t) = ae^{rt}$, where $f(t)$ is the population at time $t \geq 0$, a is the initial population, e is the mathematical constant known as Euler's number, and r is the growth rate.

Compound interest: $f(t) = P\left(1 + \frac{r}{n}\right)^{nt}$, where $f(t)$ is the account value at a certain number of time periods $t \geq 0$, P is the initial principle balance, r is the interest rate, and n is the number of times the interest is applied per time period.

General exponential growth or decay: $f(t) = a(1 + r)^t$, where $f(t)$ is the future count, a is the current or initial count, r is the growth or decay rate, and t is the time.

For example, suppose the initial population of a town was 1,200 people. The population growth is 5%. The current population is 2,400. To find out how much time has passed since the town was founded, we can use the following function:

$$2400 = 1200e^{0.05t}.$$

The general form for population growth may be represented as $f(t) = ae^{rt}$, where $f(t)$ represents the current population, a represents the initial population, r represents the growth rate, and t represents the time. Thus, substituting the initial population, current population, and rate into this form gives the equation above.

The number of years that have passed were found by first dividing both sides of the equation by 1,200. Doing so gives $2 = e^{0.05t}$. Taking the natural logarithm of both sides gives $\ln(2) = ln(e^{0.05t})$. Applying the power property of logarithms, the equation may be rewritten as $\ln(2) = 0.05t \times \ln(e)$, which simplifies as $\ln(2) = 0.05t$. Dividing both sides of this equation by 0.05 gives $t \approx 13.86$. Thus, approximately 13.86 years passed.

Logarithmic Functions

Logarithmic functions are equations that have the format $y = \log_b x$ or $f(x) = \log_b x$. The base b may be any number except one; however, the most common bases for logarithms are base 10 and base e. The log base e is the natural logarithm, or *ln*, expressed by the function $f(x) = \ln x$.

Any logarithm that does not have an assigned value of b is assumed to be base 10: $\log x = \log_{10} x$. Exponential functions and logarithmic functions are related in that one is the inverse of the other. If $f(x) = b^x$, then $f^{-1}(x) = \log_b x$. This can perhaps be expressed more clearly by the two equations: $y = b^x$ and $x = \log_b y$.

The following properties apply to logarithmic expressions:

Property	Description
$\log_b 1 = 0$	The log of 1 is equal to 0 for any base
$\log_b b = 1$	The log of the base is equal to 1
$\log_b b^p = p$	The log of the base raised to a power is equal to that power
$\log_b MN = \log_b M + \log_b N$	The log of a product is the sum of the log of each factor
$\log_b \frac{M}{N} = \log_b M - \log_b N$	The log of a quotient is equal to the log of the dividend minus the log of the divisor
$\log_b M^p = p \log_b M$	The log of a value raised to a power is equal to the power times the log of the value

The graph of an example logarithmic function, $f(x) = \log_2(x + 2)$, is below:

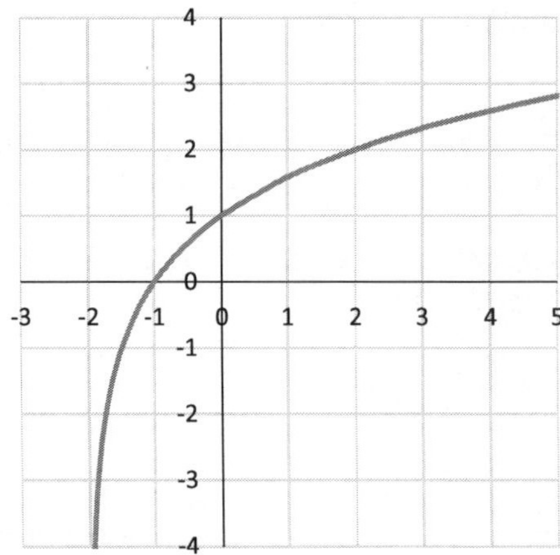

Trigonometric Functions

Trigonometric functions are periodic, meaning that they repeat the same form over and over. The basic trigonometric functions are sine (abbreviated 'sin'), cosine (abbreviated 'cos'), and tangent (abbreviated 'tan'). The simplest way to think of them is as describing the ratio of the side lengths of a right triangle in relation to the angles of the triangle.

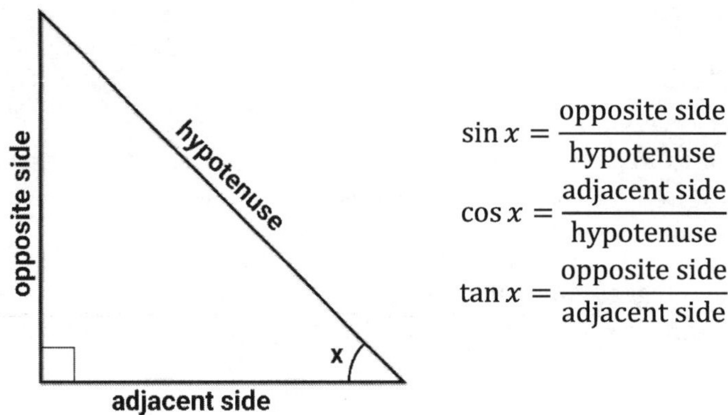

$$\sin x = \frac{\text{opposite side}}{\text{hypotenuse}}$$
$$\cos x = \frac{\text{adjacent side}}{\text{hypotenuse}}$$
$$\tan x = \frac{\text{opposite side}}{\text{adjacent side}}$$

Using sine as an example, trigonometric functions take the form $f(x) = A\sin(Bx + C) + D$, where the **amplitude** is simply equal to A. The **period** is the distance between successive peaks or troughs, essentially the length of the repeated pattern. In this form, the period is equal to ${}^{2\pi}/_{B}$. As for C, this is the **phase shift** or the horizontal shift of the function. The last term, D, is the vertical shift and determines the **midline** as $y = D$.

For instance, consider the function $f(x) = 2 + \frac{3}{2}\sin\left(\pi x + \frac{\pi}{2}\right)$. Here $A = \frac{3}{2}$, $B = \pi$, $C = \frac{\pi}{2}$, and $D = 2$, so the midline is at $y = 2$, the amplitude is $\frac{3}{2}$, and the period is ${}^{2\pi}/_{\pi} = 2$. To graph this function, we center the sine wave on the midline and extend it to a height above and below the midline equal to the amplitude—so this graph would have a minimum value of $2 - \frac{3}{2} = \frac{1}{2}$ and a maximum of $2 + \frac{3}{2} = \frac{7}{2}$. So, the function would be graphed as follows:

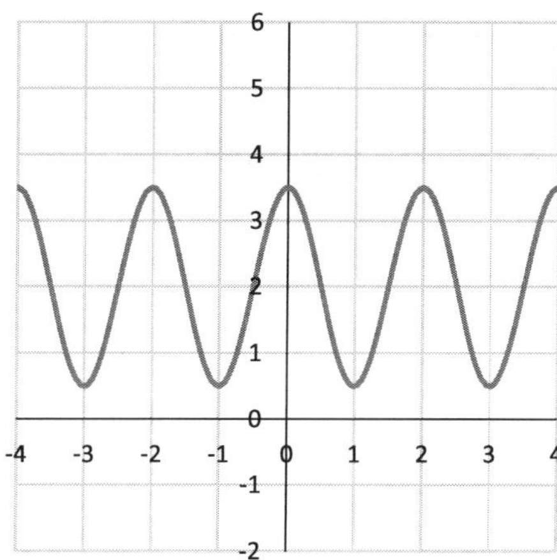

Manipulation of Functions

Translation occurs when values are added to or subtracted from the *x* or *y* values. If a constant is added to the *y* portion of each point, the graph shifts up. If a constant is subtracted from the *y* portion of each point, the graph shifts down. This is represented by the expression $f(x) \pm k$, where *k* is a constant. If a constant is added to the x portion of each point, the graph shifts left. If a constant is subtracted from the x portion of each point, the graph shifts right. This is represented by the expression $f(x \pm k)$, where *k* is a constant.

Stretching, compression, and reflection occur when different parts of a function are multiplied by different groups of constants. If the function as a whole is multiplied by a real number constant greater than 1, $(k \times f(x))$, the graph is stretched vertically. If *k* in the previous equation is greater than zero but less than 1, the graph is compressed vertically. If *k* is less than zero, the graph is reflected about the *x*-axis, in addition to being either stretched or compressed vertically if *k* is less than or greater than -1, respectively. If instead, just the *x*-term is multiplied by a constant greater than 1 $(f(k \times x))$, the graph is compressed horizontally. If *k* in the previous equation is greater than zero but less than 1, the graph is stretched horizontally. If *k* is less than zero, the graph is reflected about the *y*-axis, in addition to being either stretched or compressed horizontally if *k* is greater than or less than -1, respectively.

Algebraic Theorems

According to the **fundamental theorem of algebra**, every non-constant, single variable polynomial has exactly as many roots as the polynomial's highest exponent. For example, if x^4 is the largest exponent of a term, the polynomial will have exactly 4 roots. However, some of these roots may have multiplicity or be non-real numbers. For instance, in the polynomial function $f(x) = x^4 - 4x + 3$, the only real roots are 1 and -1. The root 1 has multiplicity of 2 and there is one non-real root $(-1 - \sqrt{2}i)$.

The **remainder theorem** is useful for determining the remainder when a polynomial is divided by a binomial. The remainder theorem states that if a polynomial function $f(x)$ is divided by a binomial $x - a$, where a is a real number, the remainder of the division will be the value of *f*(*a*). If $f(a) = 0$, then a is a root of the polynomial.

The **factor theorem** is related to the remainder theorem and states that if $f(a) = 0$ then $(x - a)$ is a factor of the function.

According to the **rational root theorem,** any rational root of a polynomial function $f(x) = a_n x^n + a_{n-1}x^{n-1} + \cdots + a_1 x + a_0$ with integer coefficients will, when reduced to its lowest terms, be a positive or negative fraction such that the numerator is a factor of a_0 and the denominator is a factor of a_n. For instance, if the polynomial function $f(x) = x^3 + 3x^2 - 4$ has any rational roots, the numerators of those roots can only be factors of 4 (1, 2, 4), and the denominators can only be factors of 1 (1). The function in this example has roots of 1 $\left(\text{or } \frac{1}{1}\right)$ and -2 $\left(\text{or } -\frac{2}{1}\right)$.

Applying the Basic Operations to Functions

For each of the basic operations, we will use these functions as examples: $f(x) = x^2$ and $g(x) = x$.

To find the sum of two functions *f* and *g*, assuming the domains are compatible, simply add the two functions together: $(f + g)(x) = f(x) + g(x) = x^2 + x$

To find the difference of two functions *f* and *g*, assuming the domains are compatible, simply subtract the second function from the first: $(f - g)(x) = f(x) - g(x) = x^2 - x$.

To find the product of two functions *f* and *g*, assuming the domains are compatible, multiply the two functions together: $(f \times g)(x) = f(x) \times g(x) = x^2 \times x = x^3$.

To find the quotient of two functions *f* and *g*, assuming the domains are compatible, divide the first function by the second: $\frac{f}{g}(x) = \frac{f(x)}{g(x)} = \frac{x^2}{x} = x\,; x \neq 0$.

The example given in each case is fairly simple, but on a given problem, if you are looking only for the value of the sum, difference, product or quotient of two functions at a particular *x*-value, it may be simpler to solve the functions individually and then perform the given operation using those values.

The composite of two functions *f* and *g*, written as $(f \circ g)(x)$ simply means that the output of the second function is used as the input of the first. This can also be written as $f\big(g(x)\big)$. In general, this can be solved by substituting $g(x)$ for all instances of *x* in $f(x)$ and simplifying. Using the example functions $f(x) = x^2 - x + 2$ and $g(x) = x + 1$, we can find that $(f \circ g)(x)$ or $f\big(g(x)\big)$ is equal to $f(x + 1) = (x + 1)^2 - (x + 1) + 2$, which simplifies to $x^2 + x + 2$.

It is important to note that $(f \circ g)(x)$ is not necessarily the same as $(g \circ f)(x)$. The process is not always commutative like addition or multiplication expressions. It *can* be commutative, but most often this is not the case.

Practice

P1. A professor wishes to invest $20,000 in a CD that compounds annually. The interest rate at his bank is 1.9%. How many years will it take for his account to reach $50,000?

P2. Suppose a new strain of bacteria, after x days, shows a growth rate of 10%. The current count for the new bacteria strain is 100. How many days will pass before the count reaches 1 million bacteria?

P3. Each of the following functions cross the x- and y-axes at the same points. Identify the most likely function type of each graph

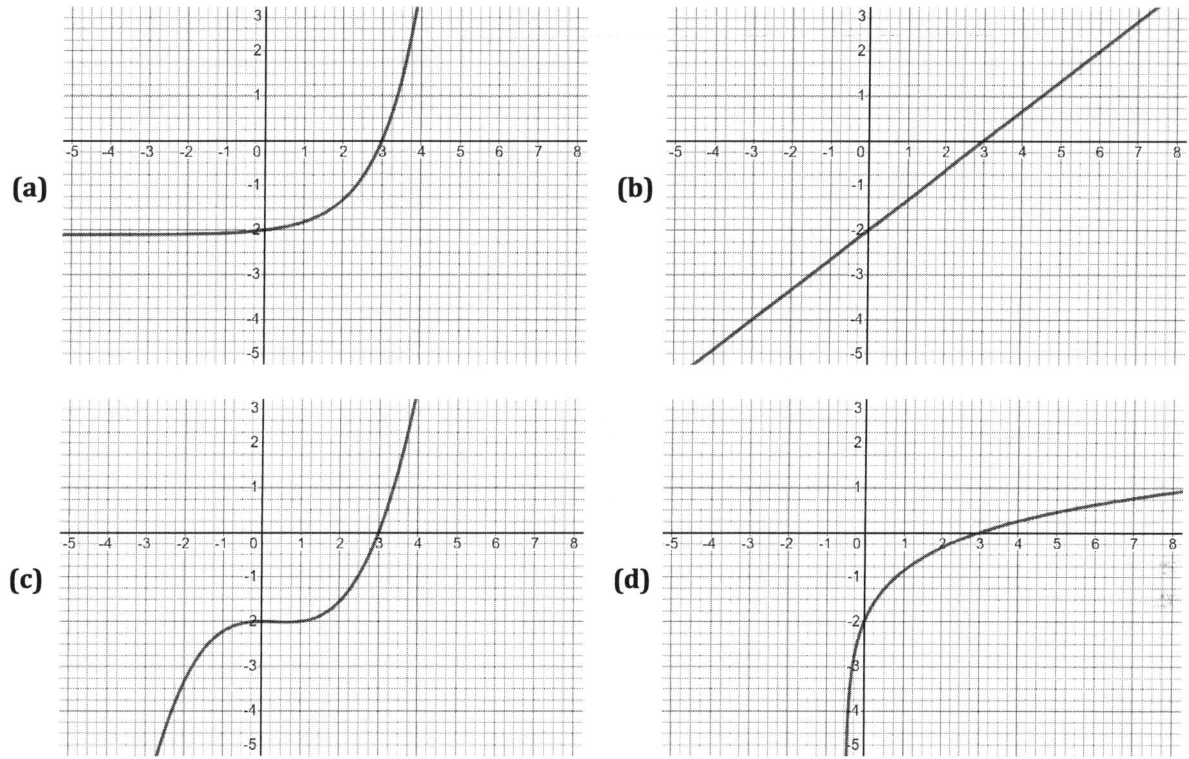

P4. Given the functions $f(x) = -3x + 3$, $g(x) = e^x + 3$, and $h(x) = x^2 - 2x + 1$, perform the following operations and write out the resulting function:

(a) Shift $g(x)$ 4 units to the left and 1 unit up, then compress the new function by a factor of $1/2$

(b) $\frac{f(x)}{h(x)}$

(c) $h(g(x))$

(d) $\frac{f(x)+h(x)}{x-1}$

PRACTICE SOLUTIONS

P1. In order to solve this problem, the compound interest formula should be evaluated for a future value of $50,000, principal of $20,000, rate of 0.019, and number of years of t. The exponential equation may then be solved by taking the logarithm of both sides. The process is shown below:

$$50{,}000 = 20{,}000\left(1 + \frac{0.019}{1}\right)^t$$

Dividing both sides of the equation by 20,000 gives $2.5 = 1.019^t$. Taking the logarithm of both sides gives $\log(2.5) = t\log(1.019)$. Dividing both sides of this equation by $\log(1.019)$ gives $t \approx 48.68$. Thus, after approximately 49 years, the professor's account will reach $50,000.

P2. The problem may be solved by writing and solving an exponential growth function, in the form, $f(x) = a(1 + r)^x$, where $f(x)$ represents the future count, a represents the current count, r represents the growth rate, and x represents the time. Once the function is evaluated for a future count of 1,000,000, a current count of 100, and a growth rate of 0.10, the exponential equation may be solved by taking the logarithm of both sides.

The problem may be modeled with the equation, $1{,}000{,}000 = 100 \times (1.10)^x$. Dividing both sides of the equation by 100 gives $10{,}000 = 1.10^x$. Taking the logarithm of both sides gives $\log(10{,}000) = x\log(1.10)$. Dividing both sides of this equation by $\log(1.10)$ gives $x \approx 96.6$. Thus, after approximately 97 days, the bacteria count will reach 1 million.

P3. (a) Exponential function - positive, increasing slope

(b) Linear function - positive, continuous slope.

(c) Polynomial function (odd degree) - positive, changing slope. Note that the graph goes off to infinity in opposite quadrants I and III, thus it is an odd degree.

(d) Logarithmic function - positive, decreasing slope

P4. (a) Shifting $g(x)$ to the left 4 units is the same as $g(x+4)$ and shifting the function up one unit is $g(x)+1$. Combining these and multiplying by ½ results in the following:

$$\begin{aligned}\frac{1}{2}(g(x+4)+1) &= \frac{1}{2}\left((e^{x+4}+3)+1\right)\\ &= \frac{e^{x+4}}{2}+2\end{aligned}$$

(b) Factor $h(x)$, noting that it is a perfect square, and be sure to note the constraint on x due to the original denominator of the rational expression:

$$\frac{f(x)}{h(x)} = \frac{-3x+3}{x^2-2x+1} = \frac{-3(x-1)}{(x-1)(x-1)} = \frac{-3}{(x-1)};x \neq 1$$

(c) Evaluate the composition as follows:

$$\begin{aligned}h(g(x)) &= (e^x+3)^2 - 2(e^x+3)+1\\ &= (e^x)^2+6e^x+9-2e^x-6+1\\ &= e^{2x}+4e^x+4\\ &= (e^x+2)^2\end{aligned}$$

(d) Note the constraint on x due to the original denominator of the rational expression:

$$\begin{aligned}\frac{f(x)+h(x)}{x-1} &= \frac{(-3x+3)+(x^2-2x+1)}{x-1}\\ &= \frac{-3(x-1)+(x-1)(x-1)}{x-1}\\ &= -3+(x-1)\\ &= x-4;x \neq 1\end{aligned}$$

Measurement and Geometry

Measurement Principles

Precision, Accuracy, and Error

Precision: How reliable and repeatable a measurement is. The more consistent the data is with repeated testing, the more precise it is. For example, hitting a target consistently in the same spot, which may or may not be the center of the target, is precision.

Accuracy: How close the data is to the correct data. For example, hitting a target consistently in the center area of the target, whether or not the hits are all in the same spot, is accuracy.

Note: it is possible for data to be precise without being accurate. If a scale is off balance, the data will be precise, but will not be accurate. For data to have precision and accuracy, it must be repeatable and correct.

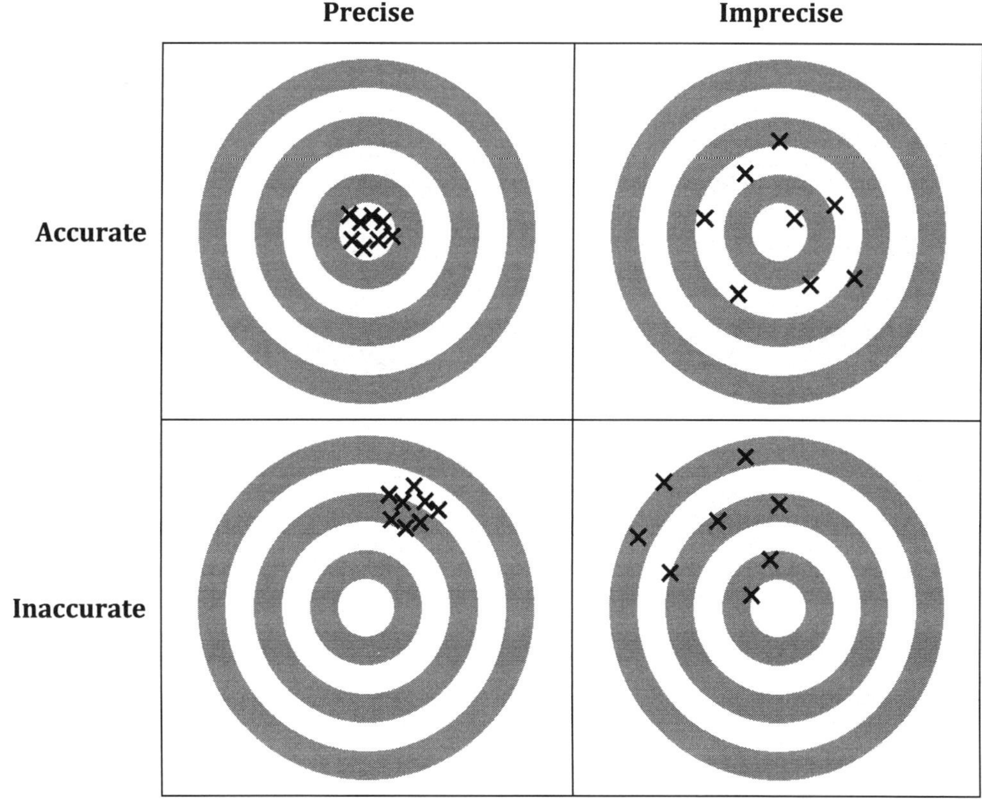

Approximate error: The amount of error in a physical measurement. Approximate error is often reported as the measurement, followed by the ± symbol and the amount of the approximate error.

Maximum possible error: Half the magnitude of the smallest unit used in the measurement. For example, if the unit of measurement is 1 centimeter, the maximum possible error is $\frac{1}{2}$ cm, written as ± 0.5 cm following the measurement. It is important to apply significant figures in reporting maximum possible error. Do not make the answer appear more accurate than the least accurate of your measurements.

Rounding and Estimation

Rounding is reducing the digits in a number while still trying to keep the value similar. The result will be less accurate, but will be in a simpler form, and will be easier to use. Whole numbers can be rounded to the nearest ten, hundred or thousand.

When you are asked to estimate the solution to a problem, you will need to provide only an approximate figure or **estimation** for your answer. In this situation, you will need to round each number in the calculation to the level indicated (nearest hundred, nearest thousand, etc.) or to a level that makes sense for the numbers involved. When estimating a sum **all numbers must be rounded to the same level.** You cannot round one number to the nearest thousand while rounding another to the nearest hundred.

Review Video: Rounding and Estimation
Visit mometrix.com/academy and enter code: 126243

Scientific Notation

Scientific notation is a way of writing large numbers in a shorter form. The form $a \times 10^n$ is used in scientific notation, where a is greater than or equal to 1, but less than 10, and n is the number of places the decimal must move to get from the original number to a. Example: The number 230,400,000 is cumbersome to write. To write the value in scientific notation, place a decimal point between the first and second numbers, and include all digits through the last non-zero digit ($a = 2.304$). To find the appropriate power of 10, count the number of places the decimal point had to move ($n = 8$). The number is positive if the decimal moved to the left, and negative if it moved to the right. We can then write 230,400,000 as 2.304×10^8. If we look instead at the number 0.00002304, we have the same value for a, but this time the decimal moved 5 places to the right ($n = -5$). Thus, 0.00002304 can be written as 2.304×10^{-5}. Using this notation makes it simple to compare very large or very small numbers. By comparing exponents, it is easy to see that 3.28×10^4 is smaller than 1.51×10^5, because 4 is less than 5.

Review Video: Scientific Notation
Visit mometrix.com/academy and enter code: 976454

Units of Measurement

Metric Measurement Prefixes

Giga-: one billion (1 *giga*watt is one billion watts)
Mega-: one million (1 *mega*hertz is one million hertz)
Kilo-: one thousand (1 *kilo*gram is one thousand grams)
Deci-: one tenth (1 *deci*meter is one tenth of a meter)
Centi-: one hundredth (1 *centi*meter is one hundredth of a meter)
Milli-: one thousandth (1 *milli*liter is one thousandth of a liter)
Micro-: one millionth (1 *micro*gram is one millionth of a gram)

Measurement Conversion

When converting between units, the goal is to maintain the same meaning but change the way it is displayed. In order to go from a larger unit to a smaller unit, multiply the number of the known amount by the equivalent amount. When going from a smaller unit to a larger unit, divide the number of the known amount by the equivalent amount.

For complicated conversions, it may be helpful to set up conversion fractions. In these fractions, one fraction is the **conversion factor**. The other fraction has the unknown amount in the numerator. So, the known value is placed in the denominator. Sometimes the second fraction has the known value from the problem in the numerator, and the unknown in the denominator. Multiply the two fractions to get the converted measurement. Note that since the numerator and the denominator of the factor are equivalent, the value of the fraction is 1. That is why we can say that the result in the new units is equal to the result in the old units even though they have different numbers.

It can often be necessary to chain known conversion factors together. As an example, consider converting 512 square inches to square meters. We know that there are 2.54 centimeters in an inch and 100 centimeters in a meter, and that we will need to square each of these factors to achieve the conversion we are looking for.

$$\frac{512\text{ in}^2}{1} \times \left(\frac{2.54\text{ cm}}{1\text{ in}}\right)^2 \times \left(\frac{1\text{ m}}{100\text{ cm}}\right)^2 = \frac{512\,\cancel{\text{in}^2}}{1} \times \left(\frac{6.4516\,\cancel{\text{cm}^2}}{1\,\cancel{\text{in}^2}}\right) \times \left(\frac{1\text{ m}^2}{10000\,\cancel{\text{cm}^2}}\right) = 0.330\text{ m}^2$$

Common Units and Equivalents

Metric Equivalents

1000 μg (microgram)	1 mg
1000 mg (milligram)	1 g
1000 g (gram)	1 kg
1000 kg (kilogram)	1 metric ton
1000 mL (milliliter)	1 L
1000 μm (micrometer)	1 mm
1000 mm (millimeter)	1 m
100 cm (centimeter)	1 m
1000 m (meter)	1 km

Distance and Area Measurement

Unit	Abbreviation	U.S. equivalent	Metric equivalent
Inch	in	1 inch	2.54 centimeters
Foot	ft	12 inches	0.305 meters
Yard	yd	3 feet	0.914 meters
Mile	mi	5280 feet	1.609 kilometers
Acre	ac	4840 square yards	0.405 hectares
Square Mile	mi^2	640 acres	2.590 square kilometers

Capacity Measurements

Unit	Abbreviation	U.S. equivalent	Metric equivalent
Fluid Ounce	fl oz	8 fluid drams	29.573 milliliters
Cup	cp	8 fluid ounces	0.237 liter
Pint	pt	16 fluid ounces	0.473 liter
Quart	qt	2 pints	0.946 liter
Gallon	gal	4 quarts	3.785 liters
Teaspoon	t or tsp	1 fluid dram	5 milliliters
Tablespoon	T or tbsp	4 fluid drams	15 or 16 milliliters
Cubic Centimeter	cc or cm^3	0.271 drams	1 milliliter

Weight Measurements

Unit	Abbreviation	U.S. equivalent	Metric equivalent
Ounce	oz	16 drams	28.35 grams
Pound	lb	16 ounces	453.6 grams
Ton	t	2,000 pounds	907.2 kilograms

VOLUME AND WEIGHT MEASUREMENT CLARIFICATIONS

Always be careful when using ounces and fluid ounces. They are not equivalent.

$$1 \text{ pint} = 16 \text{ fluid ounces} \qquad 1 \text{ fluid ounce} \neq 1 \text{ ounce}$$
$$1 \text{ pound} = 16 \text{ ounces} \qquad 1 \text{ pint} \neq 1 \text{ pound}$$

Having one pint of something does not mean you have one pound of it. In the same way, just because something weighs one pound does not mean that its volume is one pint.

In the United States, the word "ton" by itself refers to a short ton or a net ton. Do not confuse this with a long ton (also called a gross ton) or a metric ton (also spelled *tonne*), which have different measurement equivalents.

$$1 \text{ U.S. ton} = 2000 \text{ pounds} \qquad \neq \qquad 1 \text{ metric ton} = 1000 \text{ kilograms}$$

Lines and Planes

A **point** is a fixed location in space; has no size or dimensions; commonly represented by a dot. A **line** is a set of points that extends infinitely in two opposite directions. It has length, but no width or depth. A line can be defined by any two distinct points that it contains. A **line segment** is a portion of a line that has definite endpoints. A **ray** is a portion of a line that extends from a single point on that line in one direction along the line. It has a definite beginning, but no ending.

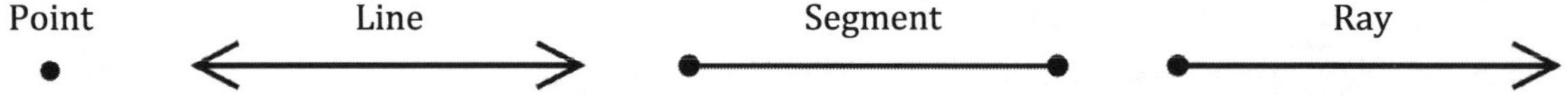

Intersecting lines are lines that have exactly one point in common. **Concurrent lines** are multiple lines that intersect at a single point. **Perpendicular lines** are lines that intersect at right angles. They are represented by the symbol ⊥. The shortest distance from a line to a point not on the line is a perpendicular segment from the point to the line. **Parallel lines** are lines in the same plane that have no points in common and never meet. It is possible for lines to be in different planes, have no points in common, and never meet, but they are not parallel because they are in different planes.

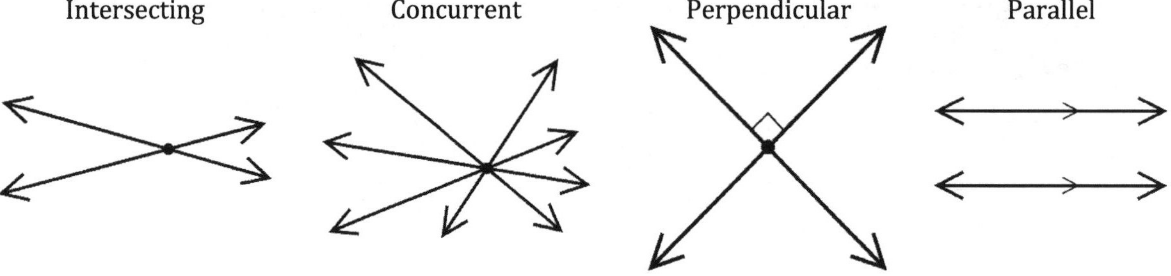

A **transversal** is a line that intersects at least two other lines, which may or may not be parallel to one another. A transversal that intersects parallel lines is a common occurrence in geometry. A **bisector** is a line or line segment that divides another line segment into two equal lengths. A **perpendicular bisector**

of a line segment is composed of points that are equidistant from the endpoints of the segment it is dividing.

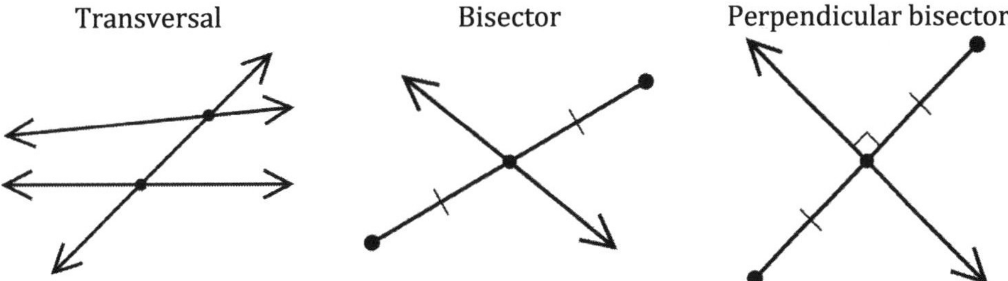

The **projection of a point on a line** is the point at which a perpendicular line drawn from the given point to the given line intersects the line. This is also the shortest distance from the given point to the line. The **projection of a segment on a line** is a segment whose endpoints are the points formed when perpendicular lines are drawn from the endpoints of the given segment to the given line. This is similar to the length a diagonal line appears to be when viewed from above.

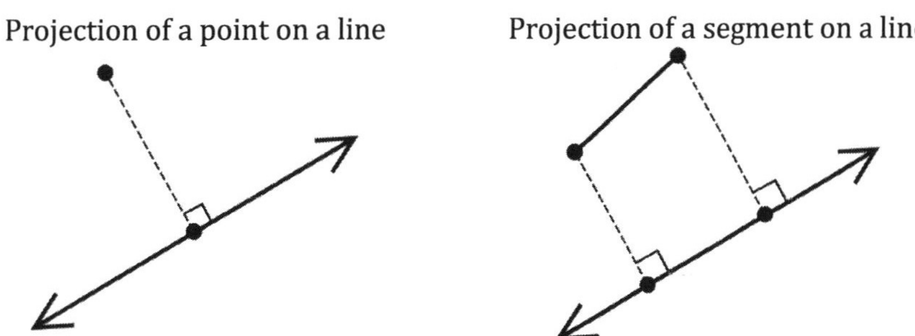

A **plane** is a two-dimensional flat surface defined by three non-collinear points. A plane extends an infinite distance in all directions in those two dimensions. It contains an infinite number of points, parallel lines and segments, intersecting lines and segments, as well as parallel or intersecting rays. A plane will never contain a three-dimensional figure or skew lines, lines that don't intersect and are not parallel. Two given planes are either parallel or they intersect at a line. A plane may intersect a circular conic surface to form **conic sections**, such as a parabola, hyperbola, circle or ellipse.

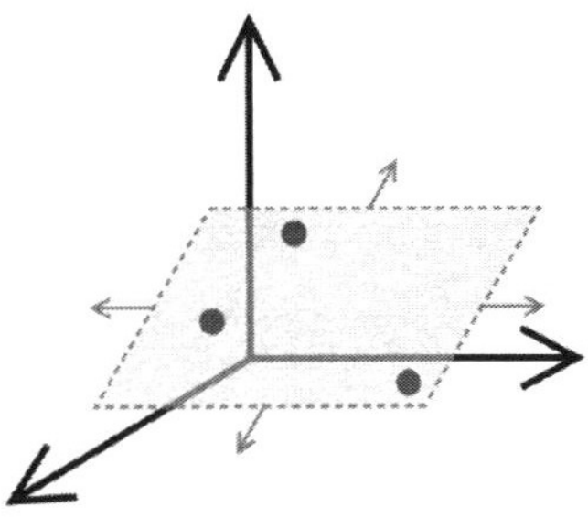

Review Video: Lines and Planes
Visit mometrix.com/academy and enter code: 554267

Angles

An **angle** is formed when two lines or line segments meet at a common point. It may be a common starting point for a pair of segments or rays, or it may be the intersection of lines. Angles are represented by the symbol $\angle$.

The **vertex** is the point at which two segments or rays meet to form an angle. If the angle is formed by intersecting rays, lines, and/or line segments, the vertex is the point at which four angles are formed. The pairs of angles opposite one another are called vertical angles, and their measures are equal.

- An **acute** angle is an angle with a degree measure less than 90°.
- A **right** angle is an angle with a degree measure of exactly 90°.
- An **obtuse** angle is an angle with a degree measure greater than 90° but less than 180°.
- A **straight angle** is an angle with a degree measure of exactly 180°. This is also a semicircle.
- A **reflex angle** is an angle with a degree measure greater than 180° but less than 360°.
- A **full angle** is an angle with a degree measure of exactly 360°.

Review Video: Geometric Symbols: Angles
Visit mometrix.com/academy and enter code: 452738

Two angles whose sum is exactly 90° are said to be **complementary**. The two angles may or may not be adjacent. In a right triangle, the two acute angles are complementary.

Two angles whose sum is exactly 180° are said to be **supplementary**. The two angles may or may not be adjacent. Two intersecting lines always form two pairs of supplementary angles. Adjacent supplementary angles will always form a straight line.

Two angles that have the same vertex and share a side are said to be **adjacent**. Vertical angles are not adjacent because they share a vertex but no common side.

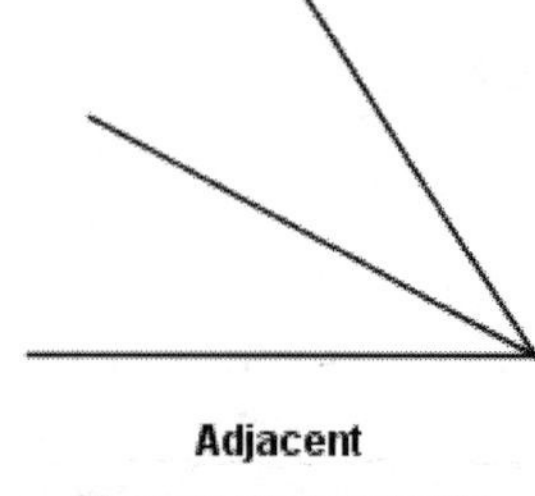

Adjacent
Share vertex and side

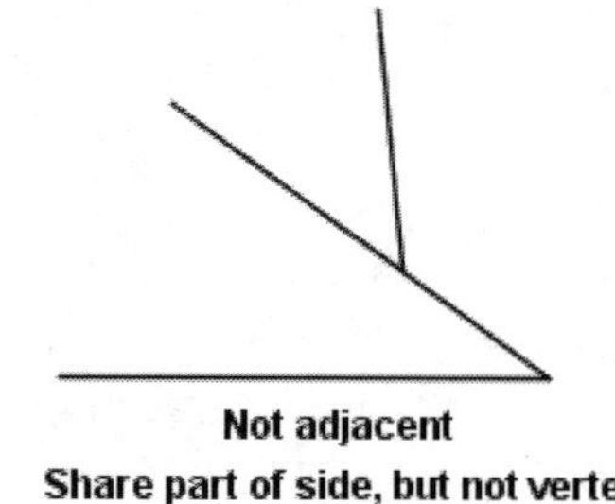

Not adjacent
Share part of side, but not vertex

When two parallel lines are cut by a transversal, the angles that are between the two parallel lines are **interior angles**. In the diagram below, angles 3, 4, 5, and 6 are interior angles.

When two parallel lines are cut by a transversal, the angles that are outside the parallel lines are **exterior angles**. In the diagram below, angles 1, 2, 7, and 8 are exterior angles.

When two parallel lines are cut by a transversal, the angles that are in the same position relative to the transversal and a parallel line are **corresponding angles**. The diagram below has four pairs of corresponding angles: angles 1 and 5; angles 2 and 6; angles 3 and 7; and angles 4 and 8. Corresponding angles formed by parallel lines are congruent.

When two parallel lines are cut by a transversal, the two interior angles that are on opposite sides of the transversal are called **alternate interior angles**. In the diagram below, there are two pairs of alternate interior angles: angles 3 and 6, and angles 4 and 5. Alternate interior angles formed by parallel lines are congruent.

When two parallel lines are cut by a transversal, the two exterior angles that are on opposite sides of the transversal are called **alternate exterior angles**.

In the diagram below, there are two pairs of alternate exterior angles: angles 1 and 8, and angles 2 and 7. Alternate exterior angles formed by parallel lines are congruent.

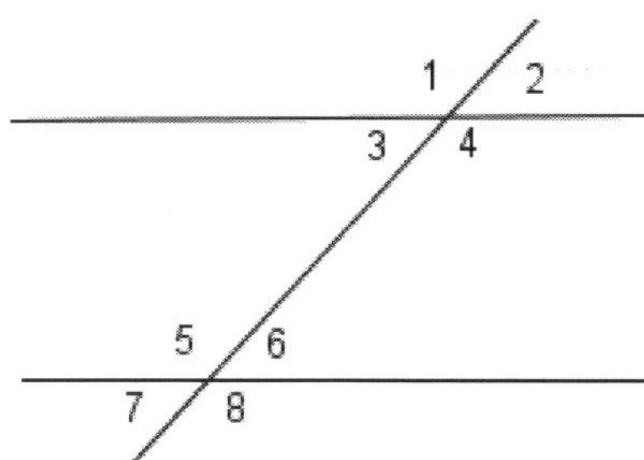

When two lines intersect, four angles are formed. The non-adjacent angles at this vertex are called vertical angles. Vertical angles are congruent. In the diagram, $\angle ABD \cong \angle CBE$ and $\angle ABC \cong \angle DBE$.

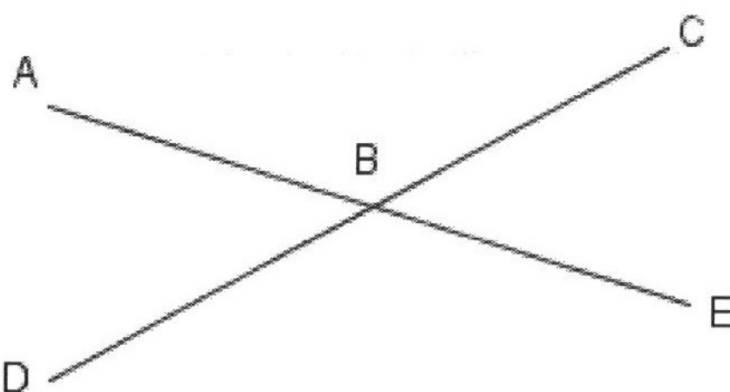

PRACTICE

P1. Find the measure of angles **(a)**, **(b)**, and **(c)** based on the figure with two parallel lines, two perpendicular lines and one transversal:

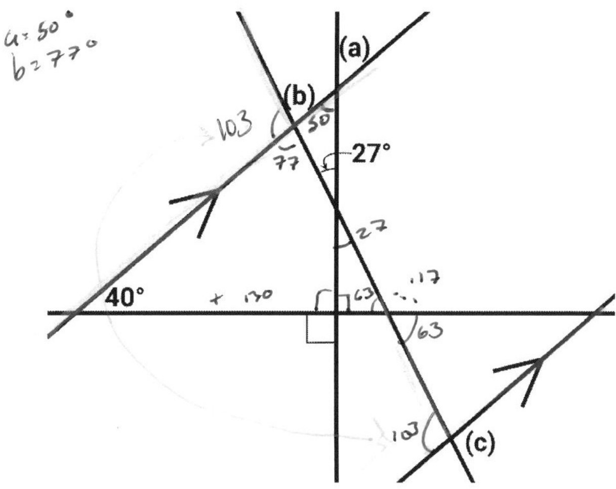

PRACTICE SOLUTIONS

P1. (a) The vertical angle paired with (a) is part of a right triangle with the 40° angle. Thus the measure can be found:

$$90° = 40° + a$$
$$a = 50°$$

(b) The triangle formed by the supplementary angle to (b) is part of a triangle with the vertical angle paired with (a) and the given angle of 27°. Since $a = 50°$:

$$180° = (180° - b) + 50° + 27°$$
$$103° = 180° - b$$
$$-77° = -b$$
$$77° = b$$

(c) As they are part of a transversal crossing parallel lines, angles (b) and (c) are supplementary. Thus $c = 103°$

$$V = \frac{1}{3}\pi r^2 h = \frac{1}{3}\pi(5\text{ yd})^2(7\text{ yd}) = \frac{35\pi}{3}\text{ yd}^3 \cong 36.65\text{ yd}^3$$

Transformations

A **rotation** is a transformation that turns a figure around a point called the **center of rotation**, which can lie anywhere in the plane. If a line is drawn from a point on a figure to the center of rotation, and another line is drawn from the center to the rotated image of that point, the angle between the two lines is the **angle of rotation**. The vertex of the angle of rotation is the center of rotation.

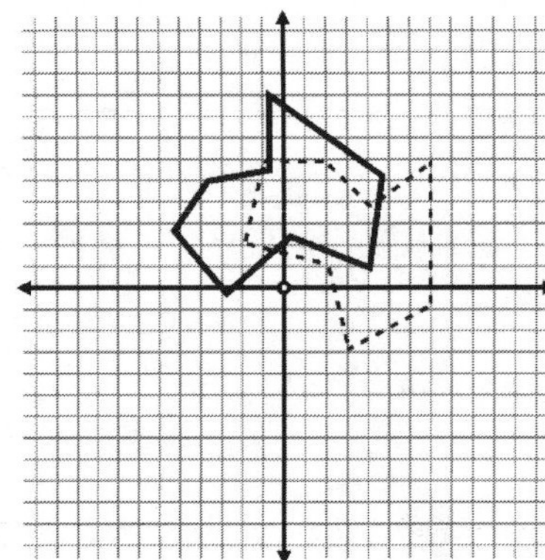

A **translation** is a transformation which slides a figure from one position in the plane to another position in the plane. The original figure and the translated figure have the same size, shape, and orientation. A **dilation** is a transformation which proportionally stretches or shrinks a figure by a **scale factor**. The dilated image is the same shape and orientation as the original image but a different size. A polygon and its dilated image are similar.

Translation

Dilation

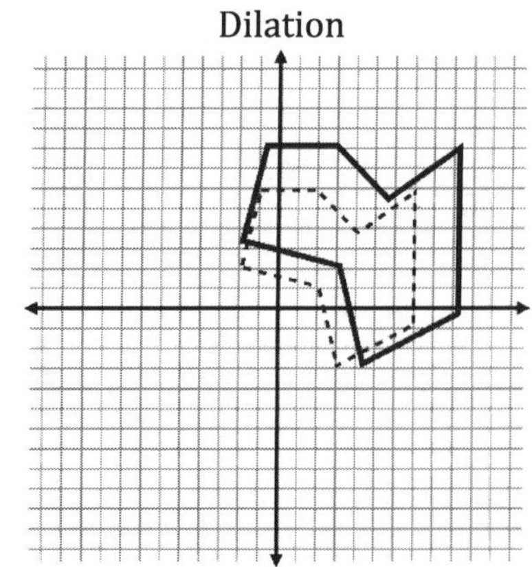

A **reflection of a figure over a line** (a "flip") creates a congruent image that is the same distance from the line as the original figure but on the opposite side. The **line of reflection** is the perpendicular bisector of any line segment drawn from a point on the original figure to its reflected image (unless the point and its reflected image happen to be the same point, which happens when a figure is reflected over one of its own sides). A **reflection of a figure over a point** (an inversion) in two dimensions is the same as the rotation of the figure 180° about that point. The image of the figure is congruent to the original figure. The **point of reflection** is the midpoint of a line segment which connects a point in the figure to its image (unless the point and its reflected image happen to be the same point, which happens when a figure is reflected in one of its own points).

Reflection of a figure over a line

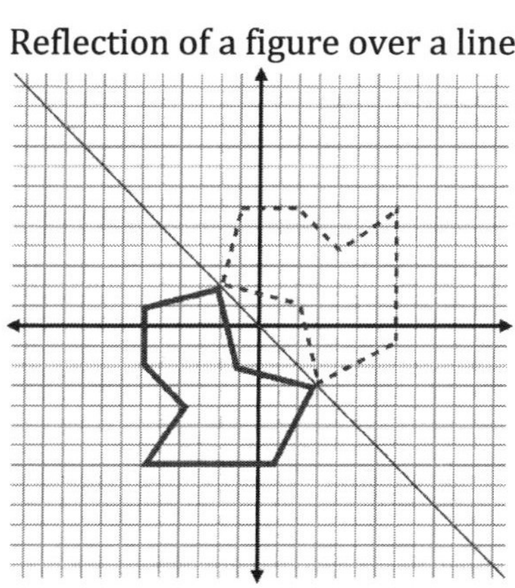

Reflection of a figure over a point

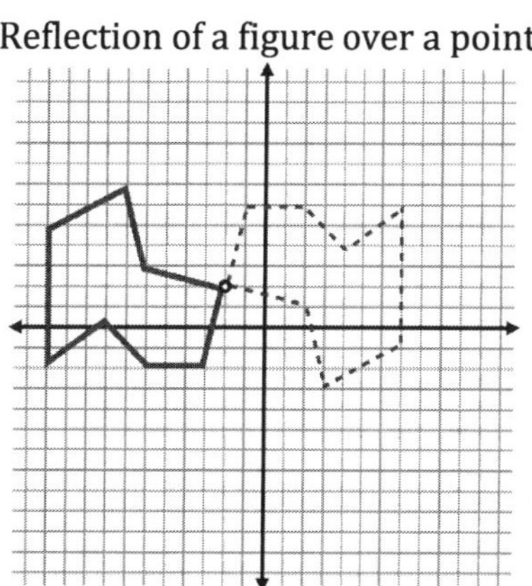

Review Video: Rotation
Visit mometrix.com/academy and enter code: 602600
Review Video: Translation
Visit mometrix.com/academy and enter code: 718628
Review Video: Dilation
Visit mometrix.com/academy and enter code: 471630
Review Video: Reflection
Visit mometrix.com/academy and enter code: 955068

PRACTICE

P1. Use the coordinate plane to reflect the figure below across the y-axis.

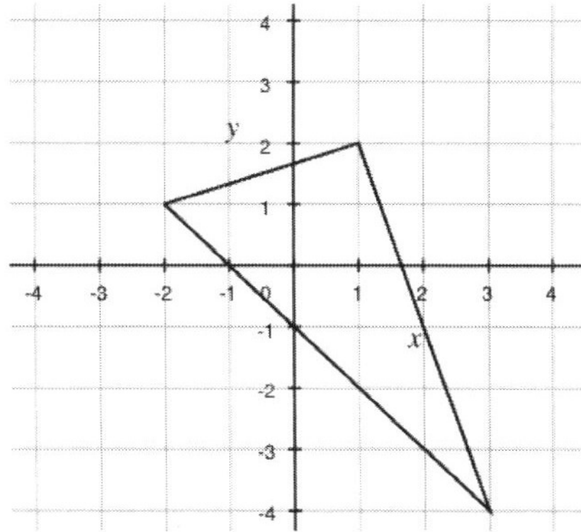

P2. Use the coordinate plane to enlarge the figure below by a factor of 2.

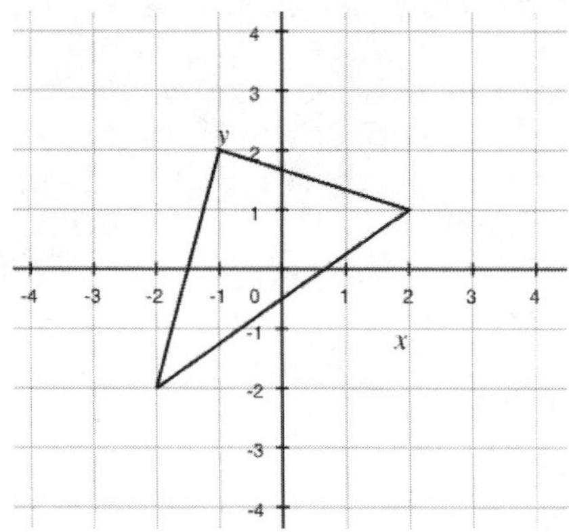

Practice Solutions

P1. To reflect the image across the y-axis, replace each x-coordinate of the points that are the vertex of the triangle, x, with its negative, $-x$.

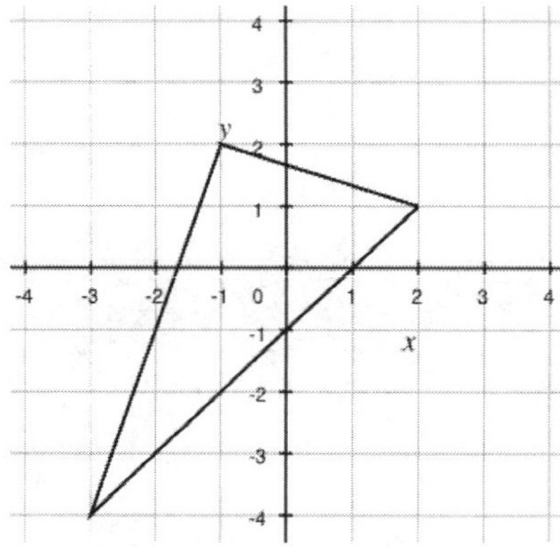

P2. An enlargement can be found by multiplying each coordinate of the coordinate pairs located at the triangle's vertices by 2. The original coordinates were $(-1, 2), (2, 1), (-2, -2)$, so the new coordinates are $(-2, 4), (4, 2), (-4, -4)$:

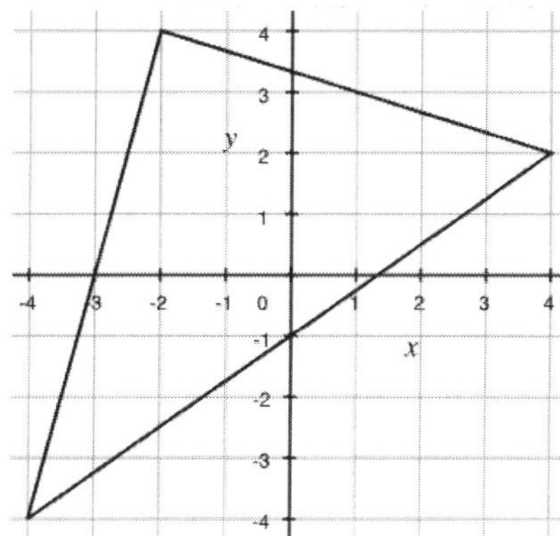

Two-Dimensional Shapes

Polygons

A **polygon** is a closed, two-dimensional figure with three or more straight line segments called **sides**. The point at which two sides of a polygon intersect is called the **vertex**. In a polygon, the number of sides is always equal to the number of vertices. A polygon with all sides congruent and all angles equal is called a **regular polygon**. Common polygons are:

Triangle = 3 sides
Quadrilateral = 4 sides
Pentagon = 5 sides
Hexagon = 6 sides
Heptagon = 7 sides
Octagon = 8 sides
Nonagon = 9 sides
Decagon = 10 sides
Dodecagon = 12 sides

More generally, an n-gon is a polygon that has n angles and n sides.

The sum of the interior angles of an n-sided polygon is $(n - 2) \times 180°$. For example, in a triangle $n = 3$. So, the sum of the interior angles is $(3 - 2) \times 180° = 180°$. In a quadrilateral, $n = 4$, and the sum of the angles is $(4 - 2) \times 180° = 360°$.

A line segment from the center of a polygon that is perpendicular to a side of the polygon is called the **apothem**. A line segment from the center of a polygon to a vertex of the polygon is called a **radius**. In a regular polygon, the apothem can be used to find the area of the polygon using the formula $A = \frac{1}{2}ap$, where a is the apothem, and p is the perimeter.

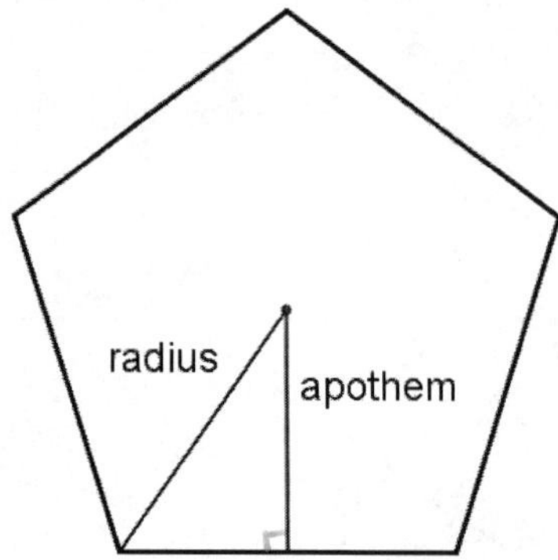

A **diagonal** is a line segment that joins two non-adjacent vertices of a polygon. The number of diagonals a polygon has can be found by using the formula:

$$\text{number of diagonals} = \frac{n(n-3)}{2}$$

Note that n is the number of sides in the polygon. This formula works for all polygons, not just regular polygons.

A **convex polygon** is a polygon whose diagonals all lie within the interior of the polygon. A **concave polygon** is a polygon with a least one diagonal that is outside the polygon. In the diagram below, quadrilateral $ABCD$ is concave because diagonal $\overline{AC}$ lies outside the polygon and quadrilateral $EFGH$ is convex because both diagonals lie inside the polygon

Concave

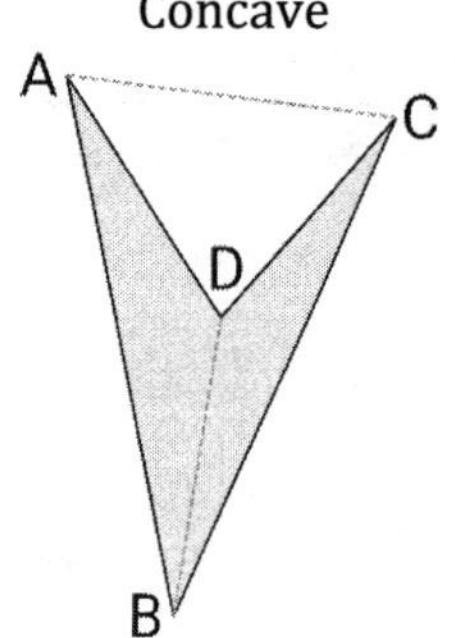

Convex

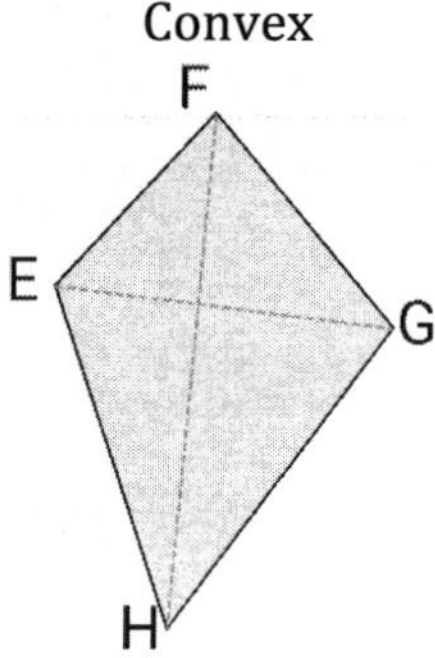

Congruent figures are geometric figures that have the same size and shape. All corresponding angles are equal, and all corresponding sides are equal. It is indicated by the symbol ≅.

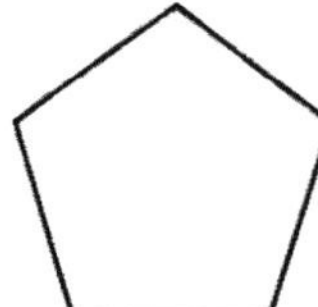

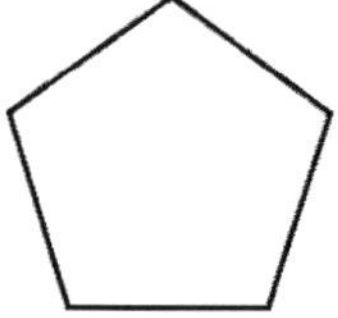

Congruent polygons

Similar figures are geometric figures that have the same shape, but do not necessarily have the same size. All corresponding angles are equal, and all corresponding sides are proportional, but they do not have to be equal. It is indicated by the symbol $\sim$.

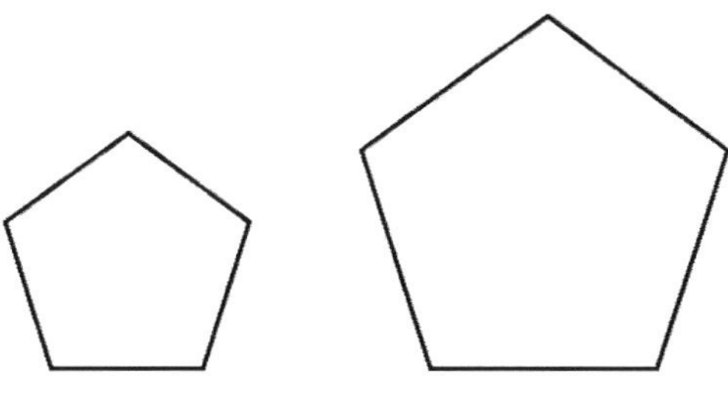

Similar polygons

Note that all congruent figures are also similar, but not all similar figures are congruent.

Review Video: Polygons, Similarity, and Congruence
Visit mometrix.com/academy and enter code: 686174

Review Video: Polygons
Visit mometrix.com/academy and enter code: 271869

LINE OF SYMMETRY

A line that divides a figure or object into congruent parts is called a **line of symmetry**. An object may have no lines of symmetry, one line of symmetry, or multiple (i.e., more than one) lines of symmetry.

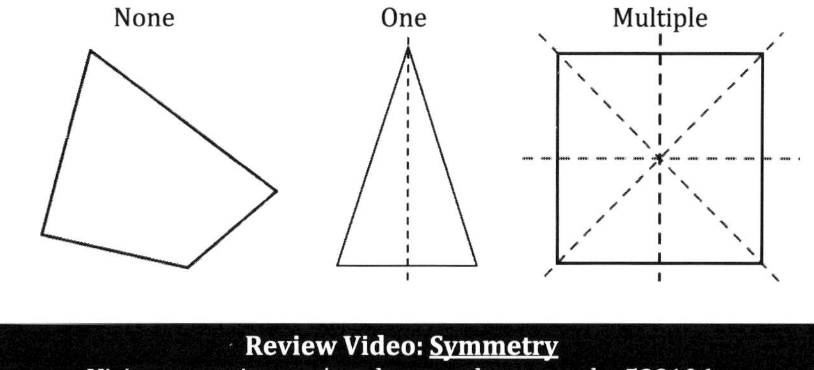

Review Video: Symmetry
Visit mometrix.com/academy and enter code: 528106

TRIANGLES

A triangle is a three-sided figure with the sum of its interior angles being 180° The **perimeter of any triangle** is found by summing the three side lengths; $P = a + b + c$. For an equilateral triangle, this is the same as $P = 3a$, where a is any side length, since all three sides are the same length.

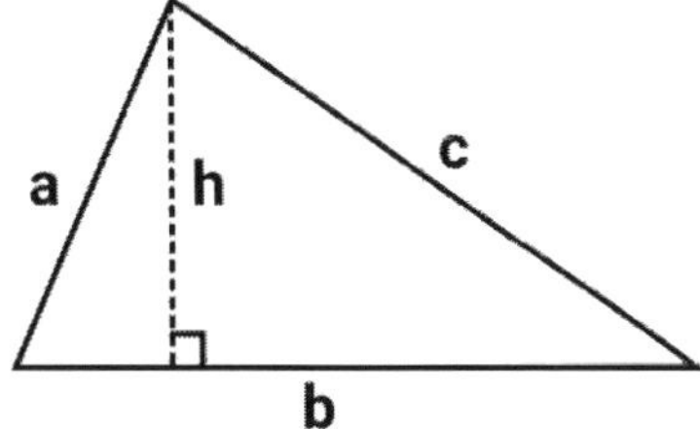

The **area of any triangle** can be found by taking half the product of one side length referred to as the base, often given the variable b and the perpendicular distance from that side to the opposite vertex called the altitude or height and given the variable h. In equation form that is $A = \frac{1}{2}bh$. Another formula that works for any triangle is $A = \sqrt{s(s-a)(s-b)(s-c)}$, where s is the semiperimeter: $\frac{a+b+c}{2}$, and a, b, and c are the lengths of the three sides. Special cases include isosceles triangles: $A = \frac{1}{2}b\sqrt{a^2 - \frac{b^2}{4}}$, where b is the unique side and a is the length of one of the two congruent sides, and equilateral triangles: $A = \frac{\sqrt{3}}{4}a^2$, where a is the length of a side.

Review Video: Area and Perimeter of a Triangle
Visit mometrix.com/academy and enter code: 853779

PARTS OF A TRIANGLE

An **altitude** of a triangle is a line segment drawn from one vertex perpendicular to the opposite side. In the diagram below, $\overline{BE}$, $\overline{AD}$, and $\overline{CF}$ are altitudes. The length of an altitude is also called the height of the triangle. The three altitudes in a triangle are always concurrent. The point of concurrency of the altitudes of a triangle, O, is called the **orthocenter**. Note that in an obtuse triangle, the orthocenter will be outside the triangle, and in a right triangle, the orthocenter is the vertex of the right angle.

A **median** of a triangle is a line segment drawn from one vertex to the midpoint of the opposite side. In the diagram below, $\overline{BH}$, $\overline{AG}$, and $\overline{CI}$ are medians. This is not the same as the altitude, except the altitude to the base of an isosceles triangle and all three altitudes of an equilateral triangle. The point of concurrency of the medians of a triangle, T, is called the **centroid**. This is the same point as the orthocenter only in an equilateral triangle. Unlike the orthocenter, the centroid is always inside the triangle. The centroid can also be considered the exact center of the triangle. Any shape triangle can be perfectly balanced on a tip placed at the centroid. The centroid is also the point that is two-thirds the distance from the vertex to the opposite side.

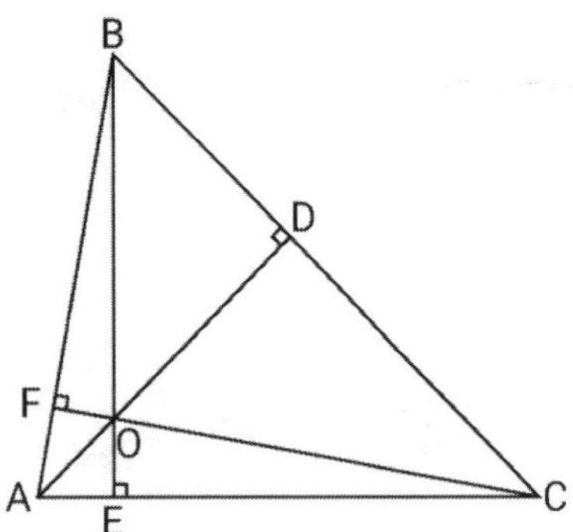

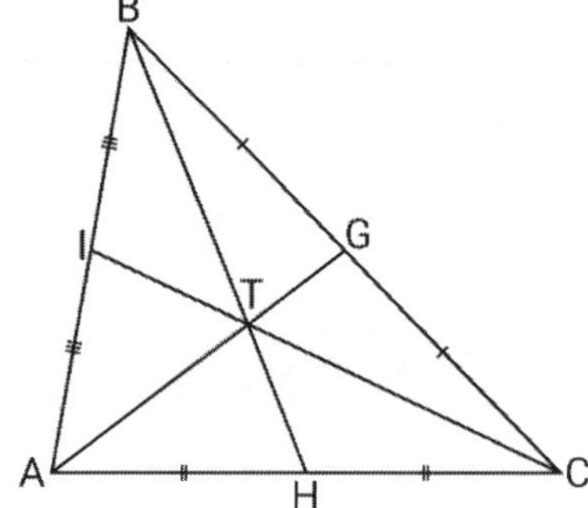

QUADRILATERALS

A **quadrilateral** is a closed two-dimensional geometric figure that has four straight sides. The sum of the interior angles of any quadrilateral is 360°.

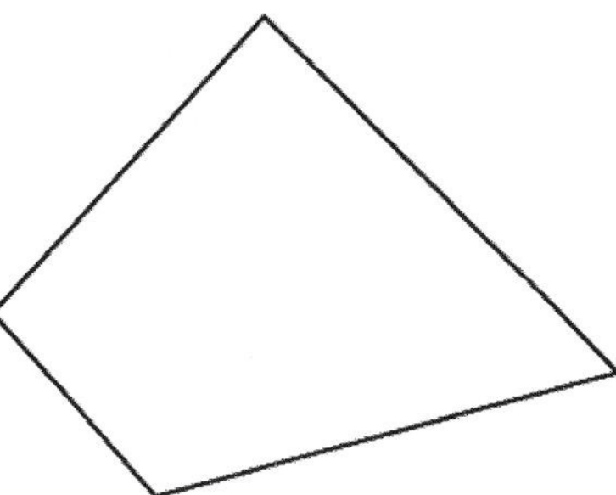

A **kite** is a quadrilateral with two pairs of adjacent sides that are congruent. A result of this is perpendicular diagonals. A kite can be concave or convex and has one line of symmetry.

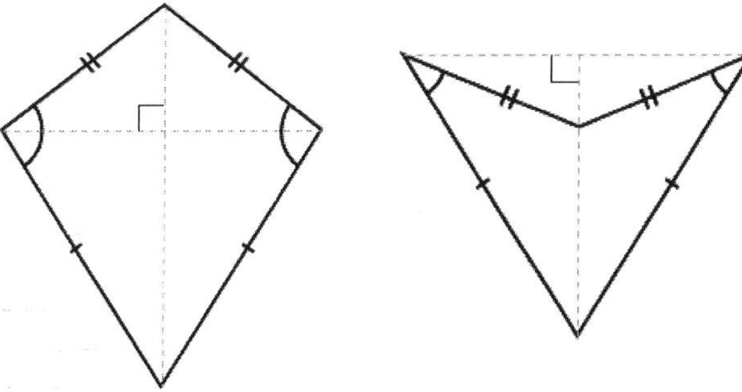

Trapezoid: A trapezoid is defined as a quadrilateral that has at least one pair of parallel sides. There are no rules for the second pair of sides. So, there are no rules for the diagonals and no lines of symmetry for a trapezoid.

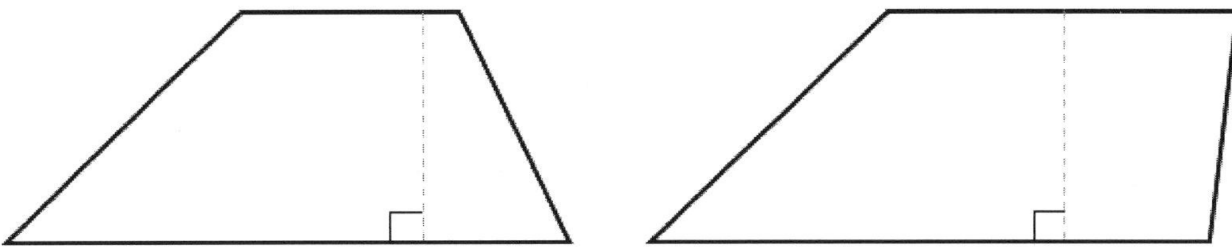

The **area of a trapezoid** is found by the formula $A = \frac{1}{2}h(b_1 + b_2)$, where h is the height (segment joining and perpendicular to the parallel bases), and b_1 and b_2 are the two parallel sides (bases). Do not use one of the other two sides as the height unless that side is also perpendicular to the parallel bases.

The **perimeter of a trapezoid** is found by the formula $P = a + b_1 + c + b_2$, where a, b_1, c, and b_2 are the four sides of the trapezoid.

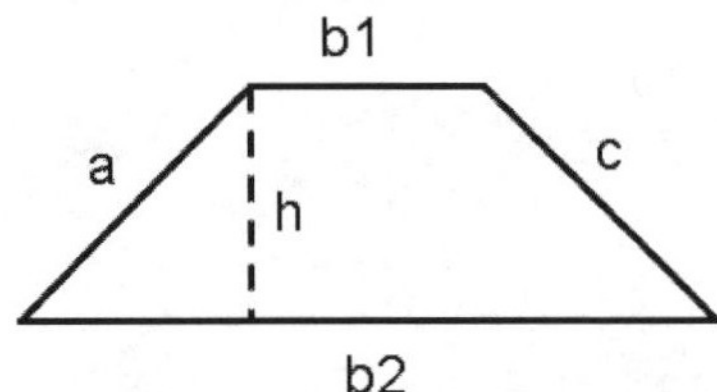

Review Video: Area and Perimeter of a Trapezoid
Visit mometrix.com/academy and enter code: 587523

Parallelogram: A quadrilateral that has two pairs of opposite parallel sides. As such it is a special type of trapezoid. The sides that are parallel are also congruent. The opposite interior angles are always congruent, and the consecutive interior angles are supplementary. The diagonals of a parallelogram divide each other. Each diagonal divides the parallelogram into two congruent triangles. A parallelogram has no line of symmetry, but does have 180-degree rotational symmetry about the midpoint.

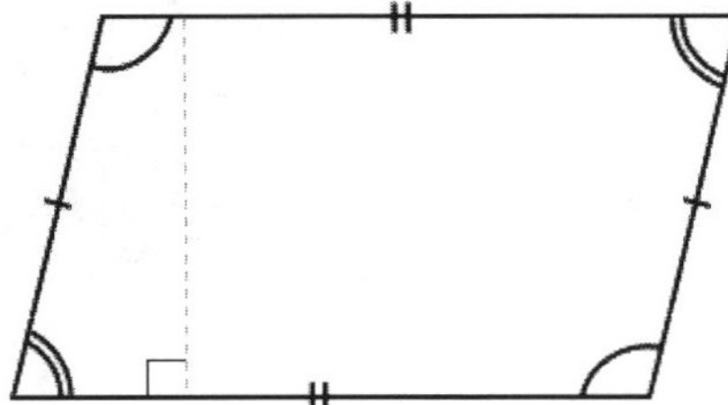

The **area of a parallelogram** is found by the formula $A = bh$, where b is the length of the base, and h is the height. Note that the base and height correspond to the length and width in a rectangle, so this formula would apply to rectangles as well. Do not confuse the height of a parallelogram with the length of the second side. The two are only the same measure in the case of a rectangle.

The **perimeter of a parallelogram** is found by the formula $P = 2a + 2b$ or $P = 2(a + b)$, where a and b are the lengths of the two sides.

Review Video: Parallelogram
Visit mometrix.com/academy and enter code: 129981

Review Video: Area and Perimeter of a Parallelogram
Visit mometrix.com/academy and enter code: 718313

Isosceles trapezoid: A trapezoid with equal base angles. This gives rise to other properties including: the two nonparallel sides have the same length, the two non-base angles are also equal, and there is one line of symmetry through the midpoints of the parallel sides.

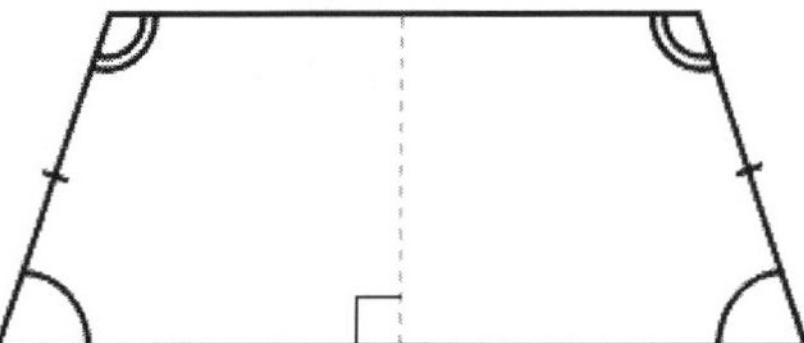

Rectangle: A quadrilateral with four right angles. All rectangles are parallelograms and trapezoids, but not all parallelograms or trapezoids are rectangles. The diagonals of a rectangle are congruent.

Rectangles have 2 lines of symmetry (through each pair of opposing midpoints) and 180-degree rotational symmetry about the midpoint.

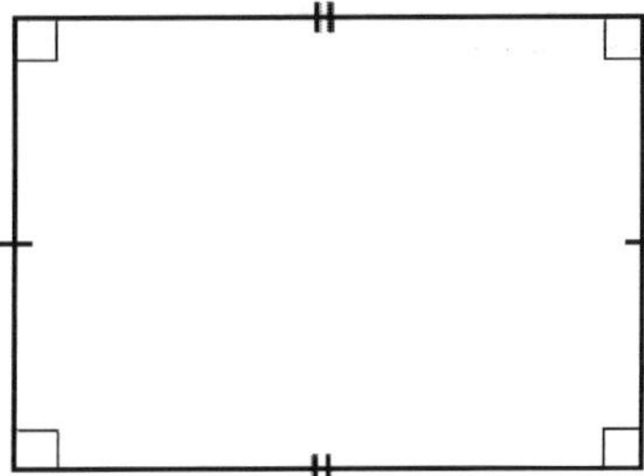

The **area of a rectangle** is found by the formula $A = lw$, where A is the area of the rectangle, l is the length (usually considered to be the longer side) and w is the width (usually considered to be the shorter side). The numbers for l and w are interchangeable.

The **perimeter of a rectangle** is found by the formula $P = 2l + 2w$ or $P = 2(l + w)$, where l is the length, and w is the width. It may be easier to add the length and width first and then double the result, as in the second formula.

Review Video: Area and Perimeter of a Rectangle
Visit mometrix.com/academy and enter code: 933707

Rhombus: A quadrilateral with four congruent sides. All rhombuses are parallelograms and kites; thus, they inherit all the properties of both types of quadrilaterals. The diagonals of a rhombus are perpendicular to each other. Rhombi have 2 lines of symmetry (along each of the diagonals) and 180-degree rotational symmetry. The **area of a rhombus** is half the product of the diagonals: $A = \frac{d_1 d_2}{2}$ and the perimeter of a rhombus is: $P = 2\sqrt{(d_1)^2 + (d_2)^2}$

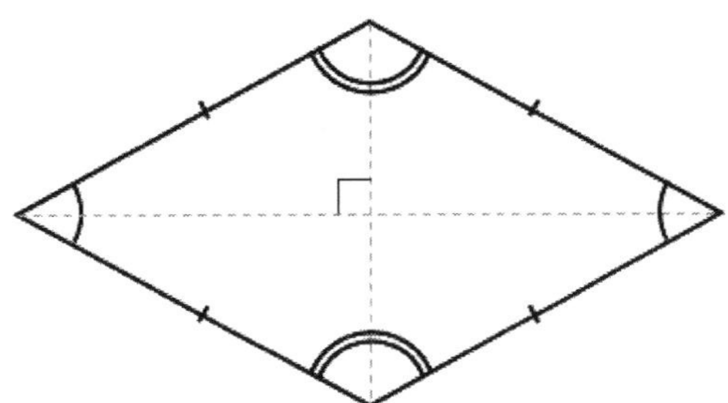

Review Video: Diagonals of Parallelograms, Rectangles, and Rhombi
Visit mometrix.com/academy and enter code: 320040

Square: A quadrilateral with four right angles and four congruent sides. Squares satisfy the criteria of all other types of quadrilaterals. The diagonals of a square are congruent and perpendicular to each other.

Squares have 4 lines of symmetry (through each pair of opposing midpoints and along each of the diagonals) as well as 90-degree rotational symmetry about the midpoint.

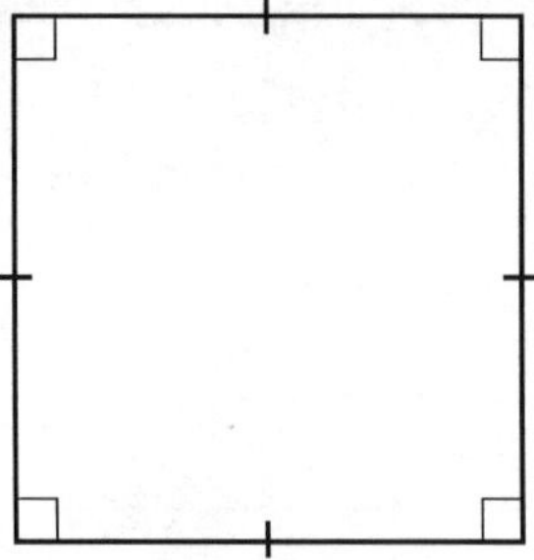

The **area of a square** is found by using the formula $A = s^2$, where s is the length of one side. The **perimeter of a square** is found by using the formula $P = 4s$, where s is the length of one side. Because all four sides are equal in a square, it is faster to multiply the length of one side by 4 than to add the same number four times. You could use the formulas for rectangles and get the same answer.

Review Video: Area and Perimeter of a Square
Visit mometrix.com/academy and enter code: 620902

The hierarchy of quadrilaterals can be shown as follows:

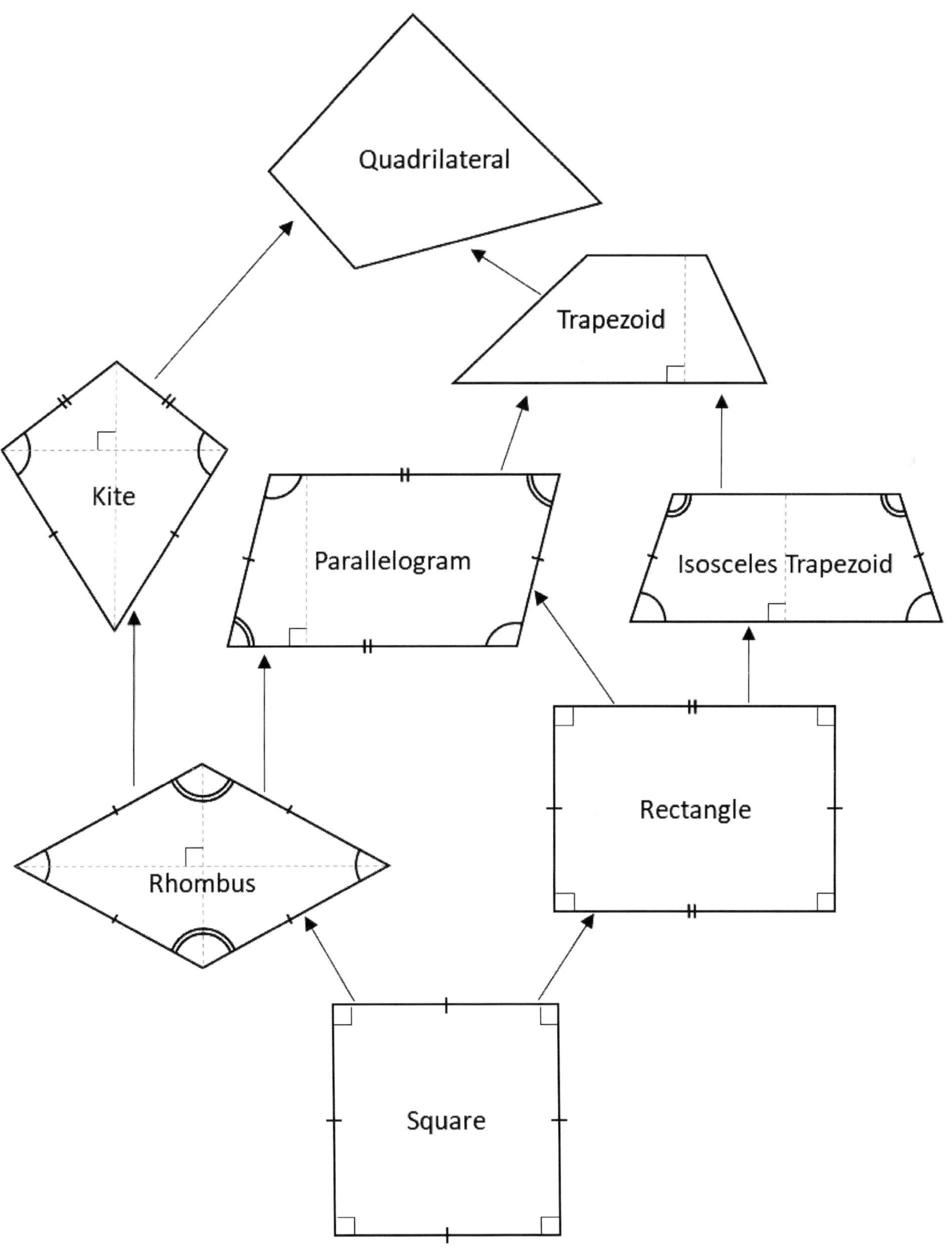

CIRCLES

The **center** of a circle is the single point from which every point on the circle is **equidistant**. The **radius** is a line segment that joins the center of the circle and any one point on the circle. All radii of a circle are equal. Circles that have the same center, but not the same length of radii are **concentric**. The **diameter** is a line segment that passes through the center of the circle and has both endpoints on the circle. The length of the diameter is exactly twice the length of the radius. Point O in the diagram below is the center of the circle, segments $\overline{OX}$, $\overline{OY}$, and $\overline{OZ}$ are radii, and segment $\overline{XZ}$ is a diameter.

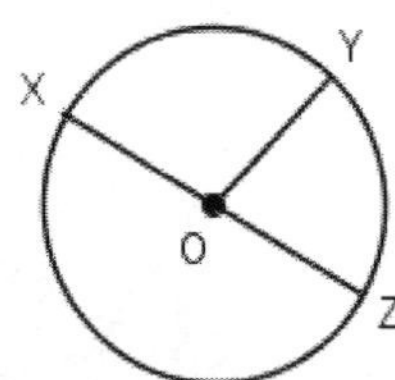

Review Video: Points of a Circle
Visit mometrix.com/academy and enter code: 420746

Review Video: The Diameter, Radius, and Circumference of Circles
Visit mometrix.com/academy and enter code: 448988

The **area of a circle** is found by the formula $A = \pi r^2$, where r is the length of the radius. If the diameter of the circle is given, remember to divide it in half to get the length of the radius before proceeding.

The **circumference** of a circle is found by the formula $C = 2\pi r$, where r is the radius. Again, remember to convert the diameter if you are given that measure rather than the radius.

Review Video: Area and Circumference of a Circle
Visit mometrix.com/academy and enter code: 243015

INSCRIBED AND CIRCUMSCRIBED FIGURES

These terms can be both used to describe a given arrangement of figures, depending on perspective. If each of the vertices of figure A lie on figure B, then it can be said that figure A is **inscribed** in figure B, but it can also be said that figure B is **circumscribed** about figure A. The following table and examples help to illustrate the concept. Note that the figures cannot both be circles, as they would be completely overlapping and neither would be inscribed or circumscribed.

Given	Description	Equivalent Description	Figures
Each of the sides of a pentagon is tangent to a circle	The circle is inscribed in the pentagon	The pentagon is circumscribed about the circle	
Each of the vertices of a pentagon lie on a circle	The pentagon is inscribed in the circle	The circle is circumscribed about the pentagon	

PRACTICE

P1. Find the area and perimeter of the following quadrilaterals:

(a) A square with side length 2.5 cm.

(b) A parallelogram with height 3 m, base 4 m, and other side 6 m.

(c) A rhombus with diagonals 15 in and 20 in.

P2. Calculate the area of a triangle with side lengths of 7 ft, 8 ft, and 9 ft.

P3. Square ABCD is inscribed in a circle with radius 20 m. What is the area of the part of the circle outside of the square?

PRACTICE SOLUTIONS

P1. (a) $A = s^2 = (2.5 \text{ cm})^2 = 6.25 \text{ cm}^2$; $P = 4s = 4 \times 2.5 \text{ cm} = 10 \text{ cm}$

(b) $A = bh = (3 \text{ m})(4 \text{ m}) = 12 \text{ m}^2$; $P = 2a + 2b = 2 \times 6 \text{ m} + 2 \times 4 \text{ m} = 20 \text{ m}$

(c) $A = \frac{d_1 d_2}{2} = \frac{(15 \text{ in})(20 \text{ in})}{2} = 150 \text{ in}^2$;
$P = 2\sqrt{(d_1)^2 + (d_2)^2} = 2\sqrt{(15 \text{ in})^2 + (20 \text{ in})^2} = 2\sqrt{625 \text{ in}^2} = 50 \text{ in}$

P2. Given only side lengths, we can use the semi perimeter to the find the area based on the formula, $A = \sqrt{s(s-a)(s-b)(s-c)}$, where s is the semiperimeter, $\frac{a+b+c}{2} = \frac{7+8+9}{2} = 12$ ft:

$$\begin{aligned} A &= \sqrt{12(12-7)(12-8)(12-9)} \\ &= \sqrt{(12)(5)(4)(3)} \\ &= 12\sqrt{5} \text{ ft}^2 \end{aligned}$$

P3. Begin by drawing a diagram of the situation, where we want to find the shaded area:

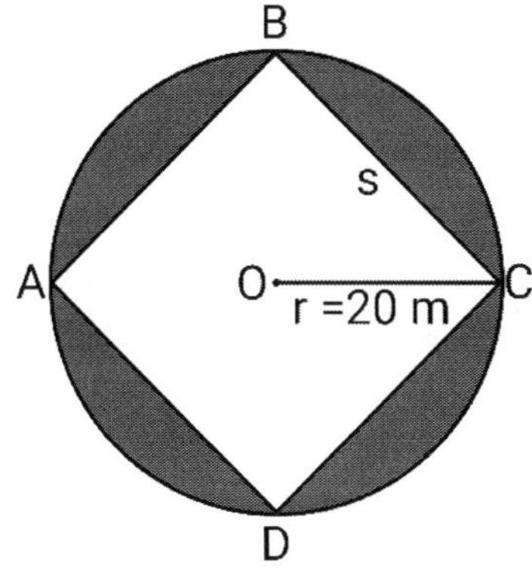

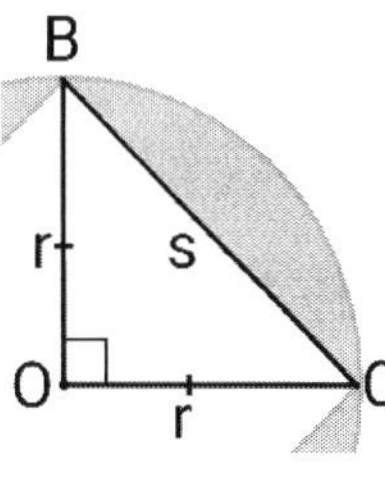

The area of the square is s^2, so the area we want to find is: $\pi r^2 - s^2$. Since the inscribed figure is a square, the triangle BCO is a 45-45-90 right triangle. Now, we can find $s^2 = r^2 + r^2 = 2r^2$. So, the shaded area is:

$$\begin{aligned} A &= \pi r^2 - s^2 \\ &= \pi r^2 - 2r^2 \\ &= (\pi - 2)r^2 \\ &= (\pi - 2) \times 400 \\ &\cong 456.6 \text{ m}^2 \end{aligned}$$

Three-Dimensional Shapes

Solids

The **surface area of a solid object** is the area of all sides or exterior surfaces. For objects such as prisms and pyramids, a further distinction is made between base surface area (B) and lateral surface area (LA). For a prism, the total surface area (SA) is $SA = LA + 2B$. For a pyramid or cone, the total surface area is $SA = LA + B$.

Review Video: How to Calculate the Volume of 3D Objects
Visit mometrix.com/academy and enter code: 163343

The **surface area of a sphere** can be found by the formula $A = 4\pi r^2$, where r is the radius. The volume is given by the formula $V = \frac{4}{3}\pi r^3$, where r is the radius. Both quantities are generally given in terms of π.

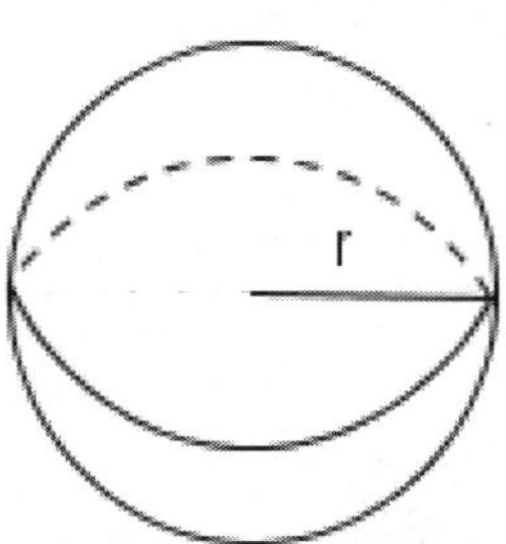

Review Video: Volume and Surface Area of a Sphere
Visit mometrix.com/academy and enter code: 786928

The **volume of any prism** is found by the formula $V = Bh$, where B is the area of the base, and h is the height (perpendicular distance between the bases). The surface area of any prism is the sum of the areas of both bases and all sides. It can be calculated as $SA = 2B + Ph$, where P is the perimeter of the base.

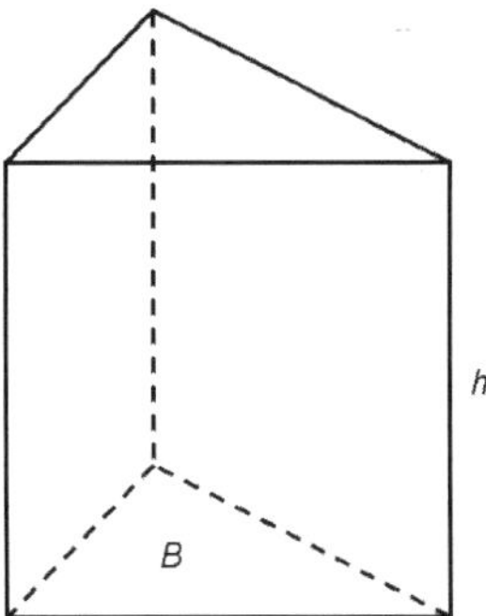

For a **rectangular prism**, the volume can be found by the formula $V = lwh$, where V is the volume, l is the length, w is the width, and h is the height. The surface area can be calculated as $SA = 2lw + 2hl + 2wh$ or $SA = 2(lw + hl + wh)$.

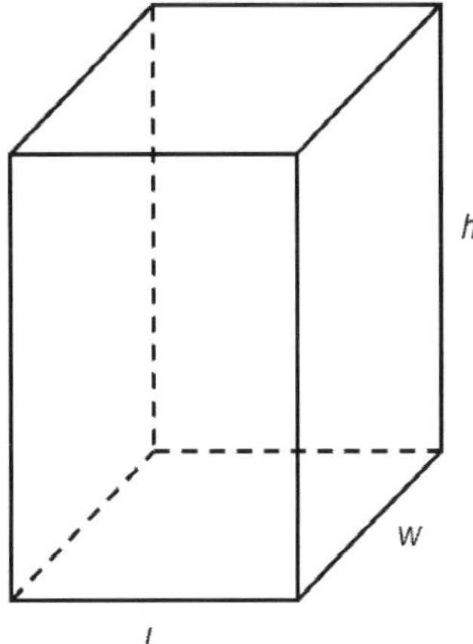

The **volume of a cube** can be found by the formula $V = s^3$, where s is the length of a side. The surface area of a cube is calculated as $SA = 6s^2$, where SA is the total surface area and s is the length of a side. These formulas are the same as the ones used for the volume and surface area of a rectangular prism, but simplified since all three quantities (length, width, and height) are the same.

Review Video: Volume and Surface Area of a Cube
Visit mometrix.com/academy and enter code: 664455

The **volume of a cylinder** can be calculated by the formula $V = \pi r^2 h$, where r is the radius, and h is the height. The surface area of a cylinder can be found by the formula $SA = 2\pi r^2 + 2\pi rh$. The first term is the base area multiplied by two, and the second term is the perimeter of the base multiplied by the height.

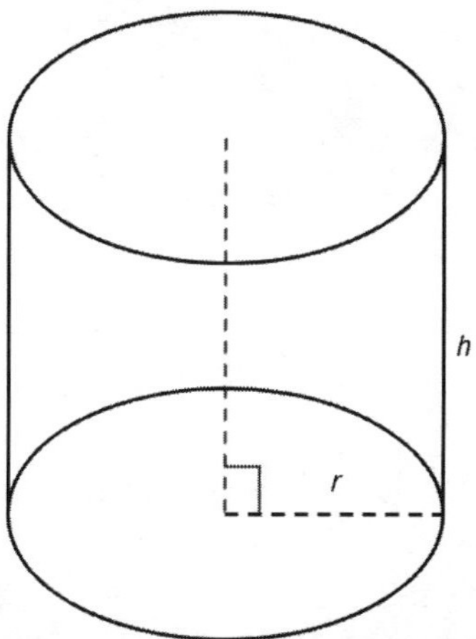

Review Video: Volume and Surface Area of a Right Circular Cylinder
Visit mometrix.com/academy and enter code: 226463

The **volume of a pyramid** is found by the formula $V = \frac{1}{3}Bh$, where B is the area of the base, and h is the height (perpendicular distance from the vertex to the base). Notice this formula is the same as $\frac{1}{3}$ times the volume of a prism. Like a prism, the base of a pyramid can be any shape.

Finding the **surface area of a pyramid** is not as simple as the other shapes we've looked at thus far. If the pyramid is a right pyramid, meaning the base is a regular polygon and the vertex is directly over the center of that polygon, the surface area can be calculated as $SA = B + \frac{1}{2}Ph_s$, where P is the perimeter of the base, and h_s is the slant height (distance from the vertex to the midpoint of one side of the base). If the pyramid is irregular, the area of each triangle side must be calculated individually and then summed, along with the base.

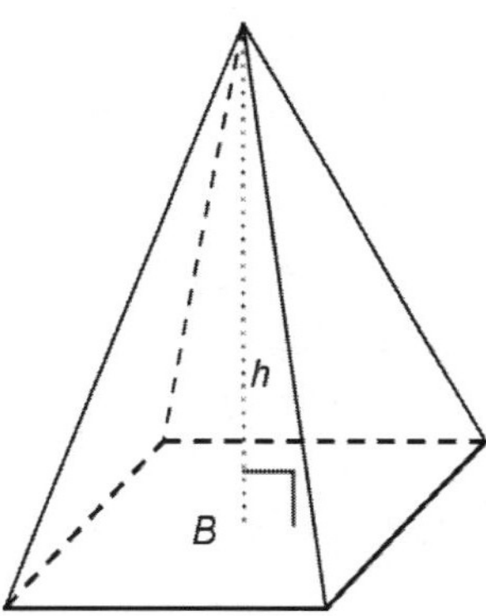

Review Video: Volume and Surface Area of a Pyramid
Visit mometrix.com/academy and enter code: 621932

The **volume of a cone** is found by the formula $V = \frac{1}{3}\pi r^2 h$, where r is the radius, and h is the height. Notice this is the same as $\frac{1}{3}$ times the volume of a cylinder. The surface area can be calculated as $SA =$

$\pi r^2 + \pi rs$, where s is the slant height. The slant height can be calculated using the Pythagorean theorem to be $\sqrt{r^2 + h^2}$, so the surface area formula can also be written as $SA = \pi r^2 + \pi r\sqrt{r^2 + h^2}$.

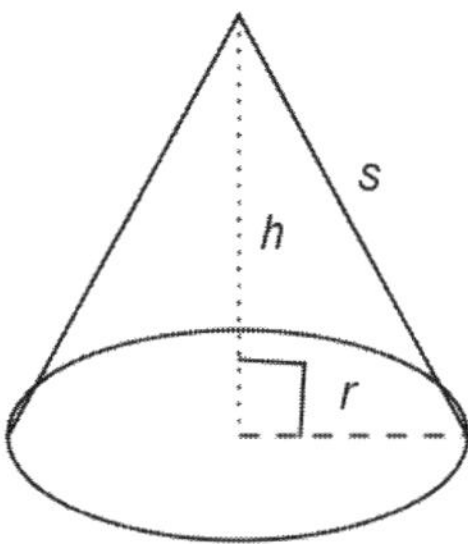

Review Video: Volume and Surface Area of a Right Circular Cone
Visit mometrix.com/academy and enter code: 573574

PRACTICE

P1. Find the surface area and volume of the following solids:

(a) A cylinder with radius 5 m and height 0.5 m.

(b) A trapezoidal prism with base area of 254 mm^2, base perimeter 74 mm, and height 10 mm.

(c) A half sphere (radius 5 yds) on the base of an inverted cone with the same radius and a height of 7 yds.

PRACTICE SOLUTIONS

P1. (a) $SA = 2\pi r^2 + 2\pi rh = 2\pi(5\text{ m})^2 + 2\pi(5\text{ m})(0.5\text{ m}) = 55\pi\text{ m}^2 \cong 172.79\text{ m}^2$;
$V = \pi r^2 h = \pi(5\text{ m})^2(0.5\text{ m}) = 12.5\pi\text{ m}^3 \cong 39.27\text{ m}^3$

(b) $SA = 2B + Ph = 2(254\text{ mm}^2) + (74\text{ mm})(10\text{ mm}) = 1248\text{ mm}^2$;
$V = Bh = (254\text{ mm}^2)(10\text{ mm}) = 2540\text{ mm}^3$

(c) We can find s, the slant height using Pythagoras' theorem, and since this solid is made of parts of simple solids, we can combine the formulas to find surface area and volume:

$$s = \sqrt{r^2 + h^2} = \sqrt{(5\text{ yd})^2 + (7\text{ yd})^2} = \sqrt{74}\text{ yd}$$

$$SA = \frac{4\pi r^2}{2} + \pi rs = \frac{4\pi(5\text{ yd})^2}{2} + \pi(5\text{ yd})(\sqrt{74}\text{ yd}) = (5\pi + 5\pi\sqrt{74})\text{ yd}^2 \cong 150.83\text{ yd}^2$$

$$V = \frac{1}{3}\pi r^2 h = \frac{1}{3}\pi(5\text{ yd})^2(7\text{ yd}) = \frac{35\pi}{3}\text{ yd}^3 \cong 36.65\text{ yd}^3$$

Triangle Classification and Properties

A **scalene triangle** is a triangle with no congruent sides. A scalene triangle will also have three angles of different measures. The angle with the largest measure is opposite the longest side, and the angle with the smallest measure is opposite the shortest side. An **acute triangle** is a triangle whose three angles are all less than 90°. If two of the angles are equal, the acute triangle is also an **isosceles triangle**. An isosceles triangle will also have two congruent angles opposite the two congruent sides. If the three angles are all equal, the acute triangle is also an **equilateral triangle**. An equilateral triangle will also have three congruent angles, each 60°. All equilateral triangles are also acute triangles. An **obtuse triangle** is a triangle with exactly one angle greater than 90°. The other two angles may or may not be equal. If the two remaining angles are equal, the obtuse triangle is also an isosceles triangle. A **right**

triangle is a triangle with exactly one angle equal to 90°. All right triangles follow the Pythagorean theorem. A right triangle can never be acute or obtuse.

The table below illustrates how each descriptor places a different restriction on the triangle:

Angles / Sides	**Acute:** All angles < 90°	**Obtuse:** One angle > 90°	**Right:** One angle = 90°
Scalene: No equal side lengths	$90° > \angle a > \angle b > \angle c$ $x > y > z$	$\angle a > 90° > \angle b > \angle c$ $x > y > z$	$90° = \angle a > \angle b > \angle c$ $x > y > z$
Isosceles: Two equal side lengths	$90° > \angle a, \angle b, or\ \angle c$ $\angle b = \angle c, \quad y = z$	$\angle a > 90° > \angle b = \angle c$ $x > y = z$	$\angle a = 90°, \angle b = \angle c = 45°$ $x > y = z$
Equilateral: Three equal side lengths	$60° = \angle a = \angle b = \angle c$ $x = y = z$		

Review Video: Introduction to Types of Triangles
Visit mometrix.com/academy and enter code: 511711

SIMILARITY AND CONGRUENCE RULES

Similar triangles are triangles whose corresponding angles are equal and whose corresponding sides are proportional. Represented by AAA. Similar triangles whose corresponding sides are congruent are also congruent triangles.

The triangles can be shown to be **congruent** in 5 ways:

- **SSS**: Three sides of one triangle are congruent to the three corresponding sides of the second triangle.
- **SAS**: Two sides and the included angle (the angle formed by those two sides) of one triangle are congruent to the corresponding two sides and included angle of the second triangle.
- **ASA**: Two angles and the included side (the side that joins the two angles) of one triangle are congruent to the corresponding two angles and included side of the second triangle.

- **AAS**: Two angles and a non-included side of one triangle are congruent to the corresponding two angles and non-included side of the second triangle.
- **HL**: The hypotenuse and leg of one right triangle are congruent to the corresponding hypotenuse and leg of the second right triangle.

Review Video: Similar Triangles
Visit mometrix.com/academy and enter code: 398538

General Rules for Triangles

The **triangle inequality theorem** states that the sum of the measures of any two sides of a triangle is always greater than the measure of the third side. If the sum of the measures of two sides were equal to the third side, a triangle would be impossible because the two sides would lie flat across the third side and there would be no vertex. If the sum of the measures of two of the sides was less than the third side, a closed figure would be impossible because the two shortest sides would never meet. In other words, for a triangle with sides lengths A, B, and C: $A + B > C, B + C > A$, and $A + C > B$

The sum of the measures of the interior angles of a triangle is always 180°. Therefore, a triangle can never have more than one angle greater than or equal to 90°.

In any triangle, the angles opposite congruent sides are congruent, and the sides opposite congruent angles are congruent. The largest angle is always opposite the longest side, and the smallest angle is always opposite the shortest side.

The line segment that joins the midpoints of any two sides of a triangle is always parallel to the third side and exactly half the length of the third side.

Practice

P1. Given the following pairs of triangles, determine whether they are similar, congruent, or neither (note that the figures are not drawn to scale):

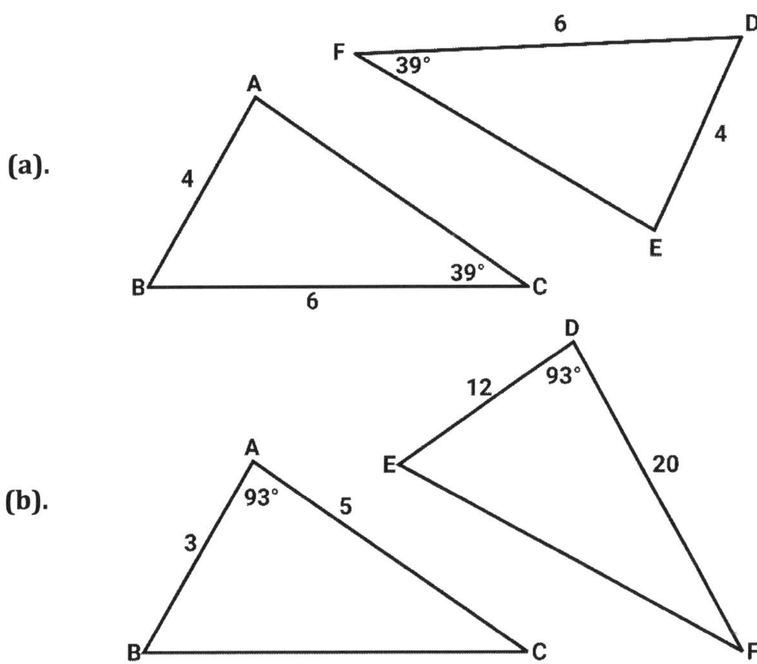

(c).

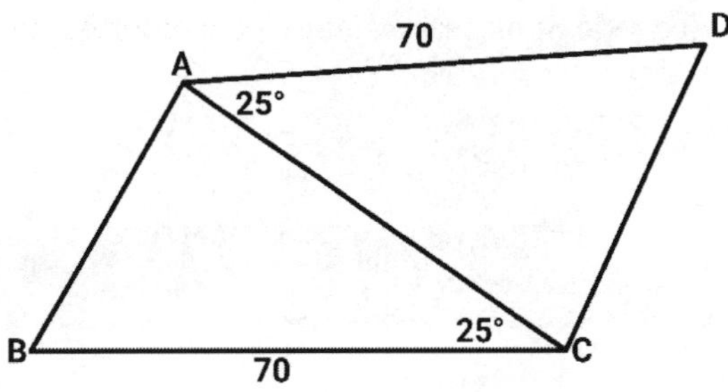

P2. Calculate the following values based on triangle MNO:

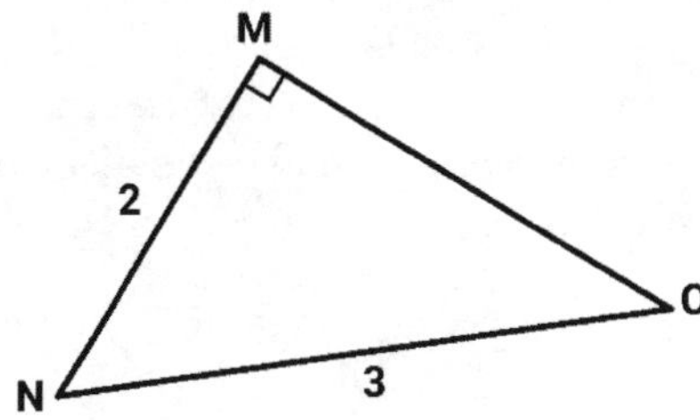

(a) length of $\overline{MO}$

(b) sin(∠NOM)

(c) area of the triangle, if the units of the measurements are in miles

Practice Solutions

P1. (a). Neither: We are given that two sides lengths and an angle are equal, however, the angle given is not between the given side lengths. That means there are two possible triangles that could satisfy the given measurements. Thus, we cannot be certain of congruence:

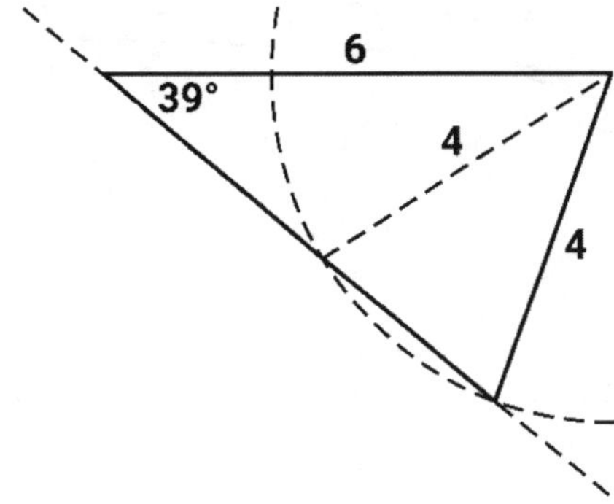

(b) Similar: Since we are given a side-angle-side of each triangle and the side lengths given are scaled evenly $\left(\frac{3}{5} \times \frac{4}{4} = \frac{12}{20}\right)$ and the angles are equal. Thus, $\Delta ABC \sim \Delta DEF$. If the side lengths were equal, then they would be congruent.

(c) Congruent: Even though we aren't given a measurement for the shared side of the figure, since it is shared it is equal. So, this is a case of SAS. Thus, $\Delta ABC \cong \Delta CDA$

P2. (a) Since triangle MNO is a right triangle, we can use the simple form of Pythagoras theorem to find the missing side length:

$$\left(\overline{\text{MO}}\right)^2 + 2^2 = 3^2$$
$$\left(\overline{\text{MO}}\right)^2 = 9 - 4$$
$$\overline{\text{MO}} = \sqrt{5}$$

(b) Recall that sine of an angle in a right triangle is the ratio of the opposite side to the hypotenuse. So, $\sin(\angle\text{NOM}) = 2/3$

(c) Since triangle MNO is a right triangle, we can use either of the legs as the height and the other as the base in the simple formula for area of a triangle:

$$A = \frac{bh}{2}$$
$$= \frac{(2\text{ mi})(\sqrt{5}\text{ mi})}{2}$$
$$= \sqrt{5}\text{ mi}^2$$

Introductory Trigonometry

Pythagorean Theorem

The side of a triangle opposite the right angle is called the **hypotenuse**. The other two sides are called the legs. The Pythagorean theorem states a relationship among the legs and hypotenuse of a right triangle: $a^2 + b^2 = c^2$, where a and b are the lengths of the legs of a right triangle, and c is the length of the hypotenuse. Note that this formula will only work with right triangles.

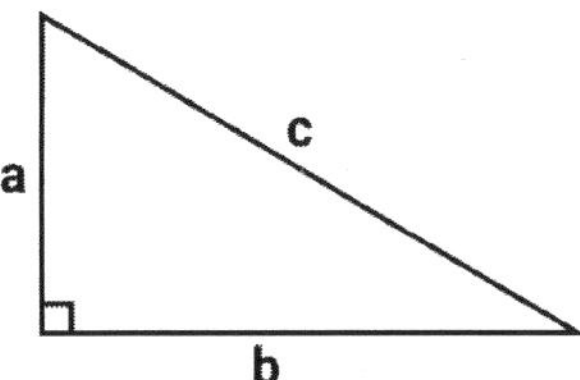

Review Video: Pythagorean Theorem
Visit mometrix.com/academy and enter code: 906576

Trigonometric Formulas

In the diagram below, angle C is the right angle, and side c is the hypotenuse. Side a is the side opposite to angle A and side b is the side opposite to angle B. Using ratios of side lengths as a means to calculate the sine, cosine, and tangent of an acute angle only works for right triangles.

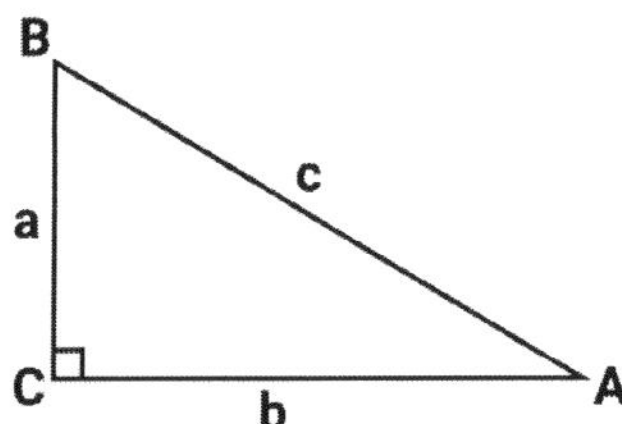

$$\sin A = \frac{\text{opposite side}}{\text{hypotenuse}} = \frac{a}{c} \qquad \csc A = \frac{1}{\sin A} = \frac{\text{hypotenuse}}{\text{opposite side}} = \frac{c}{a}$$
$$\cos A = \frac{\text{adjacent side}}{\text{hypotenuse}} = \frac{b}{c} \qquad \sec A = \frac{1}{\cos A} = \frac{\text{hypotenuse}}{\text{adjacent side}} = \frac{c}{b}$$
$$\tan A = \frac{\text{opposite side}}{\text{adjacent side}} = \frac{a}{b} \qquad \cot A = \frac{1}{\tan A} = \frac{\text{adjacent side}}{\text{opposite side}} = \frac{b}{a}$$

Laws of Sines and Cosines

The **law of sines** states that $\frac{\sin A}{a} = \frac{\sin B}{b} = \frac{\sin C}{c}$, where *A*, *B*, and *C* are the angles of a triangle, and *a*, *b*, and *c* are the sides opposite their respective angles. This formula will work with all triangles, not just right triangles.

The **law of cosines** is given by the formula $c^2 = a^2 + b^2 - 2ab(\cos C)$, where *a*, *b*, and *c* are the sides of a triangle, and *C* is the angle opposite side *c*. This is a generalized form of the Pythagorean theorem that can be used on any triangle.

Review Video: Upper Level Trig (Law of Sines)
Visit mometrix.com/academy and enter code: 206844

Review Video: Law of Cosines
Visit mometrix.com/academy and enter code: 158911

Practice

P1. Calculate the following values based on triangle MNO:

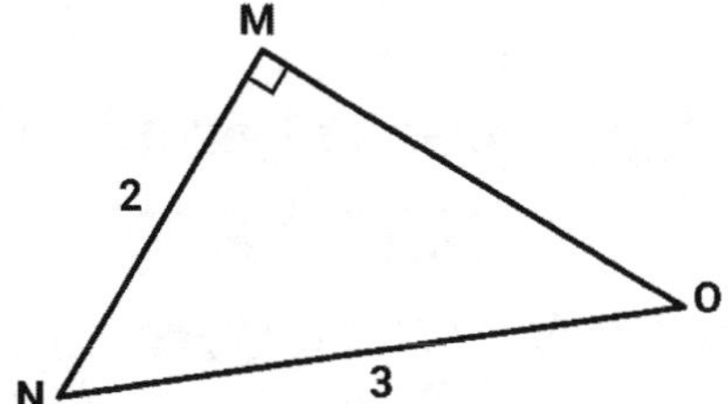

(a) length of $\overline{\text{MO}}$

(b) $\sin(\angle\text{NOM})$

(c) area of the triangle, if the units of the measurements are in miles

Practice Solutions

P1. (a) Since triangle MNO is a right triangle, we can use the simple form of Pythagoras theorem to find the missing side length:

$$\left(\overline{\text{MO}}\right)^2 + 2^2 = 3^2$$
$$\left(\overline{\text{MO}}\right)^2 = 9 - 4$$
$$\overline{\text{MO}} = \sqrt{5}$$

(b) Recall that sine of an angle in a right triangle is the ratio of the opposite side to the hypotenuse. So, $\sin(\angle\text{NOM}) = 2/3$

(c) Since triangle MNO is a right triangle, we can use either of the legs as the height and the other as the base in the simple formula for area of a triangle:

$$A = \frac{bh}{2}$$
$$= \frac{(2\text{ mi})(\sqrt{5}\text{ mi})}{2}$$
$$= \sqrt{5}\text{ mi}^2$$

Circle Properties

ARCS

An **arc** is a portion of a circle. Specifically, an arc is the set of points between and including two points on a circle. An arc does not contain any points inside the circle. When a segment is drawn from the endpoints of an arc to the center of the circle, a sector is formed. A **minor arc** is an arc that has a measure less than 180°. A **major arc** is an arc having a measure of at least 180°. Every minor arc has a corresponding major arc that can be found by subtracting the measure of the minor arc from 360°. A **semicircle** is an arc whose endpoints are the endpoints of the diameter of a circle. A semicircle is exactly half of a circle.

Arc length is the length of that portion of the circumference between two points on the circle. The formula for arc length is $s = \frac{\pi r \theta}{180°}$ where s is the arc length, r is the length of the radius, and θ is the angular measure of the arc in degrees, or $s = r\theta$, where θ is the angular measure of the arc in radians (2π radians $=$ 360 degrees).

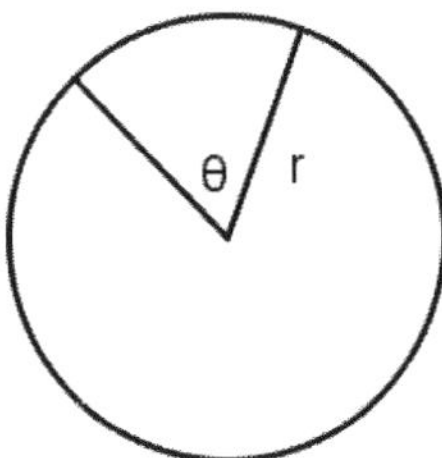

ANGLES OF CIRCLES

A **central angle** is an angle whose vertex is the center of a circle and whose legs intercept an arc of the circle. The measure of a central angle is equal to the measure of the minor arc it intercepts.

An **inscribed angle** is an angle whose vertex lies on a circle and whose legs contain chords of that circle. The portion of the circle intercepted by the legs of the angle is called the intercepted arc. The measure of the intercepted arc is exactly twice the measure of the inscribed angle. In the following diagram, angle *ABC* is an inscribed angle. $\widehat{AC} = 2(\text{m}\angle ABC)$

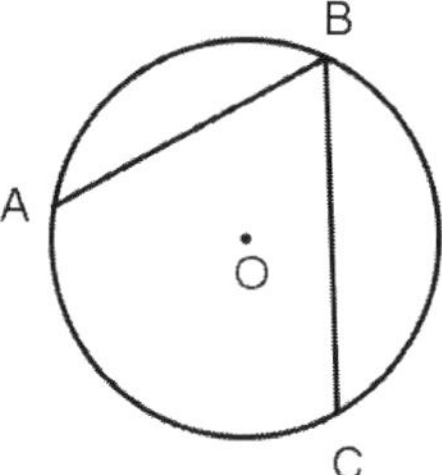

Any angle inscribed in a semicircle is a right angle. The intercepted arc is 180°, making the inscribed angle half that, or 90°. In the diagram below, angle *ABC* is inscribed in semicircle *ABC*, making angle *ABC* equal to 90°.

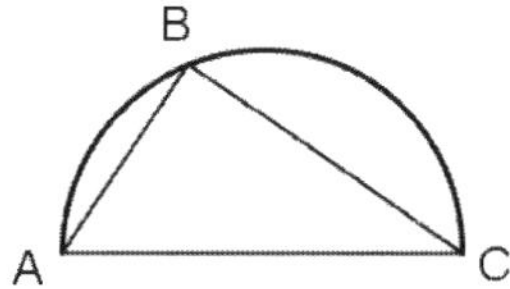

Secants, Chords, and Tangents

A **secant** is a line that intersects a circle in two points. The segment of a secant line that is contained within the circle is called a **chord**. Two secants may intersect inside the circle, on the circle, or outside the circle. When the two secants intersect on the circle, an inscribed angle is formed.When two secants intersect inside a circle, the measure of each of two vertical angles is equal to half the sum of the two intercepted arcs. Consider the following diagram where $m\angle AEB = \frac{1}{2}(\widehat{AB} + \widehat{CD})$ and $m\angle BEC = \frac{1}{2}(\widehat{BC} + \widehat{AD})$.

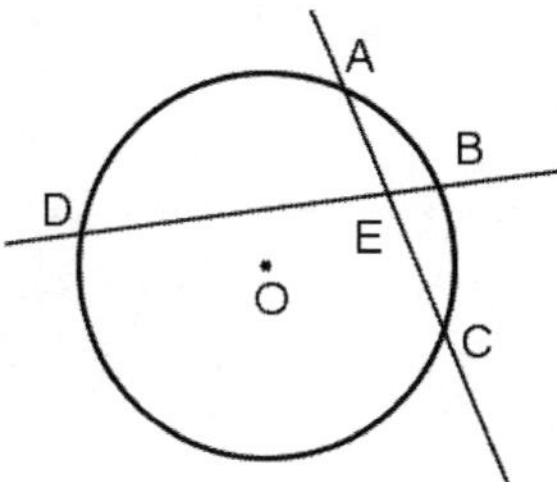

When two secants intersect outside a circle, the measure of the angle formed is equal to half the difference of the two arcs that lie between the two secants. In the diagram below, $m\angle AEB = \frac{1}{2}(\widehat{AB} - \widehat{CD})$.

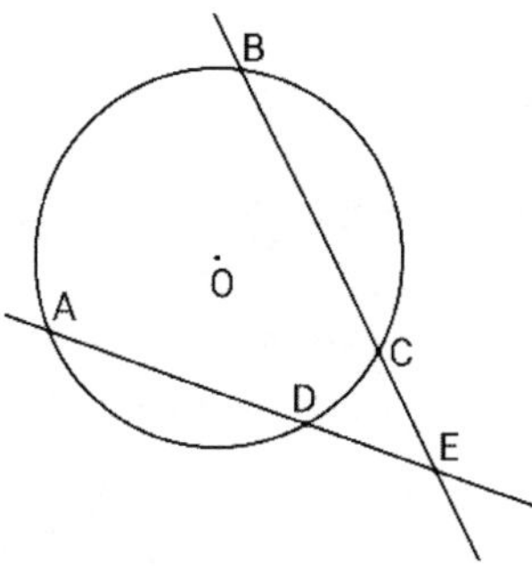

A **tangent** is a line in the same plane as a circle that touches the circle in exactly one point. The point at which a tangent touches a circle is called the **point of tangency**. While a line segment can be tangent to a circle as part of a line that is tangent, it is improper to say a tangent can be simply a line segment that touches the circle in exactly one point.

In the diagram below, $\overleftrightarrow{EB}$ is a secant and contains chord $\overline{EB}$ and $\overleftrightarrow{CD}$ is tangent to circle A. Notice that $\overline{FB}$ is not tangent to the circle. $\overline{FB}$ is a line segment that touches the circle in exactly one point, but if the segment were extended, it would touch the circle in a second point. In the diagram below, point B is the point of tangency.

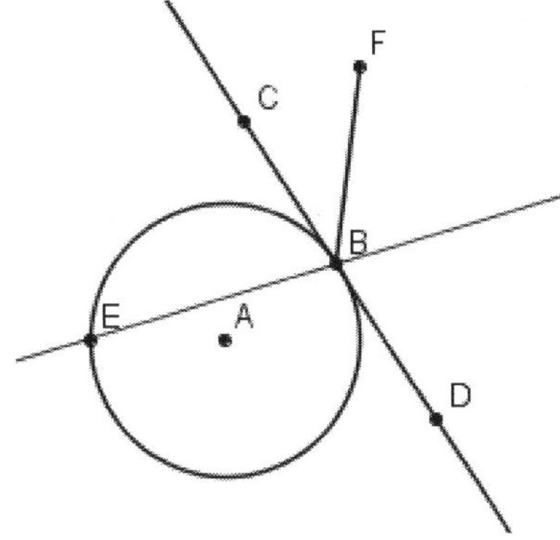

Review Video: Tangent Lines of a Circle
Visit mometrix.com/academy and enter code: 780167

SECTORS

A **sector** is the portion of a circle formed by two radii and their intercepted arc. While the arc length is exclusively the points that are also on the circumference of the circle, the sector is the entire area bounded by the arc and the two radii.

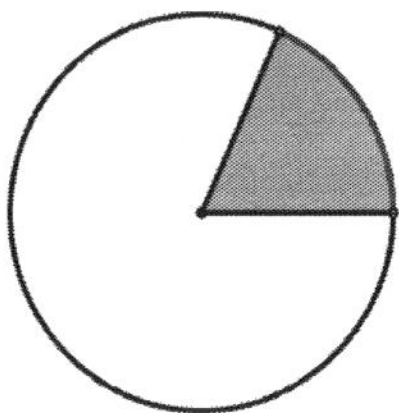

The **area of a sector** of a circle is found by the formula, $A = \frac{\theta r^2}{2}$, where A is the area, θ is the measure of the central angle in radians, and r is the radius. To find the area with the central angle in degrees, use the formula, $A = \frac{\theta \pi r^2}{360}$, where θ is the measure of the central angle and r is the radius.

PRACTICE

P1. Given that $\angle DEB = 80°$and $\widehat{BC} = 90°$, determine the following values based on the figure:

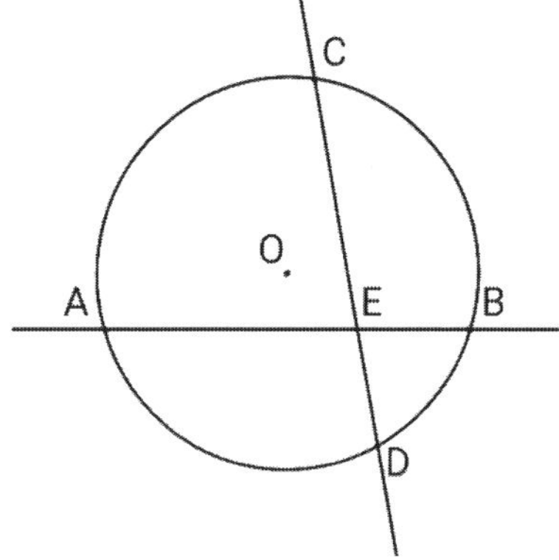

(a) $\widehat{AD}$

(b) $\widehat{DB} + \widehat{CA}$

P2. Given that $\angle OCB = 50°$, $\overleftrightarrow{EF}$ is tangent to the circle at B, and $\overline{CB} = 6$ km, determine the following values abased on the figure:

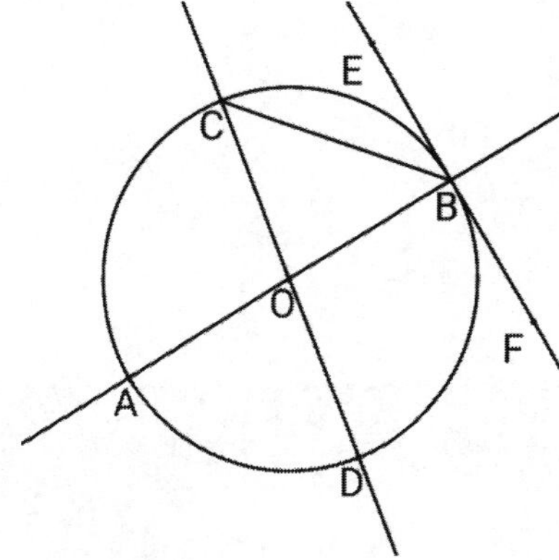

(a) The angle made between $\overleftrightarrow{CD}$ and a line tangent to the circle at A.

(b) The area of the sector of the circle between C and B.

Practice Solutions

P1. (a). Recall that when two secants intersect inside of a circle, the measure of each of two vertical angles is equal to half the sum of the two intercepted arcs. Also, since $\angle DEB$ and $\angle CEB$are supplementary, the measure of $\angle CEB = 180° - 80° = 100°$ In other words:

$$\begin{aligned}\angle CEB &= \frac{1}{2}(\widehat{BC} + \widehat{AD})\\ 100° &= \frac{1}{2}(90° + \widehat{AD})\\ 200° &= 90° + \widehat{AD}\\ 110° &= \widehat{AD}\end{aligned}$$

(b) Note that the whole circle is divided into four arcs. Thus,

$$\begin{aligned}\widehat{AD} + \widehat{DB} + \widehat{BC} + \widehat{CA} &= 360°\\ 110° + \widehat{DB} + 90° + \widehat{CA} &= 360°\\ \widehat{DB} + \widehat{CA} &= 160°\end{aligned}$$

P2. (a) A line tangent to the circle at A creates a right triangle with one vertex at O, one at A, and the final vertex where $\overleftrightarrow{CD}$ intersects the tangent line, let us call that point G.

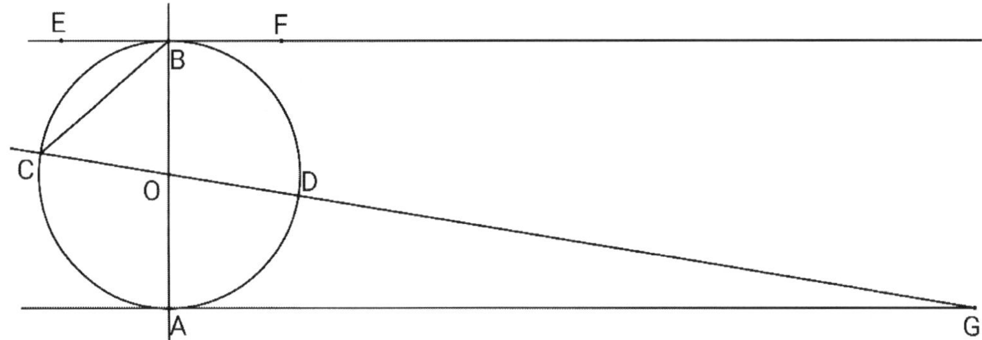

Since AB is a diameter, the line tangent at A is perpendicular to AB, so $\angle OAG = 90°$. The triangle COB has two legs that are the radius of the circle and so must be isosceles. So, $50° \times 2 + \angle COB = 180°$, which means that $\angle COB$ and the vertical angle $\angle GOA$ both equal 80°. Knowing this we can find $\angle AGO$:

$$\begin{aligned} 80° + 90° + \angle AGO &= 180° \\ \angle AGO &= 10° \end{aligned}$$

(b) We know $\angle OCB = 50°$ and that triangle COB is isosceles with two legs equal to the radius, so a perpendicular bisector of the triangle as shown will create a right triangle:

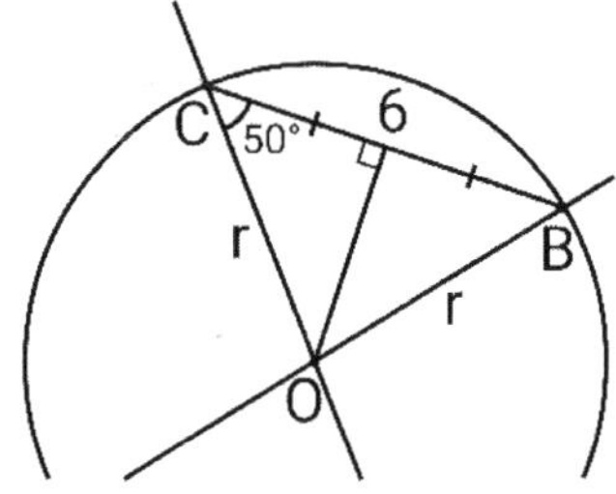

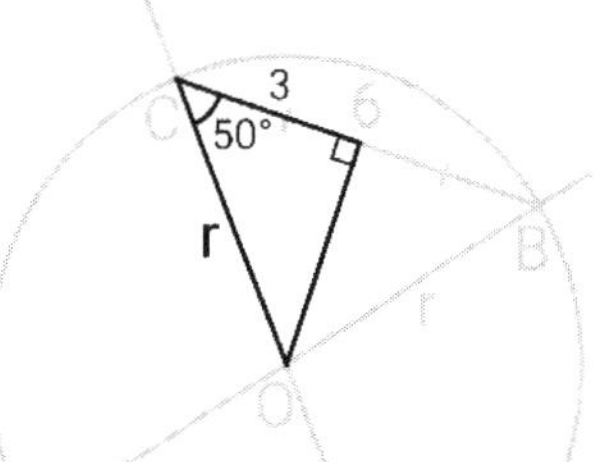

Recall that cosine of an angle in a right triangle is the ratio of the adjacent side to the hypotenuse. Thus, we can find r:

$$\begin{aligned} \cos 50° &= \frac{3}{r} \\ r &= \frac{3}{\cos 50°} \end{aligned}$$

As noted in part (a), $\angle COB = 80°$ so, the area of the sector is:

$$\begin{aligned} A &= \frac{\theta \pi r^2}{360°} \\ &= \frac{80°\pi \left(\frac{3}{\cos 50°}\right)^2}{360°} \\ &= \frac{2\pi \left(\frac{9}{\cos^2 50°}\right)}{9} \\ &= \frac{2\pi}{\cos^2 50°} \cong 15.2 \text{ km}^2 \end{aligned}$$

Conic Sections

Conic sections are a family of shapes that can be thought of as cross sections of a pair of infinite, right cones stacked vertex to vertex. This is easiest to see with a visual representation:

A three-dimensional look at representative conic sections. (Note that a hyperbola intersects both cones.)

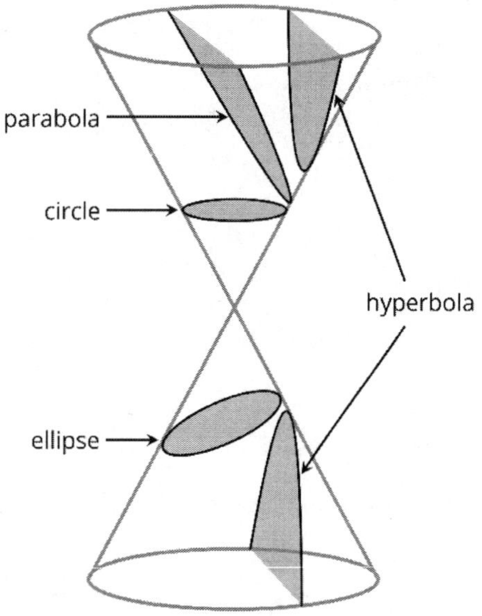

A side-on look at representative conic sections. (Note that the parabola is parallel to the slant of the cones.)

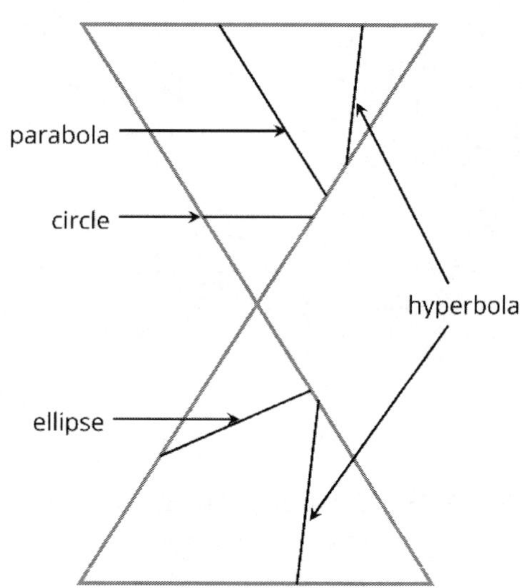

In short, a circle is a horizontal cross section, a parabola is a cross section parallel to the slant of the cone, an ellipse is a cross section at an angle *less than* the slant of the cone, and a hyperbola is a cross section at an angle *greater than* the slant of the cone.

Ellipse

An **ellipse** is the set of all points in a plane, whose total distance from two fixed points called the **foci** (singular: focus) is constant, and whose center is the midpoint between the foci.

The standard equation of an ellipse that is taller than it is wide is $\frac{(x-h)^2}{a^2} + \frac{(y-k)^2}{b^2} = 1$, where a and b are coefficients. The center is the point (h, k) and the foci are the points $(h, k + c)$ and $(h, k - c)$, where $c^2 = a^2 - b^2$ and $a^2 > b^2$.

The major axis has length $2a$, and the minor axis has length $2b$.

Eccentricity (e) is a measure of how elongated an ellipse is, and is the ratio of the distance between the foci to the length of the major axis. Eccentricity will have a value between 0 and 1. The closer to 1 the eccentricity is, the closer the ellipse is to being a circle. The formula for eccentricity is $= \frac{c}{a}$.

Parabola

A **parabola** is the set of all points in a plane that are equidistant from a fixed line, called the **directrix**, and a fixed point not on the line, called the **focus**. The **axis** is the line perpendicular to the directrix that passes through the focus.

For parabolas that open up or down, the standard equation is $(x - h)^2 = 4c(y - k)$, where h, c, and k are coefficients. If c is positive, the parabola opens up. If c is negative, the parabola opens down. The vertex is the point (h, k). The directrix is the line having the equation $y = -c + k$, and the focus is the point $(h, c + k)$.

For parabolas that open left or right, the standard equation is $(y - k)^2 = 4c(x - h)$, where k, c, and h are coefficients. If c is positive, the parabola opens to the right. If c is negative, the parabola opens to the left. The vertex is the point (h, k). The directrix is the line having the equation $x = -c + h$, and the focus is the point $(c + h, k)$.

HYPERBOLA

A **hyperbola** is the set of all points in a plane, whose distance from two fixed points, called foci, has a constant difference.

The standard equation of a horizontal hyperbola is $\frac{(x-h)^2}{a^2} - \frac{(y-k)^2}{b^2} = 1$, where a, b, h, and k are real numbers. The center is the point (h, k), the vertices are the points $(h + a, k)$ and $(h - a, k)$, and the foci are the points that every point on one of the parabolic curves is equidistant from. The foci are found using the formulas $(h + c, k)$ and $(h - c, k)$, where $c^2 = a^2 + b^2$. The asymptotes are two lines the graph of the hyperbola approaches but never reaches, and are given by the equations $y = \left(\frac{b}{a}\right)(x - h) + k$ and $y = -\left(\frac{b}{a}\right)(x - h) + k$.

The standard equation of a vertical hyperbola is $\frac{(y-k)^2}{a^2} - \frac{(x-h)^2}{b^2} = 1$, where a, b, k, and h are real numbers. The center is the point (h, k), the vertices are the points $(h, k + a)$ and $(h, k - a)$, and the foci are the points that every point on one of the hyperbolic curves is equidistant from and are found using the formulas $(h, k + c)$ and $(h, k - c)$, where $c^2 = a^2 + b^2$. The asymptotes are two lines the graph of the hyperbola approaches but never reach, and are given by the equations $y = \left(\frac{a}{b}\right)(x - h) + k$ and $y = -\left(\frac{a}{b}\right)(x - h) + k$.

Statistics, Probability, and Discrete Mathematics

Factorials

The **factorial** is a function that can be performed on any **non-negative integer**. It is represented by the ! sign written after the integer on which it is being performed. The factorial of an integer is the product of all positive integers less than or equal to the number. For example, 4! (read "4 factorial") is calculated as $4 \times 3 \times 2 \times 1 = 24$.

Since 0 is not itself a positive integer, nor does it have any positive integers less than it, 0! cannot be calculated using this method. Instead, 0! is defined by convention to equal 1. This makes sense if you consider the pattern of descending factorials:

$$\begin{aligned} 5! &= 120 \\ 4! &= \frac{5!}{5} = \frac{120}{5} = 24 \\ 3! &= \frac{4!}{4} = \frac{24}{4} = 6 \\ 2! &= \frac{3!}{3} = \frac{6}{3} = 2 \\ 1! &= \frac{2!}{2} = \frac{2}{2} = 1 \\ 0! &= \frac{1!}{1} = \frac{1}{1} = 1 \end{aligned}$$

PERMUTATIONS

For any given set of data, the individual elements in the set may be arranged in different groups containing different numbers of elements arranged in different orders. For example, given the set of integers from one to three, inclusive, the elements of the set are 1, 2, and 3: written as {1, 2, 3}. They may be arranged as follows: 1, 2, 3, 12, 21, 13, 31, 23, 32, 123, 132, 213, 231, 312, and 321. These ordered sequences of elements from the given set of data are called **permutations**. It is important to note that in permutations, the order of the elements in the sequence is important. The sequence 123 is not the same as the sequence 213. Also, no element in the given set may be used more times as an element in a permutation than it appears as an element in the original set. For example, 223 is not a permutation in the above example because the number 2 only appears one time in the given set.

To find the number of permutations of *r* items from a set of *n* items, use the formula ${}_nP_r = \frac{n!}{(n-r)!}$. When using this formula, each element of *r* must be unique. Also, this assumes that different arrangements of the same set of elements yields different outcomes. For example, 123 is not the same as 321; order is important.

A special case arises while finding the number of possible permutations of *n* items from a set of *n* items. Because $n = r$, the equation for the number of permutations becomes simply $P = n!$ The same result is true for $r = n - 1$. Both of these cases are a result of the fact that 0! and 1! are both equal to 1.

If a set contains one or more groups of **indistinguishable or interchangeable elements** (e.g., the set {1, 2, 3, 3}, which has a group of two indistinguishable 3's), there is a different formula for finding distinct permutations of all *n* elements. Use the formula $P = \frac{n!}{m_1!m_2!...m_k!}$, where *P* is the number of permutations, n is the total number of elements in the set, and m_1 through m_k are the number of identical elements in each group (e.g., for the set {1, 1, 2, 2, 2, 3, 3}, $m_1 = 2, m_2 = 3$, and $m_3 = 2$). It is important to note that each repeated number is counted as its own element for the purpose of defining n (e.g., for the set {1, 1, 2, 2, 2, 3, 3}, $n = 7$, not 3).

To find the number of possible permutations of **any number of elements** in a set of unique elements, you must apply the permutation formulas multiple times. For example, to find the total number of possible permutations of the set {1, 2, 3} first apply the permutation formula for situations where $n = r$ as follows: $P = n! = 3! = 6$. This gives the number of permutations of the three elements when all three elements are used. To find the number of permutations when only two of the three elements are used, use the formula ${}_nP_r = \frac{n!}{(n-r)!}$, where n is 3 and r is 2.

$${}_nP_r = \frac{n!}{(n-r)!} \Rightarrow {}_3P_2 = \frac{3!}{(3-2)!} = \frac{6}{1} = 6$$

To find the number of permutations when one element is used, use the formula ${}_nP_r = \frac{n!}{(n-r)!}$, where n is 3 and r is 1.

$${}_nP_r = \frac{n!}{(n-r)!} \Rightarrow {}_3P_1 = \frac{3!}{(3-1)!} = \frac{3!}{2!} = \frac{6}{2} = 3$$

Find the sum of the three formulas: $6 + 6 + 3 = 15$ total possible permutations.

Alternatively, the general formula for total possible permutations can be written as follows:

$$P_T = \sum_{i=1}^{n} \frac{n!}{(i-1)!}$$

Combinations

Combinations are essentially defined as permutations where the order in which the elements appear does not matter. Going back to the earlier example of the set {1, 2, 3}, the possible combinations that can be made from that set are 1, 2, 3, 12, 13, 23, and 123.

In a set containing n elements, the number of combinations of r items from the set can be found using the formula ${}_nC_r = \frac{n!}{r!(n-r)!}$. Notice the similarity to the formula for permutations. In effect, you are dividing the number of permutations by $r!$ to get the number of combinations, and the formula may be written ${}_nC_r = \frac{{}_nP_r}{r!}$. When finding the number of combinations, it is important to remember that the elements in the set must be unique (i.e., there must not be any duplicate items), and that no item may be used more than once in any given sequence.

Review Video: Probability - Permutation and Combination
Visit mometrix.com/academy and enter code: 907664

Practice

P1. Ichiro has 4 shirts, 1 jacket, and 5 different pairs of pants that he packed for his work trip. If wearing a jacket is optional, how many outfit combinations can he make?

P2. Determine the number of permutations and combinations of the following:

(a) Choose 3 from the set: $\{4, 5, 6, 7\}$

(b) Choose 2 from the set: $\{a, b, c, d, e\}$

(c) Choose 4 from the set: $\{a, h, m, t\}$

Practice Solutions

P1. To start with, each shirt can be matched with each pair of pants, so that would be $4 \times 5 = 20$ combinations. Since the jacket is optional each of the 20 can be either with or without the jacket, i.e. $20 \times 2 = 40$. There are 40 distinct combinations he could wear.

P2. (a) ${}_nP_r = \frac{n!}{(n-r)!} = \frac{4!}{(4-3)!} = \frac{4\times3\times2\times1}{1} = 24;\ {}_nC_r = \frac{n!}{(n-r)!r!} = \frac{4!}{(4-3)!3!} = \frac{4\times3\times2\times1}{3\times2\times1} = 4$

(b) ${}_nP_r = \frac{n!}{(n-r)!} = \frac{5!}{(5-2)!} = \frac{5\times4\times3\times2\times1}{3\times2\times1} = 20;\ {}_nC_r = \frac{n!}{(n-r)!r!} = \frac{5!}{(5-2)!2!} = \frac{5\times4\times3\times2\times1}{(3\times2\times1)\times(2\times1)} = 10$

(c) ${}_nP_r = \frac{n!}{(n-r)!} = \frac{4!}{(4-4)!} = \frac{4\times3\times2\times1}{1} = 24;\ {}_nC_r = \frac{n!}{(n-r)!r!} = \frac{4!}{(4-4)!4!} = \frac{4\times3\times2\times1}{1\times(4\times3\times2\times1)} = 1$

Probability

Probability is the likelihood of a certain outcome occurring for a given event. An **event** is a situation that produces a result; that could be something as simple as flipping a coin or as complex as launching a rocket. Determining the probability of an outcome for an event can be equally simple or complex. As such there are specific terms used in the study of probability that need to be understood:

- **Compound event** – event that involves two or more independent events (rolling a pair of dice and taking the sum)
- **Desired outcome** (or success) – an outcome that meets a particular set of criteria (a roll of 1 or 2 if we are looking for numbers less than 3)
- **Independent events** – two or more events whose outcomes do not affect one another (two coins tossed at the same time)
- **Dependent events** – two or more events whose outcomes affect one another (two cards drawn consecutively from the same deck)
- **Certain outcome** – probability of outcome is 100% or 1
- **Impossible outcome** – probability of outcome is 0% or 0
- **Mutually exclusive outcomes** – two or more outcomes whose criteria cannot all be satisfied in a single event (a coin coming up heads and tails on the same toss)
- **Random variable** – refers to all possible outcomes of a single event which may be discrete or continuous.

Review Video: Intro to Probability
Visit mometrix.com/academy and enter code: 212374

Theoretical and Experimental Probability

Theoretical probability can usually be determined without actually performing the event. The likelihood of a outcome occurring, or the probability of an outcome occurring, is given by the formula:

$$P(A) = \frac{\text{Number of acceptable outcomes}}{\text{Number of possible outcomes}}$$

Note that $P(A)$ is the probability of an outcome A occurring, and each outcome is just as likely to occur as any other outcome. If each outcome has the same probability of occurring as every other possible outcome, the outcomes are said to be equally likely to occur. The total number of acceptable outcomes must be less than or equal to the total number of possible outcomes. If the two are equal, then the outcome is certain to occur and the probability is 1. If the number of acceptable outcomes is zero, then the outcome is impossible and the probability is 0. For example, if there are 20 marbles in a bag and 5 are red, then the theoretical probability of randomly selecting a red marble is 5 out of 20, ($\frac{5}{20} = \frac{1}{4}$, 0.25, or 25%).

If the theoretical probability is unknown or too complicated to calculate, it can be estimated by an experimental probability. **Experimental probability**, also called empirical probability, is an estimate of the likelihood of a certain outcome based on repeated experiments or collected data. In other words, while theoretical probability is based on what *should* happen, experimental probability is based on what *has* happened. Experimental probability is calculated in the same way as theoretical, except that actual outcomes are used instead of possible outcomes. The more experiments performed or datapoints gathered, the better the estimate should be.

Theoretical and experimental probability do not always line up with one another. Theoretical probability says that out of 20 coin-tosses, 10 should be heads. However, if we were actually to toss 20 coins, we might record just 5 heads. This doesn't mean that our theoretical probability is incorrect; it just means that this particular experiment had results that were different from what was predicted. A practical application of empirical probability is the insurance industry. There are no set functions that define lifespan, health, or safety. Insurance companies look at factors from hundreds of thousands of individuals to find patterns that they then use to set the formulas for insurance premiums.

Review Video: Empirical Probability
Visit mometrix.com/academy and enter code: 513468

Objective and Subjective Probability

Objective probability is based on mathematical formulas and documented evidence. Examples of objective probability include raffles or lottery drawings where there is a pre-determined number of possible outcomes and a predetermined number of outcomes that correspond to an event. Other cases of objective probability include probabilities of rolling dice, flipping coins, or drawing cards. Most gambling games are based on objective probability.

In contrast, **subjective probability** is based on personal or professional feelings and judgments. Often, there is a lot of guesswork following extensive research. Areas where subjective probability is applicable include sales trends and business expenses. Attractions set admission prices based on subjective probabilities of attendance based on varying admission rates in an effort to maximize their profit.

Sample Space

The total set of all possible results of a test or experiment is called a **sample space**, or sometimes a universal sample space. The sample space, represented by one of the variables S, Ω, or U (for universal sample space) has individual elements called outcomes. Other terms for outcome that may be used interchangeably include elementary outcome, simple event, or sample point. The number of outcomes in a given sample space could be infinite or finite, and some tests may yield multiple unique sample sets. For example, tests conducted by drawing playing cards from a standard deck would have one sample space of the card values, another sample space of the card suits, and a third sample space of suit-denomination combinations. For most tests, the sample spaces considered will be finite.

An **event**, represented by the variable E, is a portion of a sample space. It may be one outcome or a group of outcomes from the same sample space. If an event occurs, then the test or experiment will generate an outcome that satisfies the requirement of that event. For example, given a standard deck of 52 playing cards as the sample space, and defining the event as the collection of face cards, then the event will occur if the card drawn is a J, Q, or K. If any other card is drawn, the event is said to have not occurred.

For every sample space, each possible outcome has a specific likelihood, or probability, that it will occur. The probability measure, also called the **distribution**, is a function that assigns a real number probability, from zero to one, to each outcome. For a probability measure to be accurate, every outcome must have a real number probability measure that is greater than or equal to zero and less than or equal to one. Also, the probability measure of the sample space must equal one, and the probability measure of the union of multiple outcomes must equal the sum of the individual probability measures.

Probabilities of events are expressed as real numbers from zero to one. They give a numerical value to the chance that a particular event will occur. The probability of an event occurring is the sum of the probabilities of the individual elements of that event. For example, in a standard deck of 52 playing cards as the sample space and the collection of face cards as the event, the probability of drawing a specific face card is $\frac{1}{52} = 0.019$, but the probability of drawing any one of the twelve face cards is $12(0.019) = 0.228$. Note that rounding of numbers can generate different results. If you multiplied 12 by the fraction $\frac{1}{52}$ before converting to a decimal, you would get the answer $\frac{12}{52} = 0.231$.

Tree Diagram

For a simple sample space, possible outcomes may be determined by using a **tree diagram** or an organized chart. In either case, you can easily draw or list out the possible outcomes. For example, to determine all the possible ways three objects can be ordered, you can draw a tree diagram:

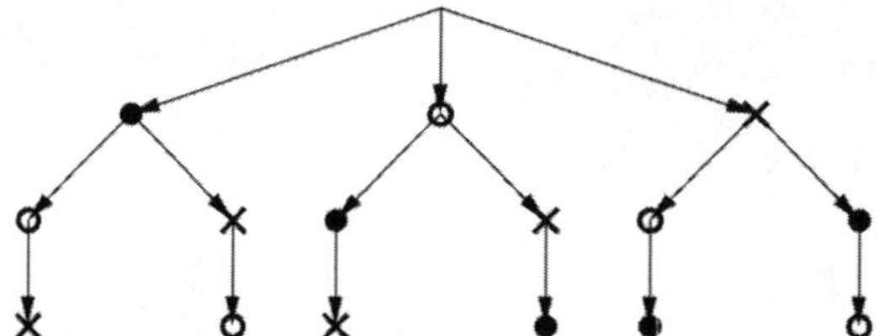

You can also make a chart to list all the possibilities:

First object	Second object	Third object
•	x	o
•	o	x
o	•	x
o	x	•
x	•	o
x	o	•

Either way, you can easily see there are six possible ways the three objects can be ordered.

If two events have no outcomes in common, they are said to be **mutually exclusive**. For example, in a standard deck of 52 playing cards, the event of all card suits is mutually exclusive to the event of all card values. If two events have no bearing on each other so that one event occurring has no influence on the probability of another event occurring, the two events are said to be independent. For example, rolling a standard six-sided die multiple times does not change that probability that a particular number will be rolled from one roll to the next. If the outcome of one event does affect the probability of the second event, the two events are said to be dependent. For example, if cards are drawn from a deck, the probability of drawing an ace after an ace has been drawn is different than the probability of drawing an ace if no ace (or no other card, for that matter) has been drawn.

In probability, the **odds in favor of an event** are the number of times the event will occur compared to the number of times the event will not occur. To calculate the odds in favor of an event, use the formula $\frac{P(A)}{1-P(A)}$, where $P(A)$ is the probability that the event will occur. Many times, odds in favor is given as a ratio in the form $\frac{a}{b}$ or a:b, where a is the probability of the event occurring and b is the complement of the event, the probability of the event not occurring. If the odds in favor are given as 2:5, that means that you can expect the event to occur two times for every 5 times that it does not occur. In other words, the probability that the event will occur is $\frac{2}{2+5} = \frac{2}{7}$.

In probability, the **odds against an event** are the number of times the event will not occur compared to the number of times the event will occur. To calculate the odds against an event, use the formula $\frac{1-P(A)}{P(A)}$, where $P(A)$ is the probability that the event will occur. Many times, odds against is given as a ratio in the form $\frac{b}{a}$ or b:a, where b is the probability the event will not occur (the complement of the event) and a is the probability the event will occur. If the odds against an event are given as 3:1, that means that you can expect the event to not occur 3 times for every one time it does occur. In other words, 3 out of every 4 trials will fail.

Permutations and Combinations

When trying to calculate the probability of an event using the $\frac{\text{desired outcomes}}{\text{total outcomes}}$ formula, you may frequently find that there are too many outcomes to individually count them. **Permutation** and **combination formulas** offer a shortcut to counting outcomes. A permutation is an arrangement of a specific number of a set of objects in a specific order. The number of **permutations** of r items given a set of n items can be calculated as ${}_nP_r = \frac{n!}{(n-r)!}$. Combinations are similar to permutations, except there are no restrictions regarding the order of the elements. While ABC is considered a different permutation than BCA, ABC and BCA are considered the same combination. The number of **combinations** of r items given a set of n items can be calculated as ${}_nC_r = \frac{n!}{r!(n-r)!}$ or ${}_nC_r = \frac{{}_nP_r}{r!}$.

Suppose you want to calculate how many different 5-card hands can be drawn from a deck of 52 cards. This is a combination since the order of the cards in a hand does not matter. There are 52 cards available, and 5 to be selected. Thus, the number of different hands is ${}_{52}C_5 = \frac{52!}{5! \times 47!} = 2{,}598{,}960$.

Review Video: Probability - Permutation and Combination
Visit mometrix.com/academy and enter code: 907664

Union and Intersection of Two Sets of Outcomes

If A and B are each a set of elements or outcomes from an experiment, then the **union** (symbol ∪) of the two sets is the set of elements found in set A or set B. For example, if $A = \{2, 3, 4\}$ and $B = \{3, 4, 5\}$, $A \cup B = \{2, 3, 4, 5\}$. Note that the outcomes 3 and 4 appear only once in the union. For statistical events, the union is equivalent to "or"; $P(A \cup B)$ is the same thing as $P(A \text{ or } B)$. The **intersection** (symbol ∩) of two sets is the set of outcomes common to both sets. For the above sets A and B, $A \cap B = \{3, 4\}$. For statistical events, the intersection is equivalent to "and"; $P(A \cap B)$ is the same thing as $P(A \text{ and } B)$. It is important to note that union and intersection operations commute. That is:

$$A \cup B = B \cup A \text{ and } A \cap B = B \cap A$$

Complement of an Event

Sometimes it may be easier to calculate the possibility of something not happening, or the **complement of an event**. Represented by the symbol $\bar{A}$, the complement of A is the probability that event A does not happen. When you know the probability of event A occurring, you can use the formula $P(\bar{A}) = 1 - P(A)$, where $P(\bar{A})$ is the probability of event A not occurring, and $P(A)$ is the probability of event A occurring.

Addition Rule

The **addition rule** for probability is used for finding the probability of a compound event. Use the formula $P(A \text{ or } B) = P(A) + P(B) - P(A \text{ and } B)$, where $P(A \text{ and } B)$ is the probability of both events occurring to find the probability of a compound event. The probability of both events occurring at the same time must be subtracted to eliminate any overlap in the first two probabilities.

Conditional Probability

Given two events A and B, the **conditional probability** $P(A|B)$ is the probability that event B will occur, given that event A has occurred. The conditional probability cannot be calculated simply from $P(A)$ and $P(B)$; these probabilities alone do not give sufficient information to determine the conditional probability. It can, however, be determined if you are also given the probability of the intersection of events A and B, $P(A \cap B)$, the probability that events A and B both occur. Specifically, $P(A|B) = \frac{P(A \cap B)}{P(B)}$.

For instance, suppose you have a jar containing two red marbles and two blue marbles, and you draw two marbles at random. Consider event A being the event that the first marble drawn is red, and event B being the event that the second marble drawn is blue. $P(A)$ is $\frac{1}{2}$, and $P(A \cap B)$ is $\frac{1}{3}$. (The latter may not be obvious, but may be determined by finding the product of $\frac{1}{2}$ and $\frac{2}{3}$). Therefore $P(A|B) = \frac{1/3}{1/2} = \frac{2}{3}$.

Conditional Probability in Everyday Situations

Conditional probability often arises in everyday situations in, for example, estimating the risk or benefit of certain activities. The conditional probability of having a heart attack given that you exercise daily may be smaller than the overall probability of having a heart attack. The conditional probability of having lung cancer given that you are a smoker is larger than the overall probability of having lung cancer. Note that changing the order of the conditional probability changes the meaning: the conditional probability of having lung cancer given that you are a smoker is a very different thing from the probability of being a smoker given that you have lung cancer. In an extreme case, suppose that a certain rare disease is caused only by eating a certain food, but even then, it is unlikely. Then the conditional probability of having that disease given that you eat the dangerous food is nonzero but low, but the conditional probability of having eaten that food given that you have the disease is 100%!

Review Video: Conditional Probability
Visit mometrix.com/academy and enter code: 397924

Independence

The conditional probability $P(A|B)$ is the probability that event B will occur given that event A occurs. If the two events are independent, we do not expect that whether or not event A occurs should have any effect on whether or not event B occurs. In other words, we expect $P(A|B) = P(A)$.

This can be proven using the usual equations for conditional probability and the joint probability of independent events. The conditional probability $P(A|B) = \frac{P(A \cap B)}{P(B)}$. If A and B are independent, then $P(A \cap B) = P(A)P(B)$. So $P(A|B) = \frac{P(A)P(B)}{P(B)} = P(A)$. By similar reasoning, if A and B are independent then $P(B|A) = P(B)$.

Two-Way Frequency Tables

If we have a two-way frequency table, it is generally a straightforward matter to read off the probabilities of any two events A and B, as well as the joint probability of both events occurring, $P(A \cap B)$. We can then find the conditional probability $P(A|B)$ by calculating $P(A|B) = \frac{P(A \cap B)}{P(B)}$. We could also check whether or not events are independent by verifying whether $P(A)P(B) = P(A \cap B)$.

For example, a certain store's recent T-shirt sales:

		Size			
		Small	**Medium**	**Large**	**Total**
Color	**Blue**	25	40	35	100
	White	27	25	22	74
	Black	8	23	15	46
	Total	60	88	72	220

Suppose we want to find the conditional probability that a customer buys a black shirt (event A), given that the shirt he buys is size small (event B). From the table, the probability $P(A)$ that a customer buys a small shirt is $\frac{60}{220} = \frac{3}{11}$. The probability $P(A \cap B)$ that he buys a small, black shirt is $\frac{8}{220} = \frac{2}{55}$. The conditional probability $P(A|B)$ that he buys a black shirt, given that he buys a small shirt, is therefore $P(A|B) = \frac{2/55}{3/11} = \frac{2}{15}$.

Similarly, if we want to check whether the event a customer buys a blue shirt, A, is independent of the event that a customer buys a medium shirt, B. From the table, $P(A) = \frac{100}{220} = \frac{5}{11}$ and $P(B) = \frac{88}{220} = \frac{4}{10}$. Also, $P(A \cap B) = \frac{40}{220} = \frac{2}{11}$. Since $\left(\frac{5}{11}\right)\left(\frac{4}{10}\right) = \frac{20}{220} = \frac{2}{11}$, $P(A)P(B) = P(A \cap B)$ and these two events are indeed independent.

Multiplication Rule

The **multiplication rule** can be used to find the probability of two independent events occurring using the formula $P(A \text{ and } B) = P(A) \times P(B)$, where $P(A \text{ and } B)$ is the probability of two independent events occurring, $P(A)$ is the probability of the first event occurring, and $P(B)$ is the probability of the second event occurring.

The multiplication rule can also be used to find the probability of two dependent events occurring using the formula $P(A \text{ and } B) = P(A) \times P(B|A)$, where $P(A \text{ and } B)$ is the probability of two dependent events occurring and $P(B|A)$ is the probability of the second event occurring after the first event has already occurred. Before using the multiplication rule, you MUST first determine whether the two events are *dependent* or *independent*.

Use a **combination of the multiplication** rule and the rule of complements to find the probability that at least one outcome of the element will occur. This given by the general formula $P(\text{at least one event occurring}) = 1 - P(\text{no outcomes occurring})$. For example, to find the probability that at least one even number will show when a pair of dice is rolled, find the probability that two odd numbers will be rolled (no even numbers) and subtract from one. You can always use a tree diagram or make a chart to list the possible outcomes when the sample space is small, such as in the dice-rolling example, but in most cases it will be much faster to use the multiplication and complement formulas.

Review Video: Multiplication Rule
Visit mometrix.com/academy and enter code: 782598

Expected Value

Expected value is a method of determining expected outcome in a random situation. It is really a sum of the weighted probabilities of the possible outcomes. Multiply the probability of an event occurring by the weight assigned to that probability (such as the amount of money won or lost). A practical application of the expected value is to determine whether a game of chance is really fair. If the sum of the weighted probabilities is equal to zero, the game is generally considered fair because the player has a fair chance to at least break even. If the expected value is less than zero, then players lose more than they win. For example, a lottery drawing might allow the player to choose any three-digit number, 000–999. The probability of choosing the winning number is 1:1000. If it costs \$1 to play, and a winning number receives \$500, the expected value is $\left(-\$1 \times \frac{999}{1{,}000}\right) + \left(\$499 \times \frac{1}{1{,}000}\right) = -\$0.50$. You can expect to lose on average 50 cents for every dollar you spend.

Review Video: Expected Value
Visit mometrix.com/academy and enter code: 643554

Expected Value and Simulators

A die roll simulator will show the results of *n* rolls of a die. The result of each die roll may be recorded. For example, suppose a die is rolled 100 times. All results may be recorded. The numbers of 1s, 2s, 3s, 4s, 5s, and 6s, may be counted. The experimental probability of rolling each number will equal the ratio of the frequency of the rolled number to the total number of rolls. As the number of rolls increases, or approaches infinity, the experimental probability will approach the theoretical probability of 1/6. Thus, the expected value for the roll of a die is shown to be $(1 \times 1/6) + (2 \times 1/6) + (3 \times 1/6) + (4 \times 1/6) + (5 \times 1/6) + (6 \times 1/6)$, or 3.5.

Practice

P1. Determine the theoretical probability of the following events:

(a) Rolling an even number on a regular 6-sided die.

(b) Not getting a red ball when selecting one from a bag of 3 red balls, 4 black balls, and 2 green balls.

(c) Rolling a standard die and then selecting a card from a standard deck that is less than the value rolled.

P2. There is a game of chance involving a standard deck of cards that has been shuffled and then laid on a table. The player wins \$10 if they can turn over 2 cards of matching color (black or red), \$50 for 2 cards with matching value (A-K), and \$100 for 2 cards with both matching color and value. What is the expected value of playing this game?

P3. Today, there were two food options for lunch at a local college cafeteria. Given the following survey data, what is the probability that a junior selected at random from the sample had a sandwich?

	Freshman	Sophomore	Junior	Senior
Salad	15	12	27	36
Sandwich	24	40	43	35
Nothing	42	23	23	30

Practice Solutions

P1. (a). The values on the faces of a regular die are 1, 2, 3, 4, 5, and 6. Since three of these are even numbers (2, 4, 6), The probability of rolling an even number is $\frac{3}{6} = \frac{1}{2} = 0.5 = 50\%$.

(b) The bag contains a total of 9 balls, 6 of which are not red, so the probability of selecting one non-red ball would be $\frac{6}{9} = \frac{2}{3} \cong 0.667 \cong 66.7\%$.

(c) In this scenario, we need to determine how many cards could satisfy the condition for each possible value of the die roll. If a one is rolled, there is no way to achieve the desired outcome, since no cards in a standard deck are less than 1. If a two is rolled, then any of the four aces would achieve the desired result. If a three is rolled, then either an ace or a two would satisfy the condition, and so on. Note that any value on the die is equally likely to occur, meaning that the probability of each roll is $\frac{1}{6}$. Putting all this in a table can help:

Roll	Cards < Roll	Probability of Card	Probability of Event
1	-	$\frac{0}{52} = 0$	$\frac{1}{6} \times 0 = 0$
2	1	$\frac{4}{52} = \frac{1}{13}$	$\frac{1}{6} \times \frac{1}{13} = \frac{1}{78}$
3	1,2	$\frac{8}{52} = \frac{2}{13}$	$\frac{1}{6} \times \frac{2}{13} = \frac{2}{78}$
4	1,2,3	$\frac{12}{52} = \frac{3}{13}$	$\frac{1}{6} \times \frac{3}{13} = \frac{3}{78}$
5	1,2,3,4	$\frac{16}{52} = \frac{4}{13}$	$\frac{1}{6} \times \frac{4}{13} = \frac{4}{78}$
6	1,2,3,4,5	$\frac{20}{52} = \frac{5}{13}$	$\frac{1}{6} \times \frac{5}{13} = \frac{5}{78}$

Assuming that each value of the die is equally likely, then the probability is the sum of the probabilities of each way to achieve the desired outcome: $\frac{0+1+2+3+4+5}{78} = \frac{15}{78} = \frac{5}{26} \cong 0.192 \cong 19.2\%$.

P2. First, determine the probability of each way of winning. In each case, the fist card simply determines which of the remaining 51 cards in the deck correspond to a win. For the color of the cards to match, there are 25 cards remaining in the deck that match the color of the first, but one of the 25 also matches the value, so only 24 are left in this category. For the value of the cards to match, there are 3 cards remaining cards in the deck that match the value of the first, but one of the three also matches the color, so only 2 are left in this category. For the cards to match both color and value, there is only one card in the deck that will work. Finally, there are 24 cards left that don't match at all.

Now we can find the expected value of playing the game, where we multiply the value of each event by the probability it will occur and sum over all of them:

$$\$10 \times \frac{24}{51} = \$4.71$$
$$\$50 \times \frac{2}{51} = \$1.96$$
$$\$100 \times \frac{1}{51} = \$1.96$$
$$\$0 \times \frac{24}{51} = \$0$$

$$\$4.71 + \$1.96 + \$1.96 = \$8.63$$

This game therefore has an expected value of $8.63 each time you play, which means if the cost to play is less than $8.63 then you would, on average, *gain* money. However, if the cost to play is more than $8.63, then you would, on average, *lose* money.

P3. With two-way tables it is often most helpful to start by totaling the rows and columns:

	Freshman	Sophomore	Junior	Senior	Total
Salad	15	12	27	36	90
Sandwich	24	40	43	35	142
Nothing	42	23	23	30	118
Total	81	75	93	101	350

Since the question is focused on juniors, we can focus on that column. There was a total of 93 juniors surveyed and 43 of them had a sandwich for lunch. Thus, the probability that a junior selected at random had a sandwich would be $\frac{43}{93} \cong 0.462 \cong 46.2\%$.

Statistics

Statistics is the branch of mathematics that deals with collecting, recording, interpreting, illustrating, and analyzing large amounts of **data**. The following terms are often used in the discussion of data and **statistics**:

- **Data** – the collective name for pieces of information (singular is datum).
- **Quantitative data** – measurements (such as length, mass, and speed) that provide information about quantities in numbers
- **Qualitative data** – information (such as colors, scents, tastes, and shapes) that cannot be measured using numbers
- **Discrete data** – information that can be expressed only by a specific value, such as whole or half numbers. For example, since people can be counted only in whole numbers, a population count would be discrete data.
- **Continuous data** – information (such as time and temperature) that can be expressed by any value within a given range
- **Primary data** – information that has been collected directly from a survey, investigation, or experiment, such as a questionnaire or the recording of daily temperatures. Primary data that has not yet been organized or analyzed is called **raw data**.
- **Secondary data** – information that has been collected, sorted, and processed by the researcher
- **Ordinal data** – information that can be placed in numerical order, such as age or weight
- **Nominal data** – information that *cannot* be placed in numerical order, such as names or places.

Data Collection

Population

In statistics, the **population** is the entire collection of people, plants, etc., that data can be collected from. For example, a study to determine how well students in the area schools perform on a standardized test would have a population of all the students enrolled in those schools, although a study may include just a small sample of students from each school. A **parameter** is a numerical value that gives information about the population, such as the mean, median, mode, or standard deviation. Remember that the symbol for the mean of a population is μ and the symbol for the standard deviation of a population is σ.

Sample

A **sample** is a portion of the entire population. Whereas a parameter helped describe the population, a **statistic** is a numerical value that gives information about the sample, such as mean, median, mode, or standard deviation. Keep in mind that the symbols for mean and standard deviation are different when they are referring to a sample rather than the entire population. For a sample, the symbol for mean is $\bar{x}$ and the symbol for standard deviation is s. The mean and standard deviation of a sample may or may not be identical to that of the entire population due to a sample only being a subset of the population. However, if the sample is random and large enough, statistically significant values can be attained. Samples are generally used when the population is too large to justify including every element or when acquiring data for the entire population is impossible.

Inferential Statistics

Inferential statistics is the branch of statistics that uses samples to make predictions about an entire population. This type of statistics is often seen in political polls, where a sample of the population is questioned about a particular topic or politician to gain an understanding about the attitudes of the entire population of the country. Often, exit polls are conducted on election days using this method. Inferential statistics can have a large margin of error if you do not have a valid sample.

Sampling Distribution

Statistical values calculated from various samples of the same size make up the **sampling distribution**. For example, if several samples of identical size are randomly selected from a large population and then the mean of each sample is calculated, the distribution of values of the means would be a sampling distribution.

The **sampling distribution of the mean** is the distribution of the sample mean, $\bar{x}$, derived from random samples of a given size. It has three important characteristics. First, the mean of the sampling distribution of the mean is equal to the mean of the population that was sampled. Second, assuming the standard deviation is non-zero, the standard deviation of the sampling distribution of the mean equals the standard deviation of the sampled population divided by the square root of the sample size. This is sometimes called the standard error. Finally, as the sample size gets larger, the sampling distribution of the mean gets closer to a normal distribution via the central limit theorem.

Survey Study

A **survey study** is a method of gathering information from a small group in an attempt to gain enough information to make accurate general assumptions about the population. Once a survey study is completed, the results are then put into a summary report.

Survey studies are generally in the format of surveys, interviews, or questionnaires as part of an effort to find opinions of a particular group or to find facts about a group.

It is important to note that the findings from a survey study are only as accurate as the sample chosen from the population.

Correlational Studies

Correlational studies seek to determine how much one variable is affected by changes in a second variable. For example, correlational studies may look for a relationship between the amount of time a student spends studying for a test and the grade that student earned on the test or between student scores on college admissions tests and student grades in college.

It is important to note that correlational studies cannot show a cause and effect, but rather can show only that two variables are or are not potentially correlated.

Experimental Studies

Experimental studies take correlational studies one step farther, in that they attempt to prove or disprove a cause-and-effect relationship. These studies are performed by conducting a series of experiments to test the hypothesis. For a study to be scientifically accurate, it must have both an experimental group that receives the specified treatment and a control group that does not get the treatment. This is the type of study pharmaceutical companies do as part of drug trials for new medications. Experimental studies are only valid when proper scientific method has been followed. In other words, the experiment must be well-planned and executed without bias in the testing process, all subjects must be selected at random, and the process of determining which subject is in which of the two groups must also be completely random.

Observational Studies

Observational studies are the opposite of experimental studies. In observational studies, the tester cannot change or in any way control all of the variables in the test. For example, a study to determine which gender does better in math classes in school is strictly observational. You cannot change a person's gender, and you cannot change the subject being studied. The big downfall of observational studies is that you have no way of proving a cause-and-effect relationship because you cannot control outside influences. Events outside of school can influence a student's performance in school, and observational studies cannot take that into consideration.

Random Samples

For most studies, a **random sample** is necessary to produce valid results. Random samples should not have any particular influence to cause sampled subjects to behave one way or another. The goal is for the random sample to be a **representative sample**, or a sample whose characteristics give an accurate picture of the characteristics of the entire population. To accomplish this, you must make sure you have a proper **sample size**, or an appropriate number of elements in the sample.

Biases

In statistical studies, biases must be avoided. **Bias** is an error that causes the study to favor one set of results over another. For example, if a survey to determine how the country views the president's job performance only speaks to registered voters in the president's party, the results will be skewed because a disproportionately large number of responders would tend to show approval, while a disproportionately large number of people in the opposite party would tend to express disapproval. **Extraneous variables** are, as the name implies, outside influences that can affect the outcome of a study. They are not always avoidable, but could trigger bias in the result.

Statistical Analysis

Measures of Central Tendency

A **measure of central tendency** is a statistical value that gives a reasonable estimate for the center of a group of data. There are several different ways of describing the measure of central tendency. Each one has a unique way it is calculated, and each one gives a slightly different perspective on the data set.

Whenever you give a measure of central tendency, always make sure the units are the same. If the data has different units, such as hours, minutes, and seconds, convert all the data to the same unit, and use the same unit in the measure of central tendency. If no units are given in the data, do not give units for the measure of central tendency.

MEAN

The **statistical mean** of a group of data is the same as the arithmetic average of that group. To find the mean of a set of data, first convert each value to the same units, if necessary. Then find the sum of all the values, and count the total number of data values, making sure you take into consideration each individual value. If a value appears more than once, count it more than once. Divide the sum of the values by the total number of values and apply the units, if any. Note that the mean does not have to be one of the data values in the set, and may not divide evenly.

$$\text{mean} = \frac{\text{sum of the data values}}{\text{quantity of data values}}$$

For instance, the mean of the data set {88, 72, 61, 90, 97, 68, 88, 79, 86, 93, 97, 71, 80, 84, 89} would be the sum of the fifteen numbers divided by 15:

$$\frac{88 + 72 + 61 + 90 + 97 + 68 + 88 + 79 + 86 + 93 + 97 + 71 + 80 + 84 + 88}{15} = \frac{1242}{15} = 82.8$$

While the mean is relatively easy to calculate and averages are understood by most people, the mean can be very misleading if used as the sole measure of central tendency. If the data set has outliers (data values that are unusually high or unusually low compared to the rest of the data values), the mean can be very distorted, especially if the data set has a small number of values. If unusually high values are countered with unusually low values, the mean is not affected as much. For example, if five of twenty students in a class get a 100 on a test, but the other 15 students have an average of 60 on the same test, the class average would appear as 70. Whenever the mean is skewed by outliers, it is always a good idea to include the median as an alternate measure of central tendency.

A **weighted mean**, or weighted average, is a mean that uses "weighted" values. The formula is weighted mean $= \frac{w_1x_1+w_2x_2+w_3x_3...+w_nx_n}{w_1+w_2+w_3+\cdots+w_n}$. Weighted values, such as $w_1, w_2, w_3, ... w_n$ are assigned to each member of the set $x_1, x_2, x_3, ... x_n$. If calculating weighted mean, make sure a weight value for each member of the set is used.

MEDIAN

The **statistical median** is the value in the middle of the set of data. To find the median, list all data values in order from smallest to largest or from largest to smallest. Any value that is repeated in the set must be listed the number of times it appears. If there are an odd number of data values, the median is the value in the middle of the list. If there is an even number of data values, the median is the arithmetic mean of the two middle values.

For example, the median of the data set {88, 72, 61, 90, 97, 68, 88, 79, 86, 93, 97, 71, 80, 84, 88} is 86 since the ordered set is {61, 68, 71, 72, 79, 80, 84, **86**, 88, 88, 88, 90, 93, 97, 97}.

The big disadvantage of using the median as a measure of central tendency is that is relies solely on a value's relative size as compared to the other values in the set. When the individual values in a set of data are evenly dispersed, the median can be an accurate tool. However, if there is a group of rather large values or a group of rather small values that are not offset by a different group of values, the information that can be inferred from the median may not be accurate because the distribution of values is skewed.

Mode

The **statistical mode** is the data value that occurs the greatest number of times in the data set. It is possible to have exactly one mode, more than one mode, or no mode. To find the mode of a set of data, arrange the data like you do to find the median (all values in order, listing all multiples of data values). Count the number of times each value appears in the data set. If all values appear an equal number of times, there is no mode. If one value appears more than any other value, that value is the mode. If two or more values appear the same number of times, but there are other values that appear fewer times and no values that appear more times, all of those values are the modes.

For example, the mode of the data set {**88**, 72, 61, 90, 97, 68, **88**, 79, 86, 93, 97, 71, 80, 84, **88**} is 88.

The main disadvantage of the mode is that the values of the other data in the set have no bearing on the mode. The mode may be the largest value, the smallest value, or a value anywhere in between in the set. The mode only tells which value or values, if any, occurred the greatest number of times. It does not give any suggestions about the remaining values in the set.

Review Video: Mean, Median, and Mode
Visit mometrix.com/academy and enter code: 286207

Dispersion

A **measure of dispersion** is a single value that helps to "interpret" the measure of central tendency by providing more information about how the data values in the set are distributed about the measure of central tendency. The measure of dispersion helps to eliminate or reduce the disadvantages of using the mean, median, or mode as a single measure of central tendency, and give a more accurate picture of the dataset as a whole. To have a measure of dispersion, you must know or calculate the range, standard deviation, or variance of the data set.

Range

The **range** of a set of data is the difference between the greatest and lowest values of the data in the set. To calculate the range, you must first make sure the units for all data values are the same, and then identify the greatest and lowest values. If there are multiple data values that are equal for the highest or lowest, just use one of the values in the formula. Write the answer with the same units as the data values you used to do the calculations.

Standard Deviation

Standard deviation is a measure of dispersion that compares all the data values in the set to the mean of the set to give a more accurate picture. To find the standard deviation of a sample, use the formula

$$s = \sqrt{\frac{\sum_{i=1}^{n}(x_i - \bar{x})^2}{n-1}}$$

Note that s is the standard deviation of a sample, x represents the individual values in the data set, $\bar{x}$ is the mean of the data values in the set, and n is the number of data values in the set. The higher the value of the standard deviation is, the greater the variance of the data values from the mean. The units associated with the standard deviation are the same as the units of the data values.

Review Video: Standard Deviation
Visit mometrix.com/academy and enter code: 419469

VARIANCE

The **variance** of a sample, or just variance, is the square of the standard deviation of that sample. While the mean of a set of data gives the average of the set and gives information about where a specific data value lies in relation to the average, the variance of the sample gives information about the degree to which the data values are spread out and tell you how close an individual value is to the average compared to the other values. The units associated with variance are the same as the units of the data values squared.

PERCENTILE

Percentiles and quartiles are other methods of describing data within a set. **Percentiles** tell what percentage of the data in the set fall below a specific point. For example, achievement test scores are often given in percentiles. A score at the 80th percentile is one which is equal to or higher than 80 percent of the scores in the set. In other words, 80 percent of the scores were lower than that score.

Quartiles are percentile groups that make up quarter sections of the data set. The first quartile is the 25th percentile. The second quartile is the 50th percentile; this is also the median of the dataset. The third quartile is the 75th percentile.

SKEWNESS

Skewness is a way to describe the symmetry or asymmetry of the distribution of values in a dataset. If the distribution of values is symmetrical, there is no skew. In general the closer the mean of a data set is to the median of the data set, the less skew there is. Generally, if the mean is to the right of the median, the data set is *positively skewed*, or right-skewed, and if the mean is to the left of the median, the data set is *negatively skewed*, or left-skewed. However, this rule of thumb is not infallible. When the data values are graphed on a curve, a set with no skew will be a perfect bell curve.

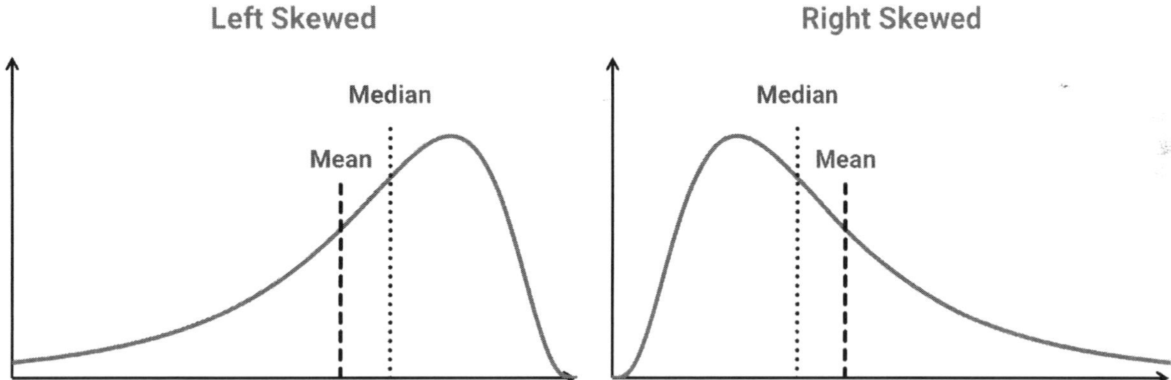

To estimate skew, use the formula:

$$\text{skew} = \frac{\sqrt{n(n-1)}}{n-2}\left(\frac{\frac{1}{n}\sum_{i=1}^{n}(x_i-\bar{x})^3}{\left(\frac{1}{n}\sum_{i=1}^{n}(x_i-\bar{x})^2\right)^{\frac{3}{2}}}\right)$$

Note that n is the datapoints in the set, x_i is the ith value in the set, and $\bar{x}$ is the mean of the set.

Review Video: Skew
Visit mometrix.com/academy and enter code: 661486

Unimodal vs. Bimodal

If a distribution has a single peak, it would be considered **unimodal.** If it has two discernible peaks it would be considered **bimodal**. Bimodal distributions may be an indication that the set of data being considered is actually the combination of two sets of data with significant differences. A **uniform distribution** is a distribution in which there is *no distinct peak or variation* in the data. No values or ranges are particularly more common than any other values or ranges.

Outlier

An outlier is an extremely high or extremely low value in the data set. It may be the result of measurement error, in which case, the outlier is not a valid member of the data set. However, it may also be a valid member of the distribution. Unless a measurement error is identified, the experimenter cannot know for certain if an outlier is or is not a member of the distribution. There are arbitrary methods that can be employed to designate an extreme value as an outlier. One method designates an outlier (or possible outlier) to be any value less than $Q_1 - 1.5(IQR)$ or any value greater than $Q_3 + 1.5(IQR)$.

Data Analysis

Simple Regression

In statistics, **simple regression** is using an equation to represent a relation between independent and a dependent variables. The independent variable is also referred to as the explanatory variable or the predictor, and is generally represented by the variable x in the equation. The dependent variable, usually represented by the variable y, is also referred to as the response variable. The equation may be any type of function – linear, quadratic, exponential, etc. The best way to handle this task is to use the regression feature of your graphing calculator. This will easily give you the curve of best fit and provide you with the coefficients and other information you need to derive an equation.

Line of Best Fit

In a scatter plot, the **line of best fit** is the line that best shows the trends of the data. The line of best fit is given by the equation $\hat{y} = ax + b$, where a and b are the regression coefficients. The regression coefficient a is also the slope of the line of best fit, and b is also the y-coordinate of the point at which the line of best fit crosses the y-axis. Not every point on the scatter plot will be on the line of best fit. The differences between the y-values of the points in the scatter plot and the corresponding y-values according to the equation of the line of best fit are the residuals. The line of best fit is also called the least-squares regression line because it is also the line that has the lowest sum of the squares of the residuals.

Correlation Coefficient

The **correlation coefficient** is the numerical value that indicates how strong the relationship is between the two variables of a linear regression equation. A correlation coefficient of –1 is a perfect negative correlation. A correlation coefficient of +1 is a perfect positive correlation. Correlation coefficients close to –1 or +1 are very strong correlations. A correlation coefficient equal to zero indicates there is no correlation between the two variables. This test is a good indicator of whether or not the equation for the line of best fit is accurate. The formula for the correlation coefficient is

$$r = \frac{\sum_{i=1}^{n}(x_i - \bar{x})(y_i - \bar{y})}{\sqrt{\sum_{i=1}^{n}(x_i - \bar{x})^2}\sqrt{\sum_{i=1}^{n}(y_i - \bar{y})^2}}$$

where r is the correlation coefficient, n is the number of data values in the set, (x_i, y_i) is a point in the set, and $\bar{x}$ and $\bar{y}$ are the means.

Z-Score

A **z-score** is an indication of how many standard deviations a given value falls from the mean. To calculate a z-score, use the formula $\frac{x-\mu}{\sigma}$, where x is the data value, μ is the mean of the data set, and σ is the standard deviation of the population. If the z-score is positive, the data value lies above the mean. If the z-score is negative, the data value falls below the mean. These scores are useful in interpreting data such as standardized test scores, where every piece of data in the set has been counted, rather than just a small random sample. In cases where standard deviations are calculated from a random sample of the set, the z-scores will not be as accurate.

Central Limit Theorem

According to the **central limit theorem**, regardless of what the original distribution of a sample is, the distribution of the means tends to get closer and closer to a normal distribution as the sample size gets larger and larger (this is necessary because the sample is becoming more all-encompassing of the elements of the population). As the sample size gets larger, the distribution of the sample mean will approach a normal distribution with a mean of the population mean and a variance of the population variance divided by the sample size.

Practice

P1. Suppose the class average on a final exam is 87, with a standard deviation of 2 points. Find the z-score of a student that got an 82.

P2. Given the following graph, determine the range of patient ages:

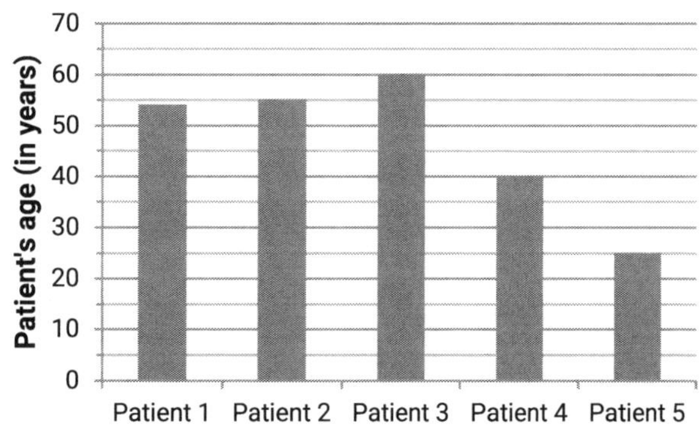

P3. Calculate the sample standard deviation for the dataset $\{10, 13, 11, 5, 8, 18\}$

Practice Solutions

P1. Using the formula for z-score: $z = \frac{82-87}{2} = -2.5$

P2. Patient 1 is 54 years old; Patient 2 is 55 years old; Patient 3 is 60 years old; Patient 4 is 40 years old; and Patient 5 is 25 years old. The range of patient ages is the age of the oldest patient minus the age of the youngest patient. In other words, $60 - 25 = 35$. The range of ages is 35 years.

P3. To find the standard deviation, first find the mean:

$$\frac{10 + 13 + 12 + 5 + 8 + 18}{6} = \frac{66}{6} = 11$$

Now, apply the formula for sample standard deviation:

$$s = \sqrt{\frac{\sum_{i=1}^{n}(x_i - \bar{x})^2}{n-1}} = \sqrt{\frac{\sum_{i=1}^{6}(x_i - 11)^2}{6-1}}$$
$$= \frac{\sqrt{(10-11)^2 + (13-11)^2 + (12-11)^2 + (5-11)^2 + (8-11)^2 + (18-11)^2}}{5}$$
$$= \frac{\sqrt{(-1)^2 + 2^2 + 1^2 + (-6)^2 + (-3)^2 + 7^2}}{5}$$
$$= \frac{\sqrt{1+4+1+36+9+49}}{5}$$
$$= \frac{\sqrt{100}}{5} = \frac{10}{5} = 2$$

Displaying Information

Frequency Tables

Frequency tables show how frequently each unique value appears in the set. A **relative frequency table** is one that shows the proportions of each unique value compared to the entire set. Relative frequencies are given as percentages; however, the total percent for a relative frequency table will not necessarily equal 100 percent due to rounding. An example of a frequency table with relative frequencies is below.

Favorite Color	Frequency	Relative Frequency
Blue	4	13%
Red	7	22%
Green		9%
Purple	6	19%
Cyan	12	38%

Review Video: Data Interpretation of Graphs
Visit mometrix.com/academy and enter code: 200439

Circle Graphs

Circle graphs, also known as *pie charts*, provide a visual depiction of the relationship of each type of data compared to the whole set of data. The circle graph is divided into sections by drawing radii to create central angles whose percentage of the circle is equal to the individual data's percentage of the whole set. Each 1% of data is equal to 3.6° in the circle graph. Therefore, data represented by a 90° section of the circle graph makes up 25% of the whole. When complete, a circle graph often looks like a pie cut into uneven wedges. The pie chart below shows the data from the frequency table referenced earlier where people were asked their favorite color.

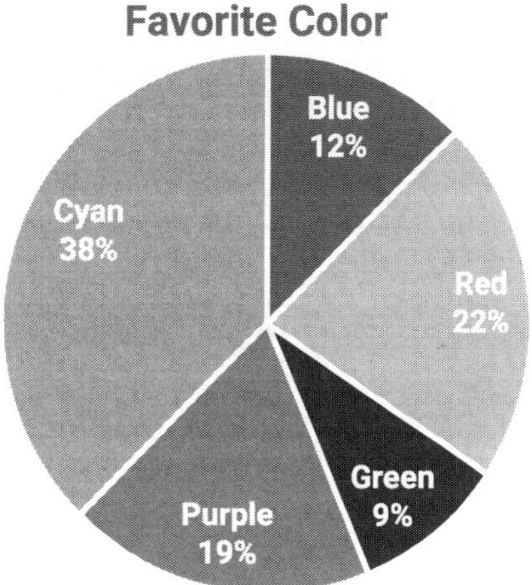

Review Video: Pie Chart
Visit mometrix.com/academy and enter code: 895285

PICTOGRAPHS

A **pictograph** is a graph, generally in the horizontal orientation, that uses pictures or symbols to represent the data. Each pictograph must have a key that defines the picture or symbol and gives the quantity each picture or symbol represents. Pictures or symbols on a pictograph are not always shown as whole elements. In this case, the fraction of the picture or symbol shown represents the same fraction of the quantity a whole picture or symbol stands for. For example, a row with $3\frac{1}{2}$ ears of corn, where each ear of corn represents 100 stalks of corn in a field, would equal $3\frac{1}{2} \times 100 = 350$ stalks of corn in the field.

LINE GRAPHS

Line graphs have one or more lines of varying styles (solid or broken) to show the different values for a set of data. The individual data are represented as ordered pairs, much like on a Cartesian plane. In this case, the x- and y-axes are defined in terms of their units, such as dollars or time. The individual plotted points are joined by line segments to show whether the value of the data is increasing (line sloping upward), decreasing (line sloping downward) or staying the same (horizontal line). Multiple sets of data can be graphed on the same line graph to give an easy visual comparison. An example of this would be graphing achievement test scores for different groups of students over the same time period to see which group had the greatest increase or decrease in performance from year-to-year (as shown below).

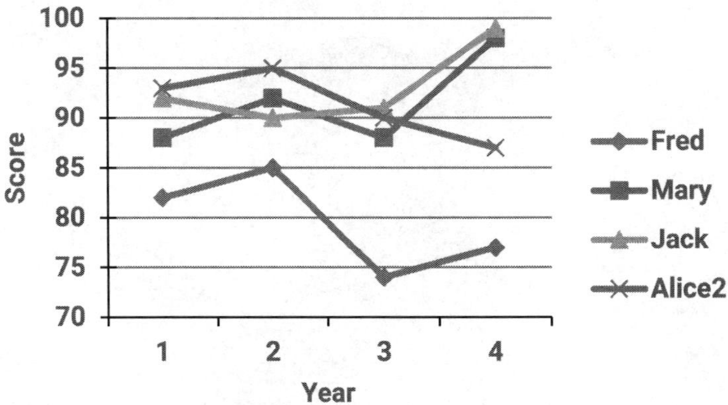

Review Video: Line Graphs
Visit mometrix.com/academy and enter code: 480147

Line Plots

A **line plot**, also known as a *dot plot*, has plotted points that are not connected by line segments. In this graph, the horizontal axis lists the different possible values for the data, and the vertical axis lists the number of times the individual value occurs. A single dot is graphed for each value to show the number of times it occurs. This graph is more closely related to a bar graph than a line graph. Do not connect the dots in a line plot or it will misrepresent the data.

Review Video: Line Plot
Visit mometrix.com/academy and enter code: 754610

Stem and Leaf Plots

A **stem and leaf plot** is useful for depicting groups of data that fall into a range of values. Each piece of data is separated into two parts: the first, or left, part is called the stem; the second, or right, part is called the leaf. Each stem is listed in a column from smallest to largest. Each leaf that has the common stem is listed in that stem's row from smallest to largest. For example, in a set of two-digit numbers, the digit in the tens place is the stem, and the digit in the ones place is the leaf. With a stem and leaf plot, you can easily see which subset of numbers (10s, 20s, 30s, etc.) is the largest. This information is also readily available by looking at a histogram, but a stem and leaf plot also allows you to look closer and see exactly which values fall in that range. Using all of the test scores from above, we can assemble a stem and leaf plot like the one below.

Test Scores

7	4	8							
8	2	5	7	8	8				
9	0	0	1	2	2	3	5	8	9

Bar Graphs

A **bar graph** is one of the few graphs that can be drawn correctly in two different configurations – both horizontally and vertically. A bar graph is similar to a line plot in the way the data is organized on the graph. Both axes must have their categories defined for the graph to be useful. Rather than placing a single dot to mark the point of the data's value, a bar, or thick line, is drawn from zero to the exact value of the data, whether it is a number, percentage, or other numerical value. Longer bar lengths correspond to greater data values. To read a bar graph, read the labels for the axes to find the units being reported. Then look where the bars end in relation to the scale given on the corresponding axis and determine the associated value.

The bar chart below represents the responses from our favorite color survey.

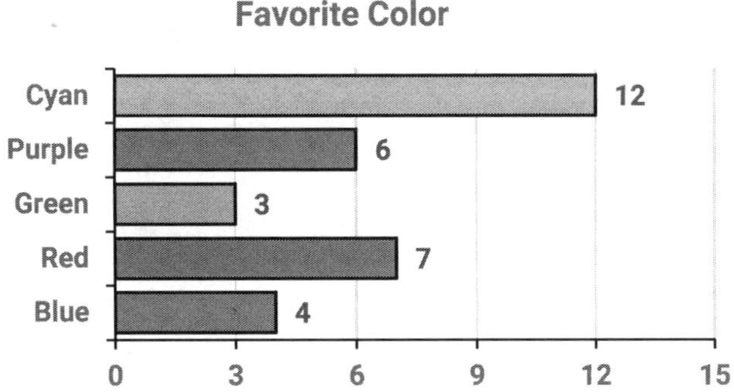

Review Video: Bar Graph
Visit mometrix.com/academy and enter code: 226729

Histograms

At first glance, a **histogram** looks like a vertical bar graph. The difference is that a bar graph has a separate bar for each piece of data and a histogram has one continuous bar for each *range* of data. For example, a histogram may have one bar for the range 0–9, one bar for 10–19, etc. While a bar graph has numerical values on one axis, a histogram has numerical values on both axes. Each range is of equal size, and they are ordered left to right from lowest to highest. The height of each column on a histogram represents the number of data values within that range. Like a stem and leaf plot, a histogram makes it easy to glance at the graph and quickly determine which range has the greatest quantity of values. A simple example of a histogram is below.

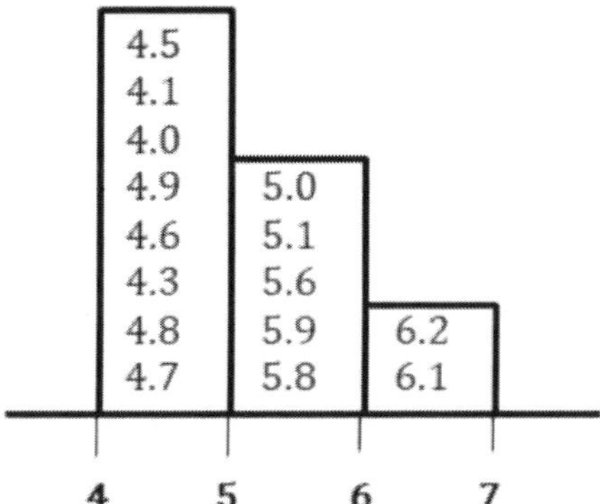

Review Video: Histogram
Visit mometrix.com/academy and enter code: 735897

Bivariate Data

Bivariate data is simply data from two different variables. (The prefix *bi-* means *two.*) In a *scatter plot,* each value in the set of data is plotted on a grid similar to a Cartesian plane, where each axis represents one of the two variables. By looking at the pattern formed by the points on the grid, you can often determine whether or not there is a relationship between the two variables, and what that relationship is, if it exists. The variables may be directly proportionate, inversely proportionate, or show no proportion at all. It may also be possible to determine if the data is linear, and if so, to find an equation to relate the two variables. The following scatter plot shows the relationship between preference for brand "A" and the age of the consumers surveyed.

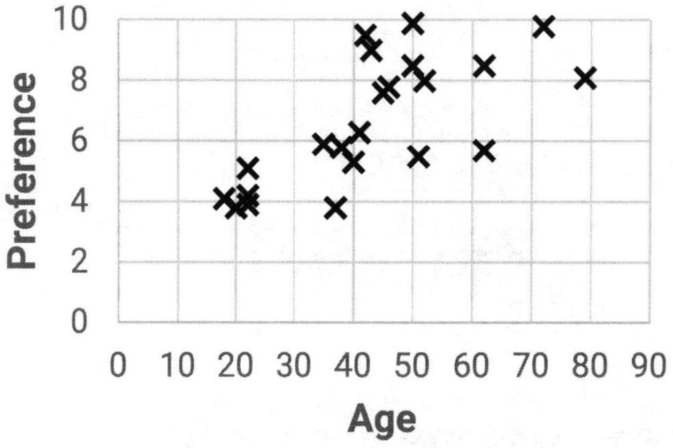

Scatter Plots

Scatter plots are also useful in determining the type of function represented by the data and finding the simple regression. Linear scatter plots may be positive or negative. Nonlinear scatter plots are generally exponential or quadratic. Below are some common types of scatter plots:

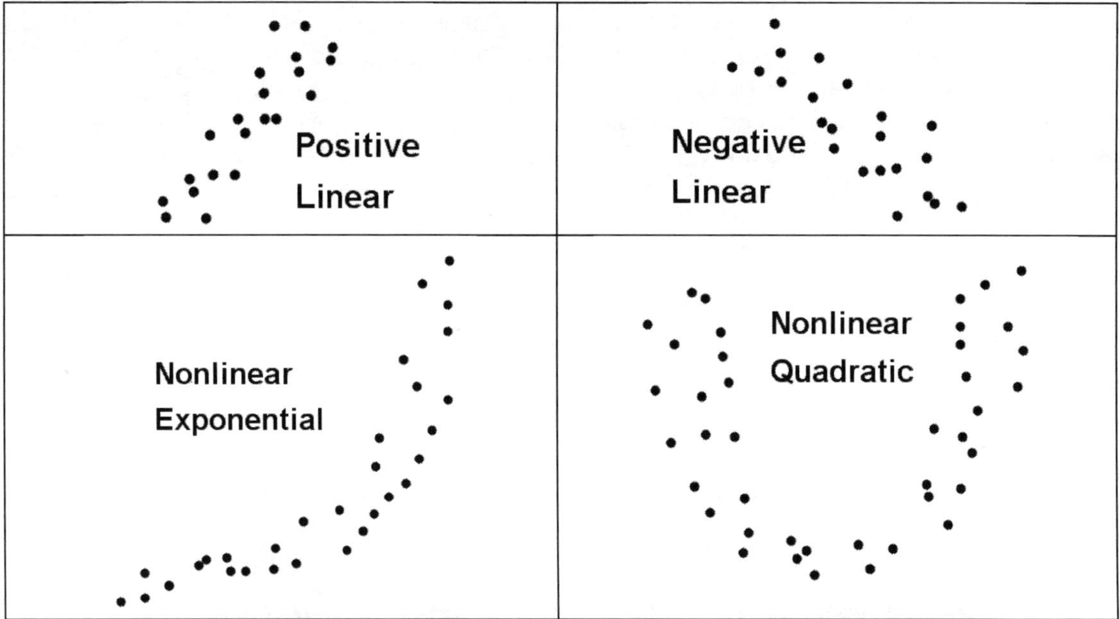

Review Video: Scatter Plot
Visit mometrix.com/academy and enter code: 596526

5-Number Summary

The **5-number summary** of a set of data gives a very informative picture of the set. The five numbers in the summary include the minimum value, maximum value, and the three quartiles. This information gives the reader the range and median of the set, as well as an indication of how the data is spread about the median.

Box and Whisker Plots

A **box-and-whisker plot** is a graphical representation of the 5-number summary. To draw a box-and-whiskers plot, plot the points of the 5-number summary on a number line. Draw a box whose ends are through the points for the first and third quartiles. Draw a vertical line in the box through the median to divide the box in half. Draw a line segment from the first quartile point to the minimum value, and from the third quartile point to the maximum value.

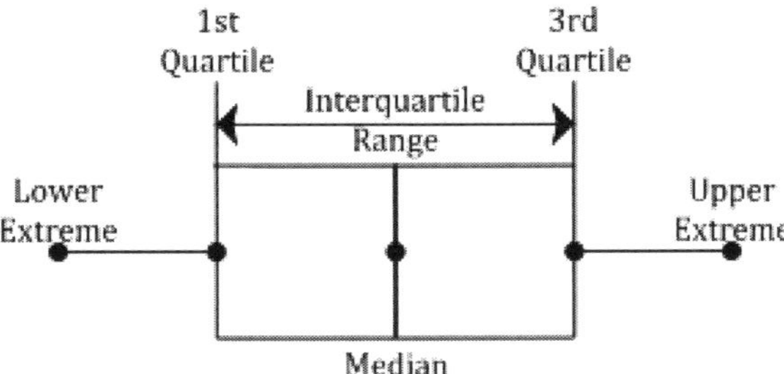

68-95-99.7 Rule

The **68–95–99.7 rule** describes how a normal distribution of data should appear when compared to the mean. This is also a description of a normal bell curve. According to this rule, 68 percent of the data values in a normally distributed set should fall within one standard deviation of the mean (34 percent above and 34 percent below the mean), 95 percent of the data values should fall within two standard deviations of the mean (47.5 percent above and 47.5 percent below the mean), and 99.7 percent of the data values should fall within three standard deviations of the mean, again, equally distributed on either side of the mean. This means that only 0.3 percent of all data values should fall more than three standard deviations from the mean. On the graph below, the normal curve is centered on the y-axis. The x-axis labels are how many standard deviations away from the center you are. Therefore, it is easy to see how the 68-95-99.7 rule can apply.

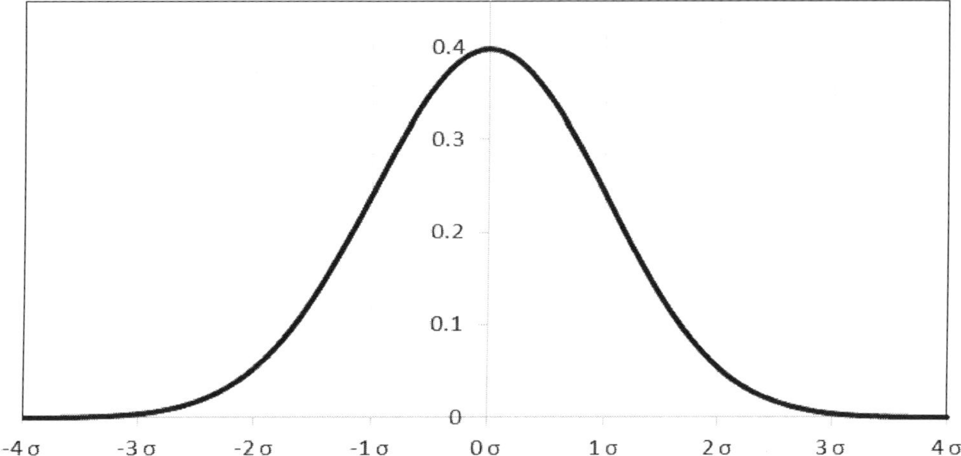

NES Practice Test

Number Sense and Operations

1. In the base-5 number system, what is the sum of 303 and 2222?

a. 2030
b. 2525
c. 3030
d. 3530

2. Kim's current monthly rent is $800. She is moving to another apartment complex, where the monthly rent will be $1,100. What is the percent increase in her monthly rent amount?

a. 25.5%
b. 27%
c. 35%
d. 37.5%

3. Which of the following statements is true?

a. The set of whole numbers is a subset of the set of natural numbers.
b. The set of integers is a subset of the set of natural numbers.
c. The set of integers is a subset of the set of rational numbers.
d. The set of rational numbers is a subset of the set of integers.

4. Which of the following represents 55 in the base-2 system?

a. 110
b. 1101
c. 101,111
d. 110,111

5. Marlon pays $45 for a jacket that has been marked down 25%. What was the original cost of the jacket?

a. $80
b. $75
c. $65
d. $60

6. Which of the following statements is true?

a. A number is divisible by 6 if the number is divisible by both 2 and 3.
b. A number is divisible by 4 if the sum of all digits is divisible by 8.
c. A number is divisible by 3 if the last digit is divisible by 3.
d. A number is divisible by 7 if the sum of the last two digits is divisible by 7.

7. Which of the following is an irrational number?

a. $4.\overline{2}$
b. $\sqrt{2}$
c. $\frac{4}{5}$
d. $\frac{21}{5}$

8. Robert buys a car for $24,210. The price of the car has been marked down by 10%. What was the original price of the car?

a. $25,900
b. $26,300
c. $26,900
d. $27,300

9. Carlos spends $\frac{1}{8}$ of his monthly salary on utility bills. If his utility bills total $320, what is his monthly salary?

a. $2,440
b. $2,520
c. $2,560
d. $2,600

10. Which of the following is closed under the operation of division?

a. whole numbers
b. integers
c. nonzero rational numbers
d. irrational numbers

11. Which of the following accurately describes the set of integers?

a. the set of counting numbers
b. the set of counting numbers, plus zero
c. the set of numbers that may be written as the ratio of $\frac{a}{b}$, where $b \neq 0$
d. the set of counting numbers, zero, and the negations of the counting numbers

12. Which of the following correctly compares the sets of rational and irrational numbers?

a. The set of rational numbers is a subset of the set of irrational numbers.
b. The set of irrational numbers is a subset of the set of rational numbers.
c. The sets of irrational and rational numbers are disjoint.
d. The sets of irrational and rational numbers are equal.

13. Which of the following illustrates the multiplicative inverse property?

a. The product of a and 1 is a.
b. The product of $\frac{1}{a}$ and a is 1.
c. The variable a, raised to the negative 1 power, is equal to the ratio of 1 to a.
d. The product of a and $-a$ is $-a^2$.

14. For any natural numbers, a, b, and c, assume $a|b$ and $a|c$. Which of the following statements is *not* necessarily true?

a. $b|c$
b. $a|(b-c)$
c. $a|bc$
d. $a|(b+c)$

15. Which of the following equations may be used to convert $0.\overline{4}$ to a fraction?

a. $10x - x = 4.\overline{4} - 0.\overline{4}$
b. $100x - x = 4.\overline{4} - 0.\overline{4}$
c. $10x - x = 44.\overline{4} - 4.\overline{4}$
d. $100x - 10x = 4.\overline{4} - 0.\overline{4}$

16. Jason decides to donate 1% of his annual salary to a local charity. If his annual salary is $45,000, how much will he donate?

a. $4.50
b. $45
c. $450
d. $4,500

17. Kendra uses the pie chart below to represent the allocation of her annual income. Her annual income is $40,000.

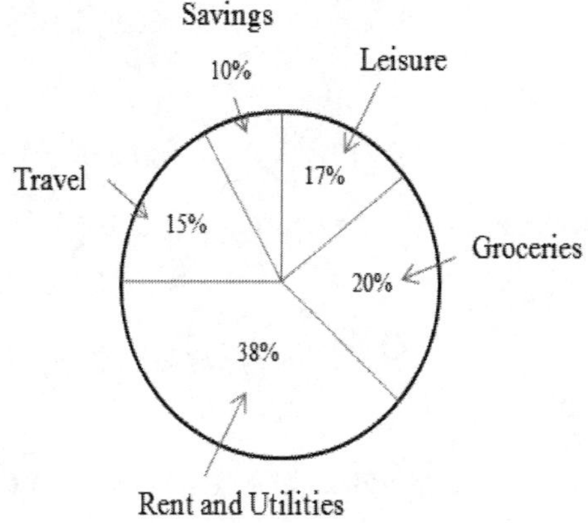

Which of the following statements is true?

a. The amount of money she spends on travel and savings is more than $11,000.
b. The amount of money she spends on rent and utilities is approximately $15,000.
c. The amount of money she spends on groceries and savings is more than $13,000.
d. The amount of money she spends on leisure is less than $5,000.

18. Which of the following correctly represents the expanded form of 0.867?

a. $8 \times \frac{1}{10^0} + 6 \times \frac{1}{10^1} + 7 \times \frac{1}{10^2}$
b. $8 \times \frac{1}{10^2} + 6 \times \frac{1}{10^3} + 7 \times \frac{1}{10^4}$
c. $8 \times \frac{1}{10^3} + 6 \times \frac{1}{10^2} + 7 \times \frac{1}{10^1}$
d. $8 \times \frac{1}{10^1} + 6 \times \frac{1}{10^2} + 7 \times \frac{1}{10^3}$

19. Which expression is represented by the diagram below?

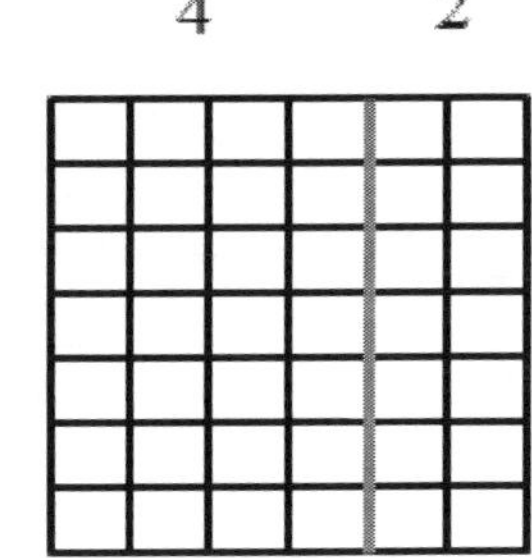

a. $7 + (4 + 2)$
b. $7 \times (4 \times 2)$
c. $7 + (4 \times 2)$
d. $7 \times (4 + 2)$

20. $b|a$ if

a. $a = b \times q$
b. $a = b + q$
c. $b = a \times q$
d. $b = a + q$

21. Which of the following sets is *not* closed under subtraction?

a. integers
b. real numbers
c. natural numbers
d. rational numbers

22. A dress is marked down 45%. The cost, after taxes, is $39.95. If the tax rate is 8.75%, what was the original price of the dress?

a. $45.74
b. $58.61
c. $66.79
d. $72.31

23. Amy saves $450 every 3 months. How much does she save after 3 years?

a. $4,800
b. $5,200
c. $5,400
d. $5,800

24. The table below shows the average amount of rainfall Houston receives during the summer and autumn months.

Month	Amount of Rainfall (in inches)
June	5.35
July	3.18
August	3.83
September	4.33
October	4.5
November	4.19

What percentage of rainfall received during this timeframe, is received during the month of October?

a. 13.5%
b. 15.1%
c. 16.9%
d. 17.7%

25. Which of the following represents 30,490?

a. 3.049×10^{-4}
b. 3.049×10^{3}
c. 30.490×10^{3}
d. 3.049×10^{4}

Algebra and Functions

26. Which of the following formulas may be used to represent the sequence 1, 2, 4, 8, 16, ...?

a. $y = 2x$
b. $y = x + 2$
c. $y = 2^{x-1}$
d. $y = x^2$

27. Which of the following formulas may be used to represent the sequence 8, 13, 18, 23, 28, ...?

a. $a_n = 5n + 3; n \in \mathbb{N}$
b. $a_n = n + 5; n \in \mathbb{N}$
c. $a_n = n + 8; n \in \mathbb{N}$
d. $a_n = 5n + 8; n \in \mathbb{N}$

28. Which of the following graphs does *not* represent a function?

a.

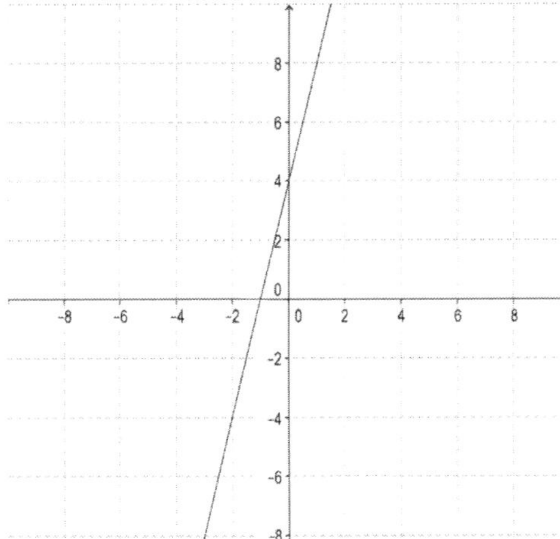

c.

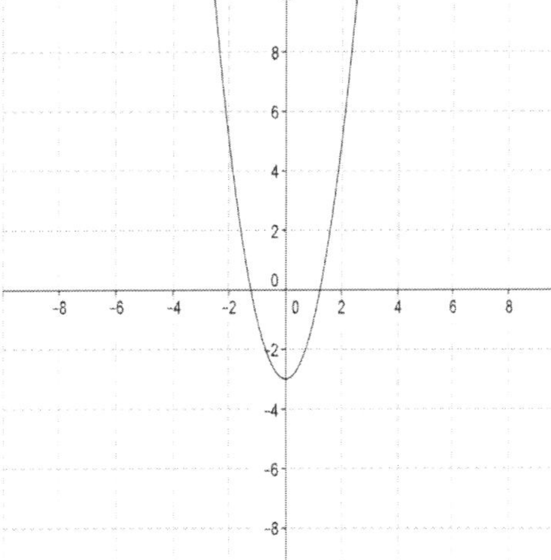

b.

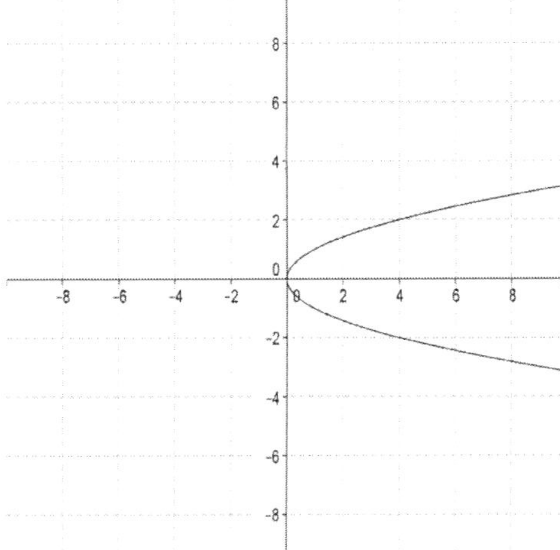

d.

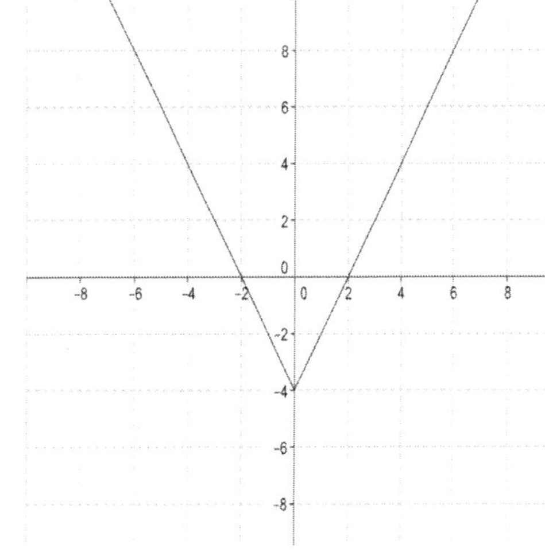

29. Which of the following represents a proportional relationship?

a.

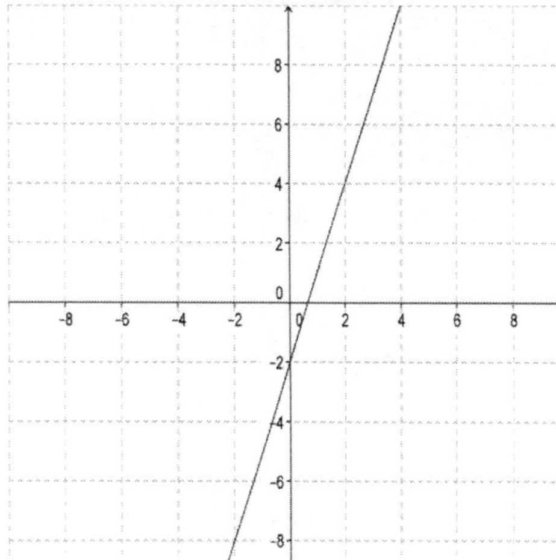

c.

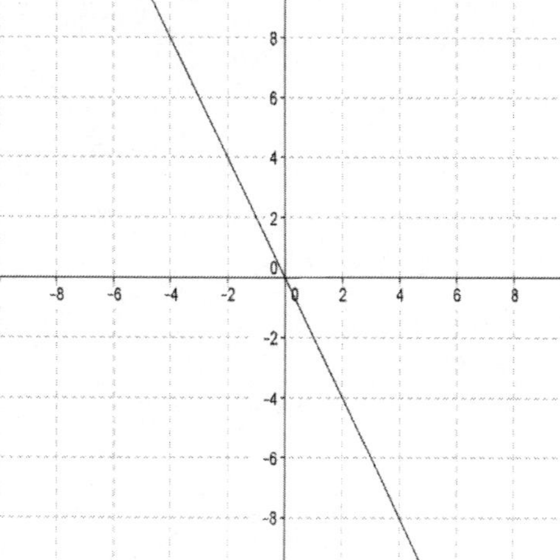

b.

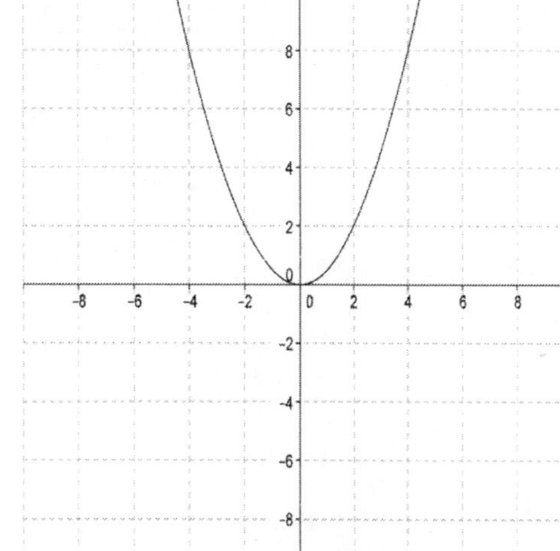

d.

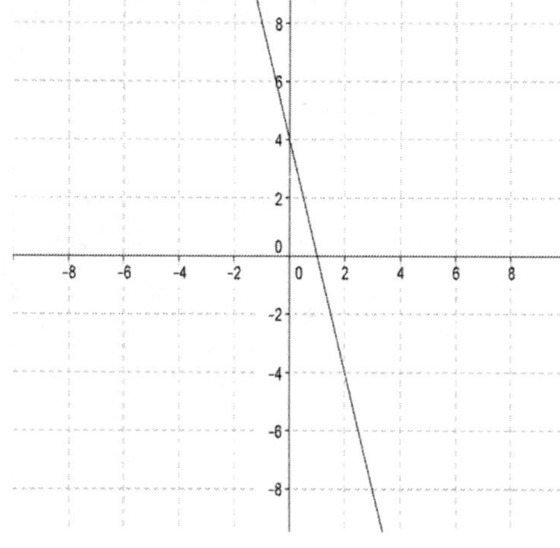

30. Which of the following represents the graph of $y = (x - 4)^2 + 3$?

a.

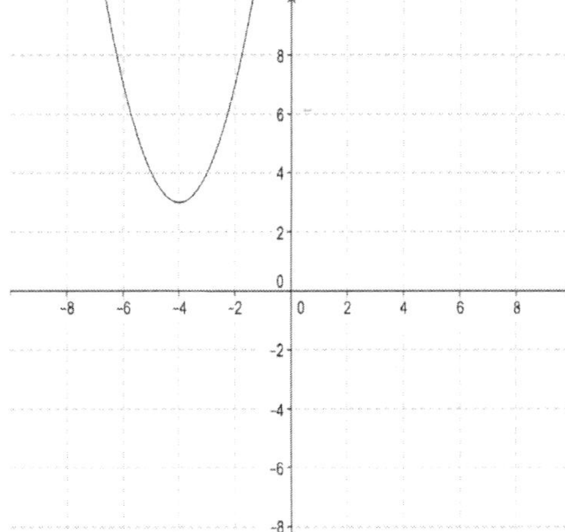

c.

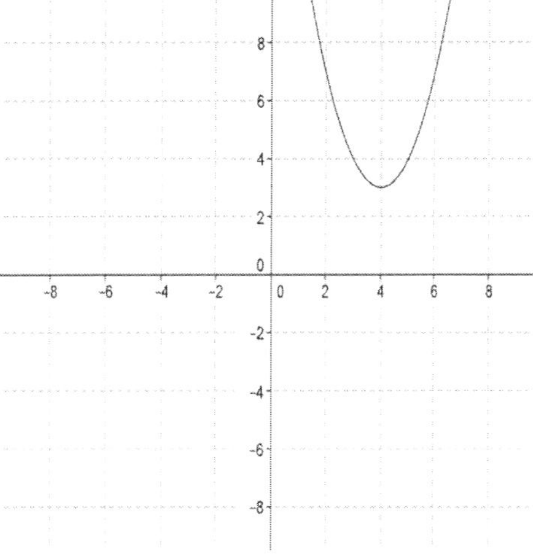

b.

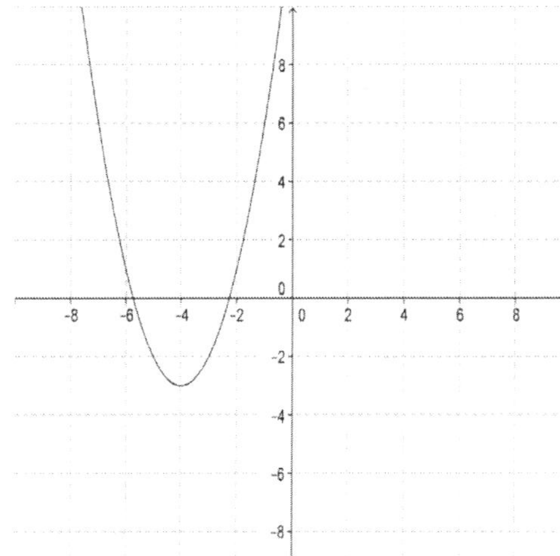

d.

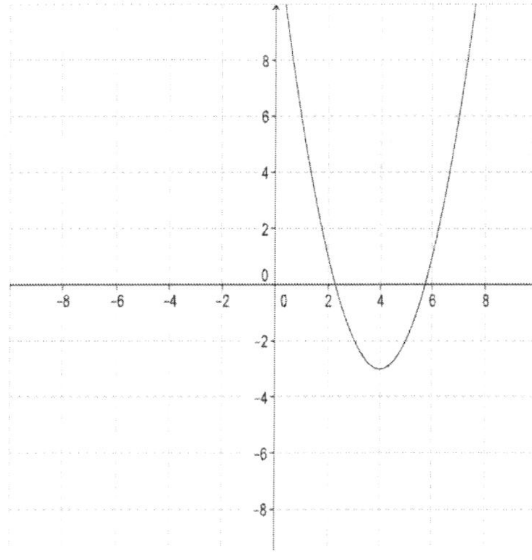

31. The expression $2x^2 - 4x - 30$ is equal to the product of $(x - 5)$ and which other factor?

a. $(2x - 10)$
b. $(2x + 25)$
c. $(2x + 7)$
d. $(2x + 6)$

32. What is the constant of proportionality represented by the table below?

x	y
2	-8
5	-20
7	-28
10	-40
11	-44

a. −12
b. −8
c. −6
d. −4

33. Which of the following represents an inverse proportional relationship?

a. $y = 3x$
b. $y = \frac{1}{3}x$
c. $y = \frac{3}{x}$
d. $y = 3x^2$

34. Which of the following expressions is equivalent to $-3x(x-2)^2$?

a. $-3x^3 + 6x^2 - 12x$
b. $-3x^3 - 12x^2 + 12x$
c. $-3x^2 + 6x$
d. $-3x^3 + 12x^2 - 12x$

35. Which of the following graphs represents the solution to $y \geq 3x - 6$?

a.
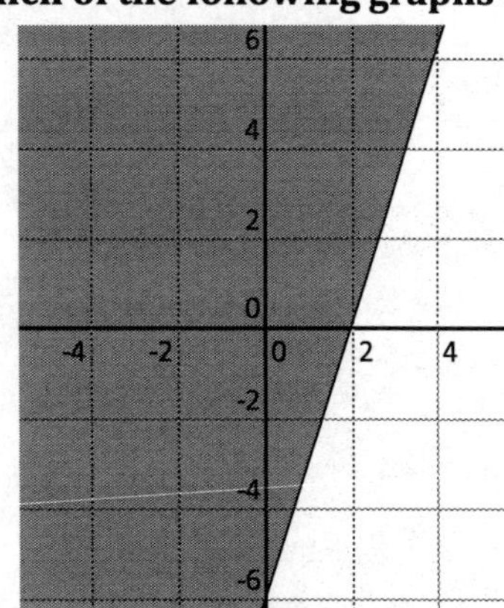

c.
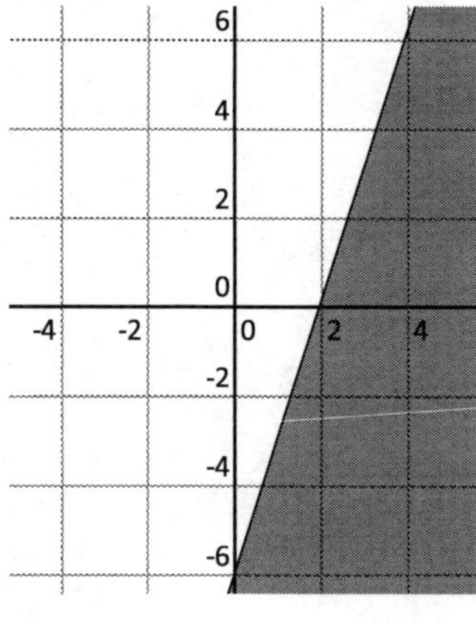

b.
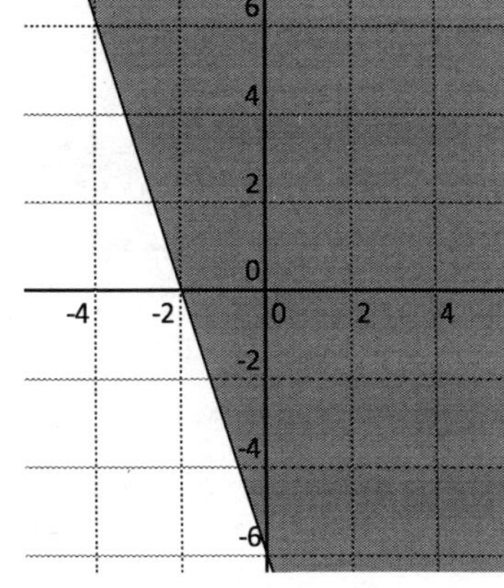

d.
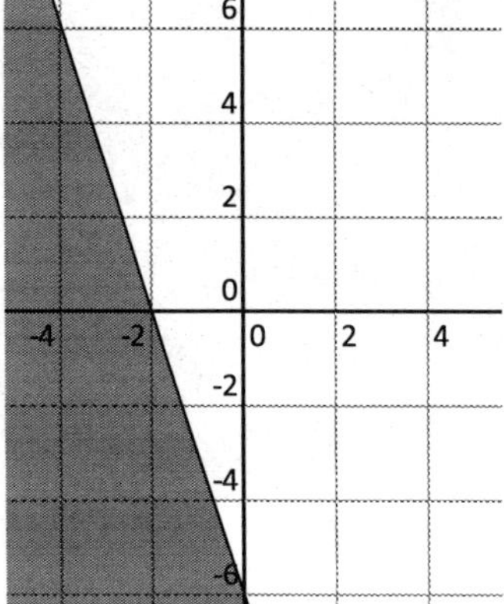

36. If $f(x) = \frac{x^3 - 2x + 1}{3x}$, what is $f(2)$?

a. $\frac{1}{3}$
b. $\frac{1}{2}$
c. $\frac{5}{6}$
d. $\frac{5}{2}$

37. The variables x and y are in a linear relationship. The table below shows a few sample values. Which of the following graphs correctly represents the linear equation relating x and y?

x	y
−2	−11
−1	−8
0	−5
1	−2
2	1

a.

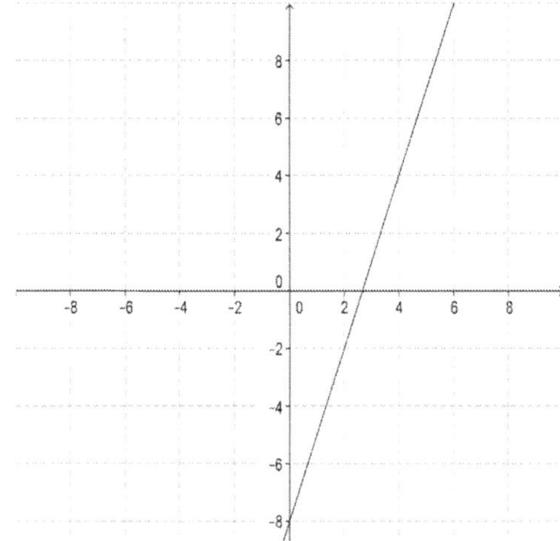

c.

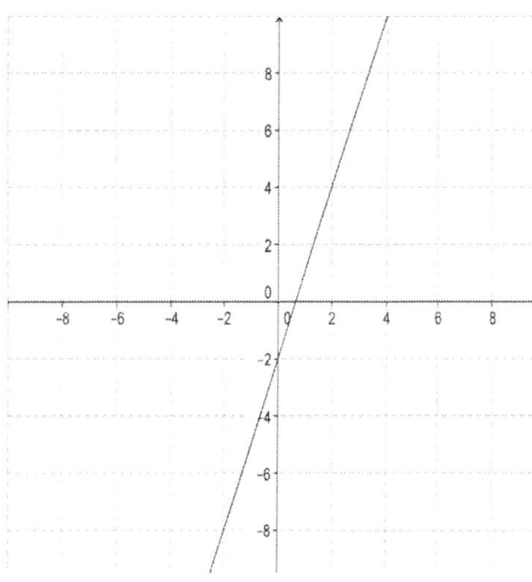

b.

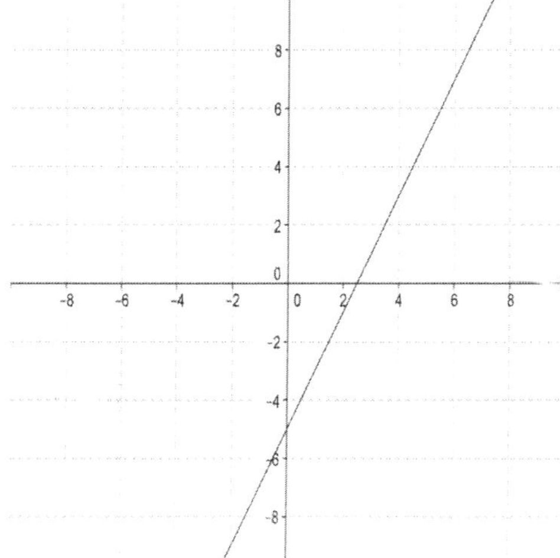

d.

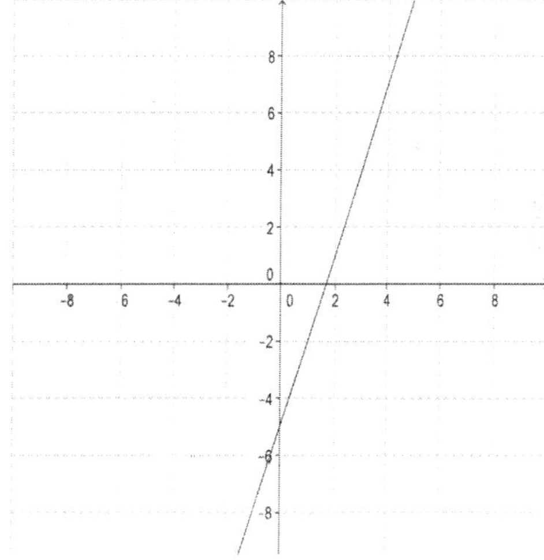

38. Which of the following is the graph of the equation $y = -4x - 6$?

a.

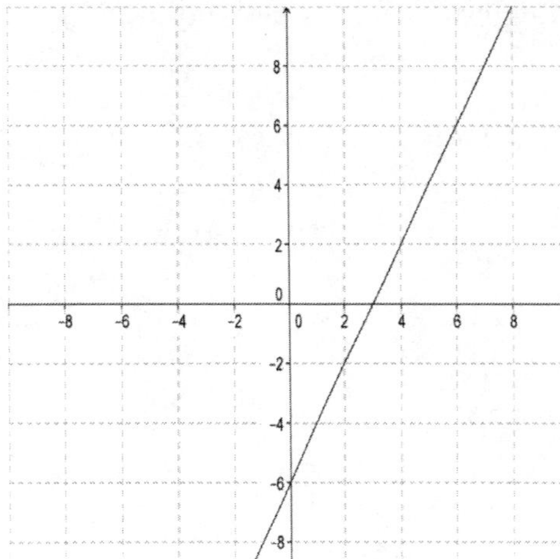

b.

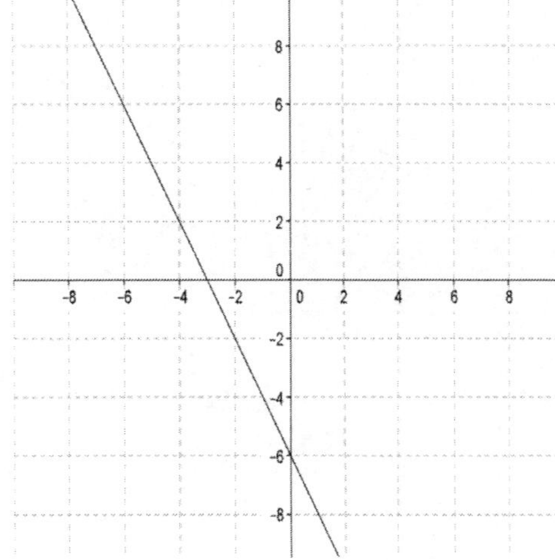

c.

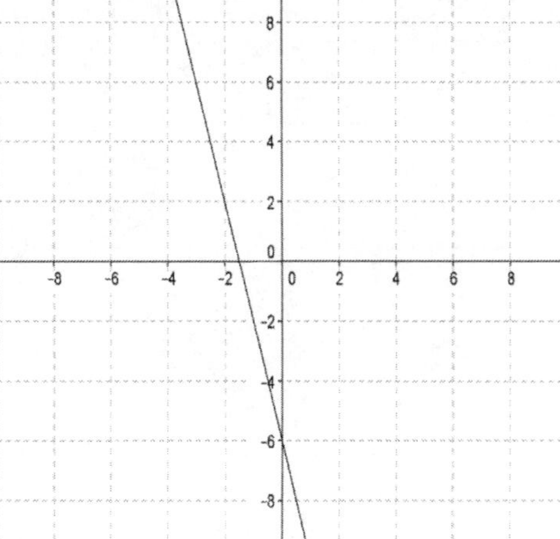

d.

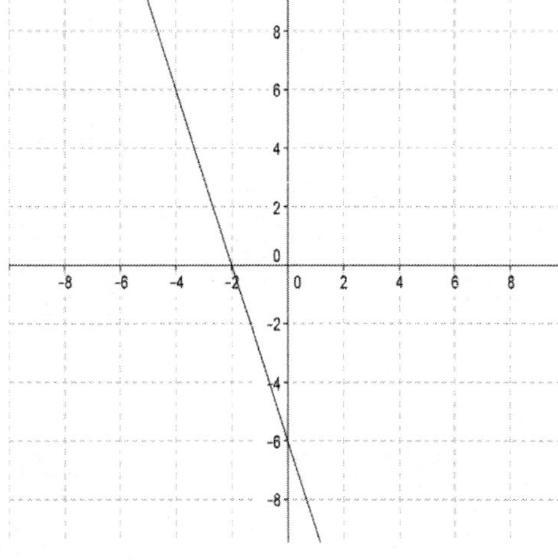

39. Given the graph below, what is the average rate of change from $f(2)$ to $f(5)$?

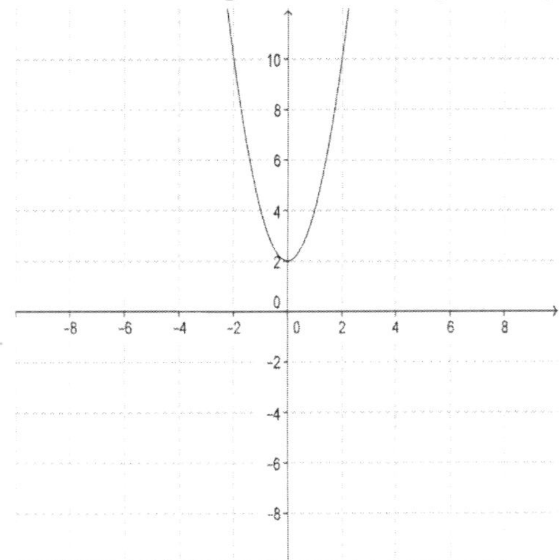

a. 2
b. 14
c. 21
d. 42

40. Elijah pays a $30 park entrance fee, plus $4 for every ticket purchased. Which of the following equations represents the cost?

a. $y = 30x + 4$
b. $y = 34x$
c. $y = 4x + 30$
d. $y = 34x + 30$

41. What is the solution to the system of linear equations graphed below?

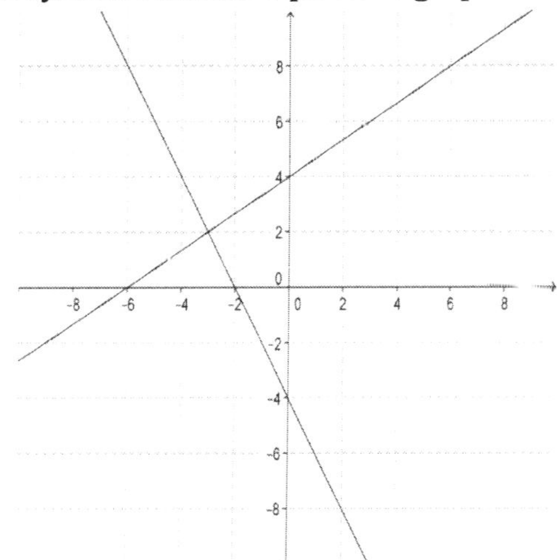

a. (2, −3)
b. (−3, −2)
c. (−2, 3)
d. (−3, 2)

42. What is the solution to the system of linear equations below?

$$4x - 2y = -38$$

$$2x + 3y = 17$$

a. $(-5, 9)$
b. $(-2, 11)$
c. $(-3, 7)$
d. $(-4, 11)$

43. Which of the following graphs represents the solution to the system of inequalities below?

$$2x - 3y \geq -11$$
$$-2x + 4y \geq 14$$

a.
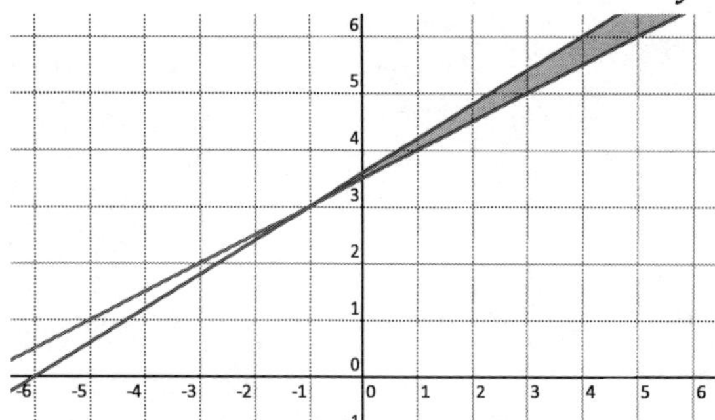

c.
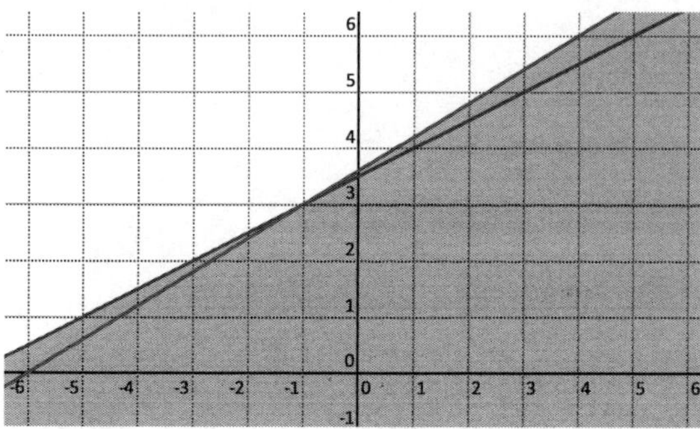

b.
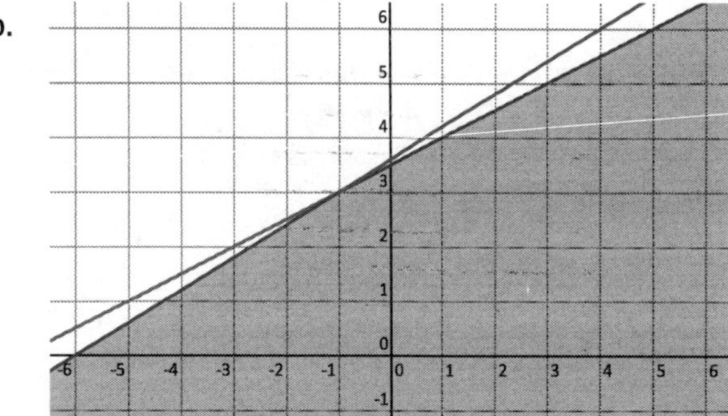

d.
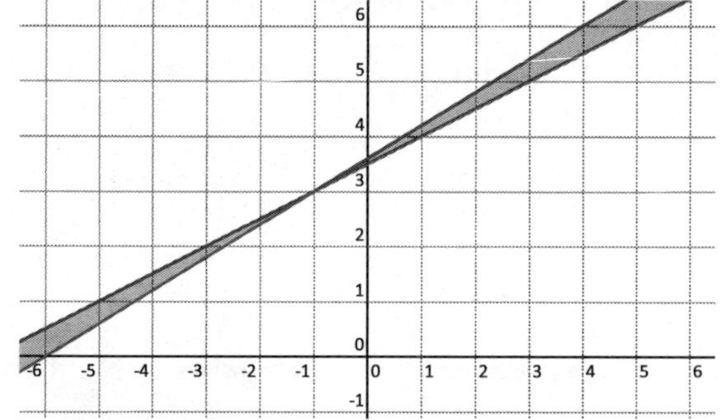

44. Robert drops a ball from his balcony. The height of the ball is modeled by the function $f(x) = -2x^2 + x + 11$, where $f(x)$ represents the height of the ball and x represents the number of seconds. Which of the following best represents the number of seconds that will pass before the ball reaches the ground?

a. 1.4
b. 1.9
c. 2.1
d. 2.6

45. Which type of function is represented by the table of values below?

x	y
−2	0.25
−1	0.5
0	1
1	2
2	4

a. linear
b. quadratic
c. cubic
d. exponential

46. What linear equation includes the data in the table below?

x	y
−3	1
1	−11
3	−17
5	−23
9	−35

a. $y = -3x - 11$
b. $y = -6x - 8$
c. $y = -3x - 8$
d. $y = -12x - 11$

47. Which of the following equations represents a line perpendicular to the one graphed below and passing through the point (3, 2)?

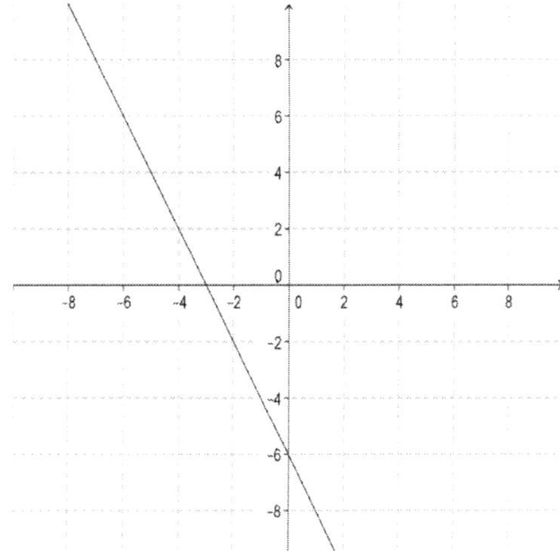

a. $y = \frac{1}{2}x + 2$
b. $y = \frac{1}{2}x + \frac{1}{2}$
c. $y = \frac{3}{2}x + \frac{1}{2}$
d. $y = 2x + 2$

48. Which of the following equations represents a line parallel to the one graphed below and passing through the point $(-1, 4)$?

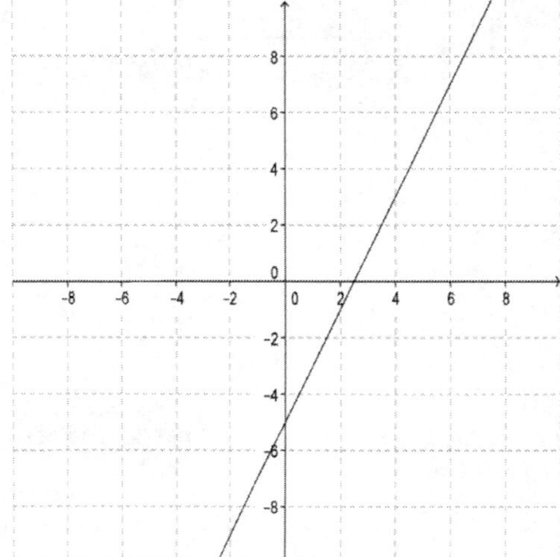

a. $y = 2x - 2$
b. $y = 3x + 6$
c. $y = 3x - 4$
d. $y = 2x + 6$

49. Hannah's monthly gym membership cost is represented by the graph shown below. Which of the following statements is correct?

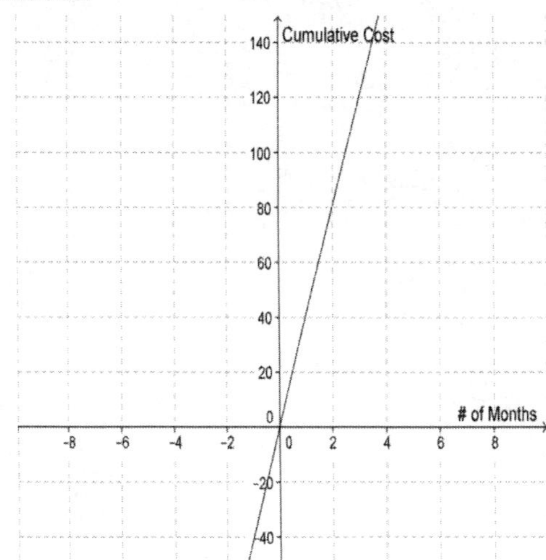

a. The cost is linear, but not proportional.
b. The cost is linear and proportional.
c. The cost is proportional, but not linear.
d. The cost represents an inverse proportional relationship.

50. Amanda saves \$0.02 during Month 1. During each subsequent month, she plans to save twice as much as she did the previous month. Which of the following equations represents the amount she will save during the *n*th month?

a. $a_n = 0.02 \times 2^{n-1}$
b. $a_n = 0.02 + 2^n$
c. $a_n = 0.02 \times 2^n$
d. $a_n = 2n - 1.98$

51. Kevin saves \$3 during Month 1. During each subsequent month, he plans to save 4 more dollars than he saved during the previous month. Which of the following equations represents the amount he will save during the *n*th month?

a. $a_n = 3n - 1$
b. $a_n = 3n + 4$
c. $a_n = 4n + 3$
d. $a_n = 4n - 1$

52. What is $\lim_{n\to\infty} \frac{n^2+1}{n}$?

a. 0
b. 1
c. 2
d. There is no limit.

53. What is $\lim_{n\to\infty} \frac{5n+2}{n}$?

a. 0
b. 2
c. 5
d. There is no limit.

54. The initial term of a sequence is 3. Each term in the sequence is $\frac{2}{3}$ the amount of the previous term. What is the sum of the terms, as *n* approaches infinity?

a. 6
b. 9
c. 12
d. 15

55. Mandy can buy 4 containers of yogurt and 3 boxes of crackers for \$9.55. She can buy 2 containers of yogurt and 2 boxes of crackers for \$5.90. How much does one box of crackers cost?

a. \$1.75
b. \$2.00
c. \$2.25
d. \$2.50

56. What is the derivative of $f(x) = 9x^2$?

a. $3x$
b. $9x$
c. 18x
d. $18x^2$

57. Which of the following functions converges?

a. $f(x) = \frac{x^2}{x}$
b. $f(x) = 2x$
c. $f(x) = \frac{4x}{x} + 1000$
d. $f(x) = \frac{3x^2+100}{x}$

58. McKenzie shades $\frac{1}{5}$ of a piece of paper. Then, she shades an additional area $\frac{1}{5}$ the size of what she just shaded. Next, she shades another area $\frac{1}{5}$ as large as the previous one. As she continues the process to infinity, what is the limit of the shaded fraction of the paper?

a. $\frac{1}{5}$
b. $\frac{1}{4}$
c. $\frac{1}{3}$
d. $\frac{1}{2}$

59. Which of the following functions has a limit of 0?

a. $f(x) = 2x$
b. $f(x) = \frac{4}{x}$
c. $f(x) = \frac{x}{8}$
d. $f(x) = \frac{3x+1}{x}$

60. What is the derivative of $g(x) = x^{ab}$?

a. $ab \times x^{ab}$
b. $ab \times x^{ab-1}$
c. $a \times x^{ab}$
d. $b \times x^{ab-1}$

61. Which of the following graphs represents an inverse proportional relationship?

a.
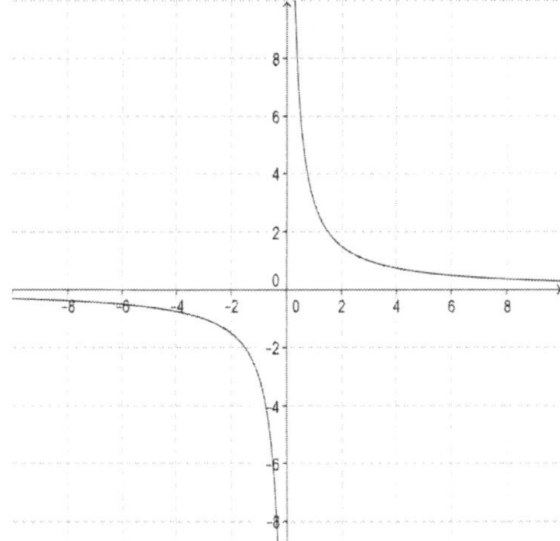

c.
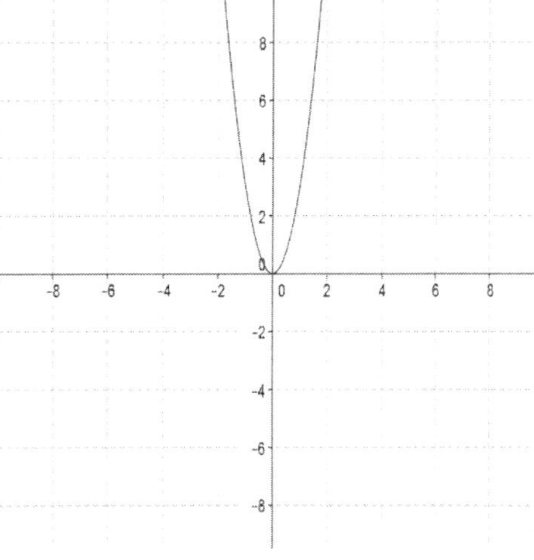

b.
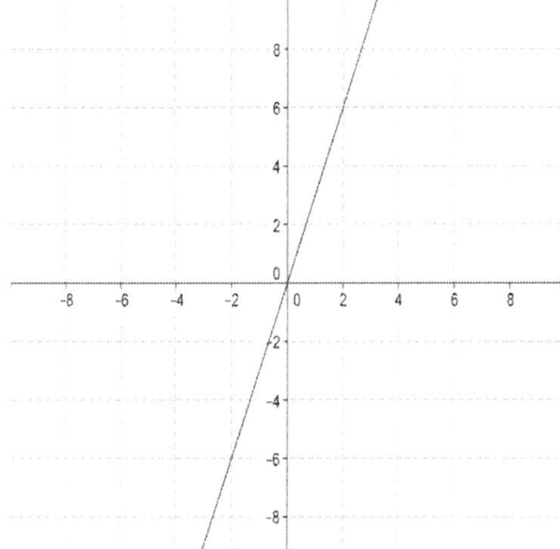

d.
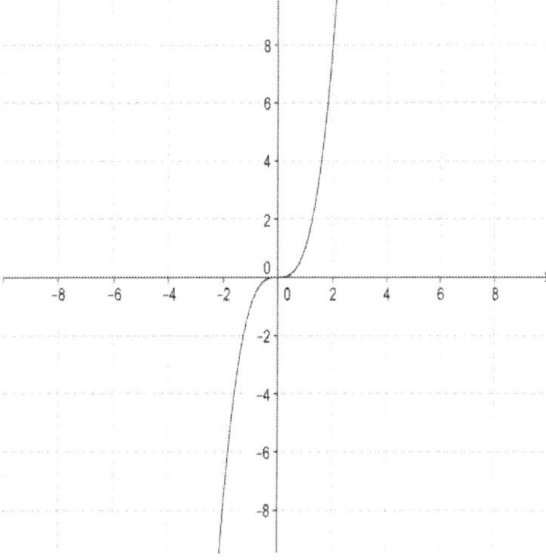

62. What is the sum of the first 50 even, positive integers?

a. 1,250
b. 2,025
c. 2,550
d. 3,250

63. The graph of the parent function $y = x^2$ is shifted 5 units to the left and 4 units down. Which of the following equations represents the transformed function?

a. $y = (x - 5)^2 - 4$
b. $y = (x + 5)^2 - 4$
c. $y = (x - 5)^2 + 4$
d. $y = (x + 5)^2 + 4$

64. Which of the following represents a function?

a. $\{(2, 9), (3, 4), (6, 8), (-1, 5), (3, -1)\}$
b. $\{(8, 7), (7, 9), (2, 1), (4, 3), (3, 6)\}$
c. $\{(-4, 6), (2, 1), (-4, -2), (3, 8), (9, 2)\}$
d. $\{(2, 6), (6, 5), (5, 9), (2, 0), (-3, 1)\}$

65. A car is accelerated. Which of the following accurately describes the appearance of the position-time graph?

a. It is a line with a positive slope.
b. It is a line with a negative slope.
c. It is a curve with an increasing slope.
d. It is a curve with a decreasing slope.

66. Tom needs to buy ink cartridges and printer paper. Each ink cartridge costs $30. Each ream of paper costs $5. He has $100 to spend. Which of the following inequalities may be used to find the combinations of ink cartridges and printer paper that he may purchase?

a. $30c + 5p \leq 100$
b. $30c + 5p < 100$
c. $30c + 5p > 100$
d. $30c + 5p \geq 100$

67. Hannah spends at least $16 on 4 packages of coffee. Which of the following inequalities represents the possible costs?

a. $16 \geq 4p$
b. $16 < 4p$
c. $16 > 4p$
d. $16 \leq 4p$

68. $f(x) = \frac{x+1}{2x}$. What is the equation of the horizontal asymptote?

a. $y = \frac{1}{4}$
b. $y = \frac{1}{2}$
c. $y = 0$
d. $y = 2$

69. $g(x) = \frac{x}{x+3}$. What is the equation of the horizontal asymptote?

a. $y = 0$
b. $y = 0.5$
c. $y = 1$
d. $y = 3$

70. What is $\lim_{x \to -\infty} \frac{4x^2}{x+2}$?

a. −4000
b. −400
c. 0
d. There is no limit.

71. What is $\lim_{x \to -2} (3x^3 - 6x^2 + 4)$?

a. −44
b. −42
c. 4
d. 52

72. Jackson can decorate a cake in 3 hours. Eli can decorate the same cake in 2 hours. If they work together, how long will it take them to decorate the cake?

a. 0.8 hours
b. 1.2 hours
c. 1.5 hours
d. 1.8 hours

73. Robert needs to buy milk and bread. Each gallon of milk costs $3. Each loaf of bread costs $2. He intends to spend at least $20. Which of the following graphs represents the possible combinations of gallons of milk and loaves of bread that he may purchase?

a.
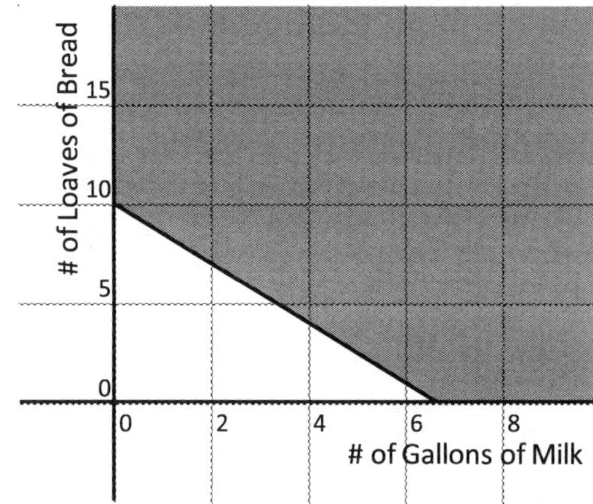

c.
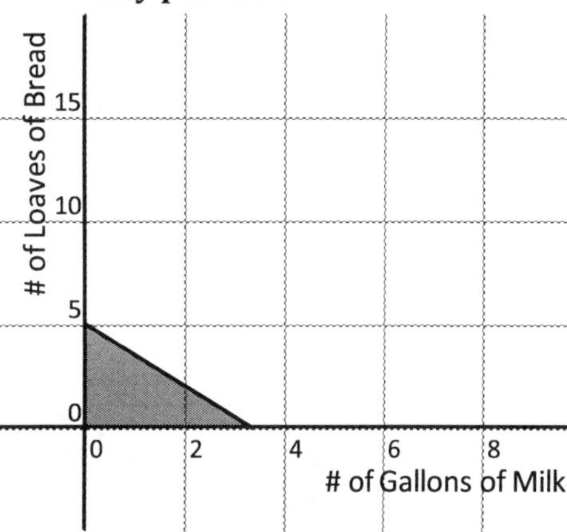

b.
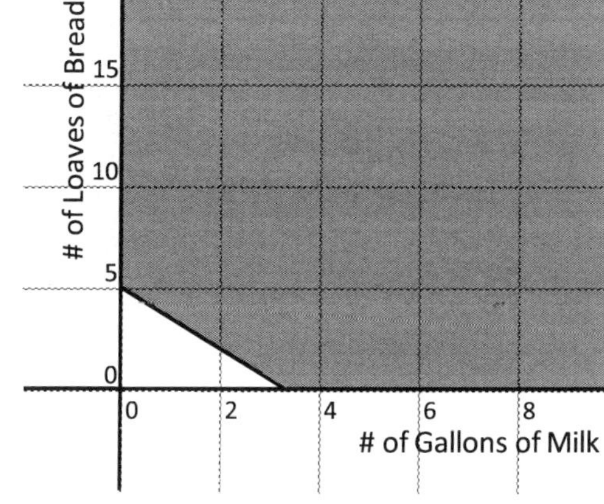

d.
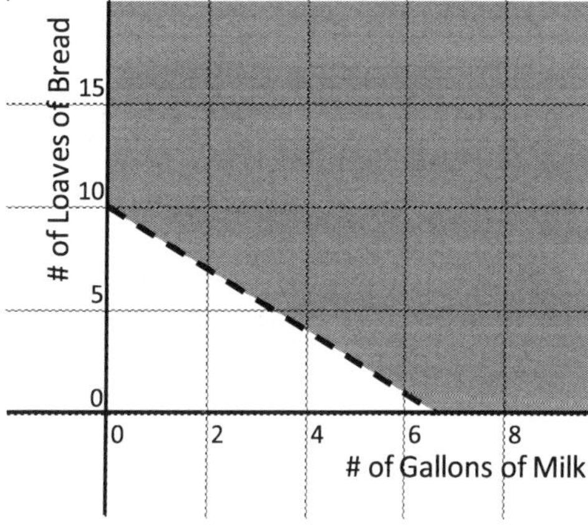

74. Kayla has a $75 budget to purchase gifts for her colleagues. She wants to buy coffee mugs and note pads. She may purchase a maximum of 30 items. Each coffee mug costs $6 and each note pad costs $3. Which of the following graphs correctly shows the possible combinations of coffee mugs and note pads that she may buy?

a.

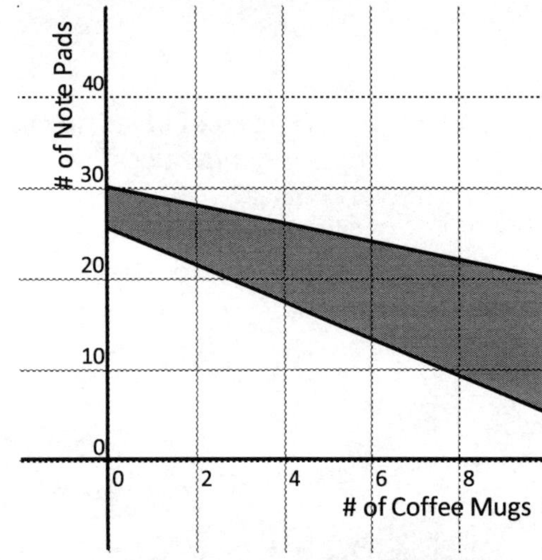

c.

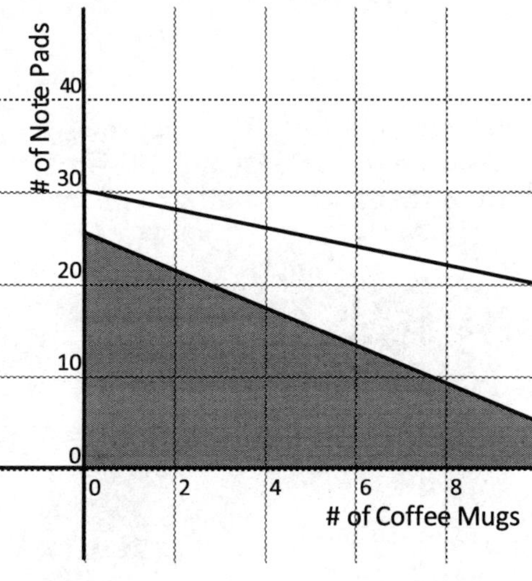

b.

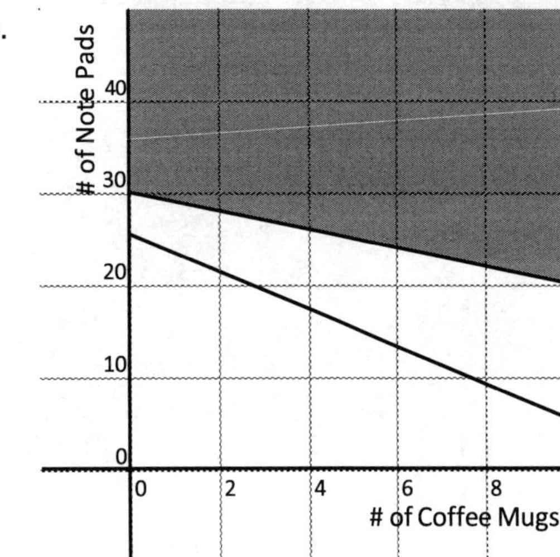

d.

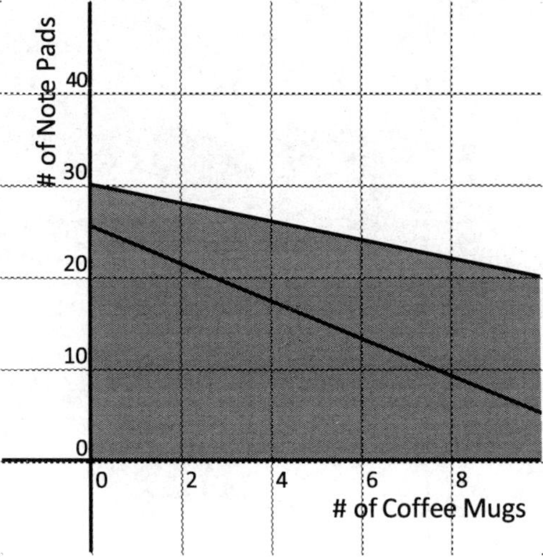

75. Which of the following tables contains points in an exponential function?

a.

x	y
−2	−24
1	12
3	36
5	60
8	96

c.

x	y
−1	−1
1	1
3	27
5	125
6	216

b.

x	y
−2	12
0	0
2	12
4	48
6	108

d.

x	y
−1	0.5
0	1
3	8
5	32
6	64

Measurement and Geometry

76. A city is at an elevation of 6,700 feet. Which of the following best represents the elevation in miles?

a. 0.77 miles
b. 1.27 miles
c. 1.56 miles
d. 1.89 miles

77. A can has a radius of 1.5 inches and a height of 3 inches. Which of the following best represents the volume of the can?

a. 17.2 in^3
b. 19.4 in^3
c. 21.2 in^3
d. 23.4 in^3

78. A ball has a diameter of 7 inches. Which of the following best represents the volume?

a. 165.7 in^3
b. 179.6 in^3
c. 184.5 in^3
d. 192.3 in^3

79. A gift box has a length of 14 inches, a height of 8 inches, and a width of 6 inches. How many square inches of wrapping paper are needed to wrap the box?

a. 56
b. 244
c. 488
d. 672

80. Aidan has a plastic container in the shape of a square pyramid. He wants to fill the container with chocolate candies. If the base has a side length of 6 inches and the height of the container is 9 inches, how many cubic inches of space may be filled with candies?

a. 98
b. 102
c. 108
d. 112

81. Eric has a beach ball with a radius of 9 inches. He is planning to wrap the ball with wrapping paper. Which of the following is the best estimate for the number of square feet of wrapping paper he will need?

a. 4.08
b. 5.12
c. 7.07
d. 8.14

82. Each base of a triangular prism has a base length of 9 cm and a height of 12 cm. The height of the prism is 15 cm. What is the volume of the prism?

a. 652 cm^3
b. 720 cm^3
c. 792 cm^3
d. 810 cm^3

83. The two prisms shown below are similar. What is the measurement of *x*?

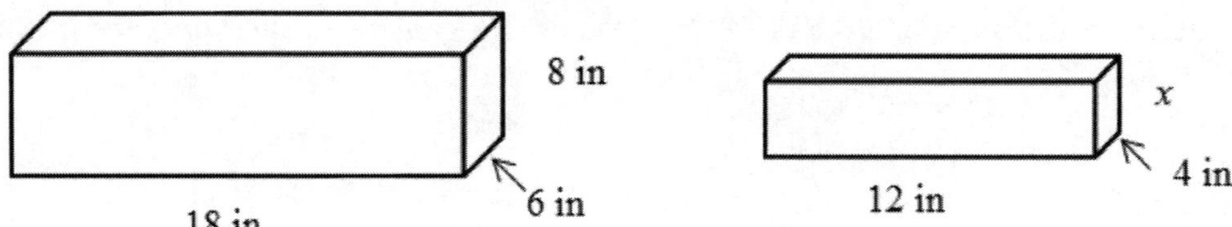

a. $4\frac{3}{4}$ in
b. $5\frac{1}{3}$ in
c. $5\frac{2}{3}$ in
d. $5\frac{3}{4}$ in

84. Given that the two horizontal lines in the diagram below are parallel, which pair of angles is congruent?

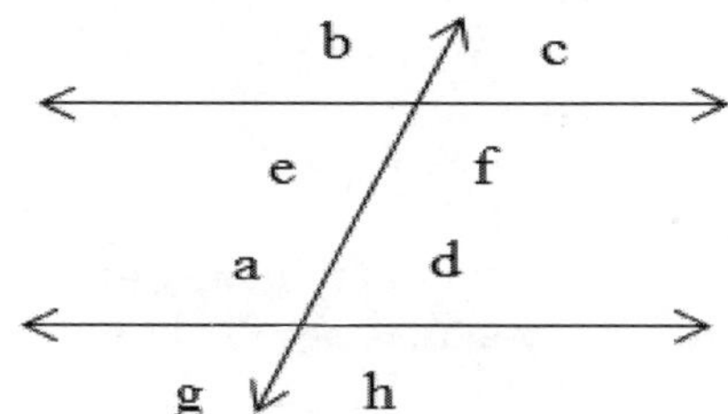

a. ∠e and ∠b
b. ∠d and ∠h
c. ∠g and ∠c
d. ∠d and ∠f

85. Given the diagram below, which of the following theorems may be used to verify that lines *a* and *b* are parallel?

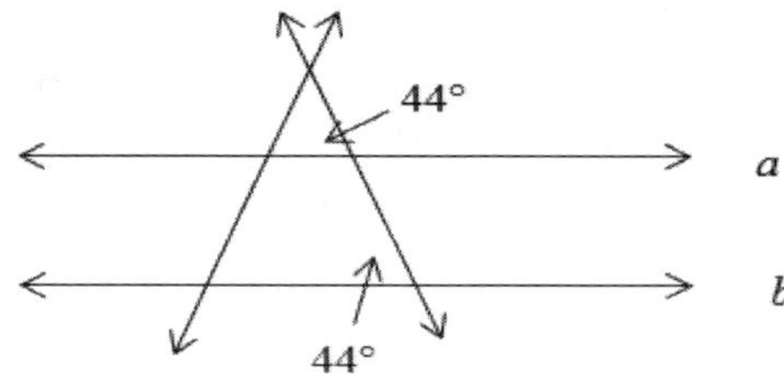

a. Alternate Interior Angles Converse Theorem
b. Alternate Exterior Angles Converse Theorem
c. Consecutive Interior Angles Converse Theorem
d. Corresponding Angles Converse Theorem

86. Given the diagram below, what is the measure of the inscribed angle?

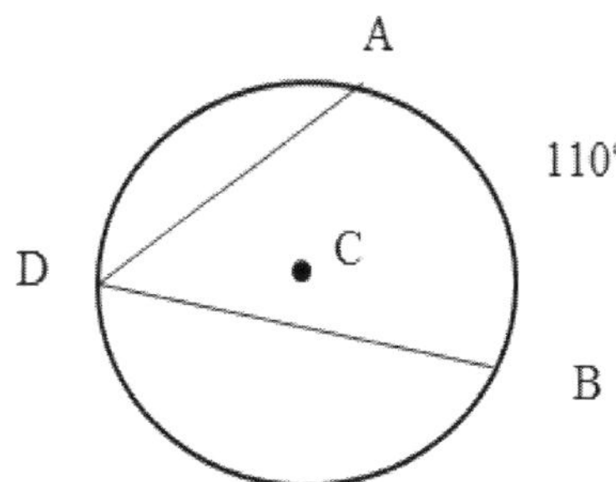

a. 37°
b. 45°
c. 55°
d. 57°

87. A tree with a height of 15 feet casts a shadow that is 5 feet in length. A man standing at the base of the shadow formed by the tree is 6 feet tall. How long is the shadow cast by the man?

a. 1.5 feet
b. 2 feet
c. 2.5 feet
d. 3 feet

88. Which of the following best represents the measurement of *x*, shown in the triangle below?

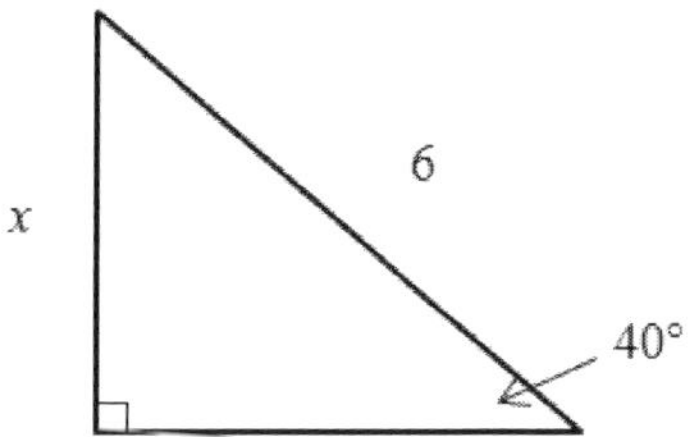

a. 2.6
b. 3.1
c. 3.9
d. 4.4

89. What is the area of the shaded region in the figure shown below?

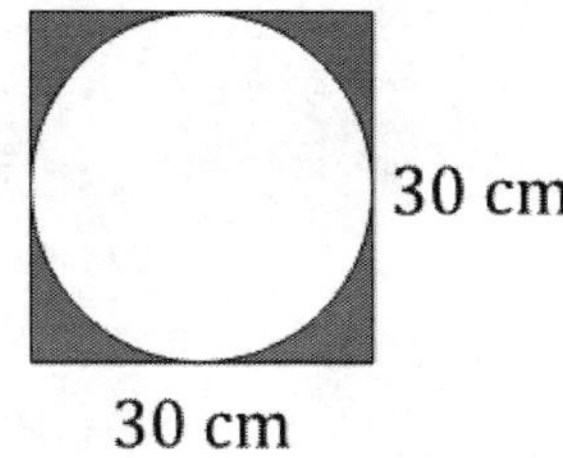

a. 177 cm^2
b. 181 cm^2
c. 187 cm^2
d. 193 cm^2

90. Which of the following postulates proves the congruence of the triangles below?

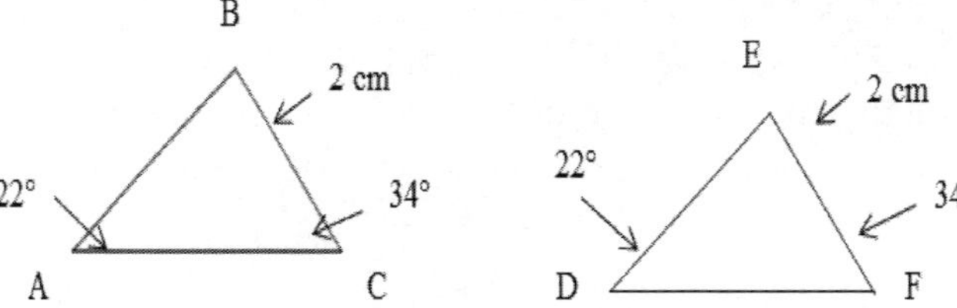

a. ASA
b. AAS
c. SAS
d. SSS

91. A man standing on a flat, level surface casts a shadow that is 6.2 ft in length. The man is 5.8 ft tall. Which of the following best represents the distance from the top of his head to the end of the shadow?

a. 7 ft
b. 7.5 ft
c. 8 ft
d. 8.5 ft

92. A cylindrical carrot stick is sliced with a knife. Which of the following shapes is *not* a possible cross-section?

a. circle
b. rectangle
c. ellipse
d. triangle

93. What is the value of x, shown in the diagram below?

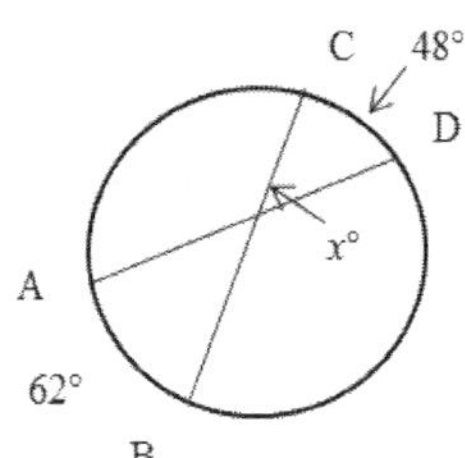

a. 16
b. 24
c. 48
d. 55

94. What is the value of x, shown in the diagram below?

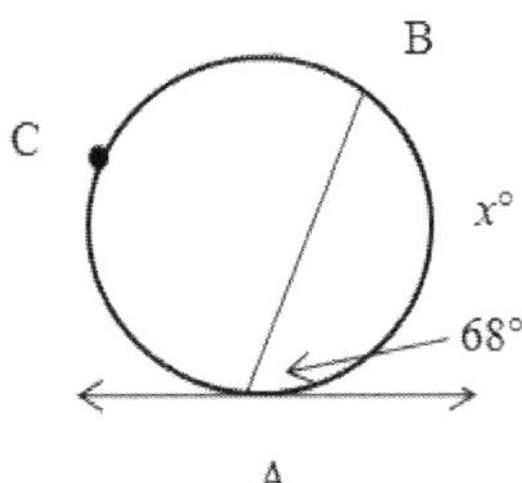

a. 68°
b. 76°
c. 128°
d. 136°

95. Which of the following represents the net of a triangular prism?

a.
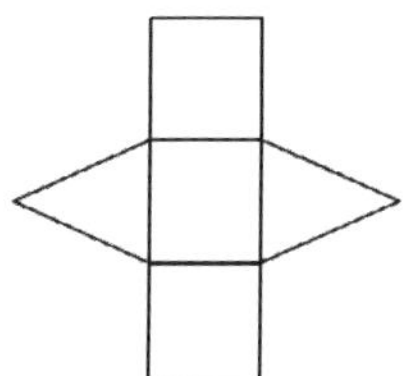

c.
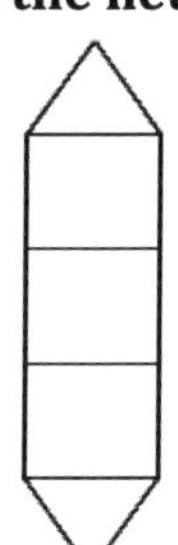

b.
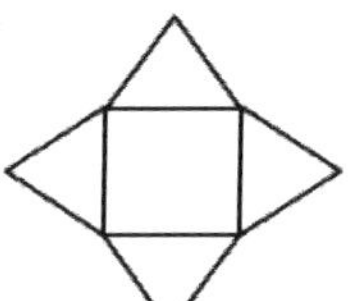

d.
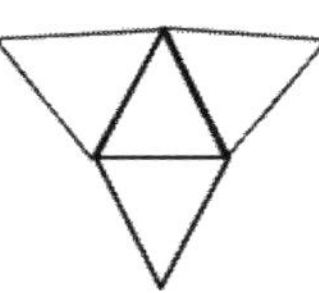

96. A convex three-dimensional figure has 9 edges and 6 vertices. How many faces does it have?

a. 4
b. 5
c. 6
d. 8

97. Given that the two horizontal lines in the diagram below are parallel, which of the following statements is correct?

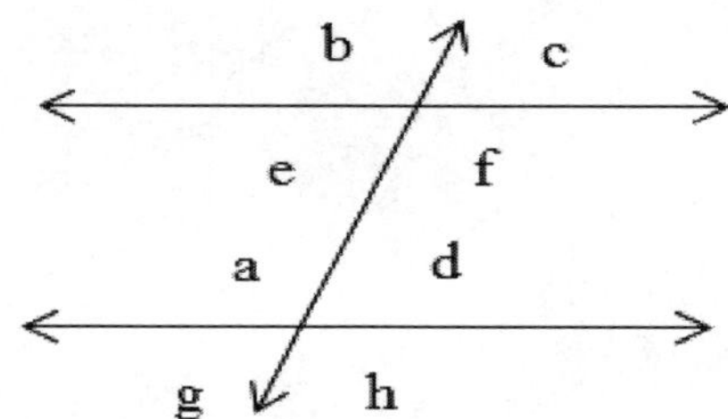

a. ∠b and ∠g are complementary.
b. ∠d and ∠c are supplementary.
c. ∠a and ∠e are supplementary.
d. ∠e and ∠h are congruent.

98. Which of the following postulates may be used to prove the similarity of ΔABC and ΔADE?

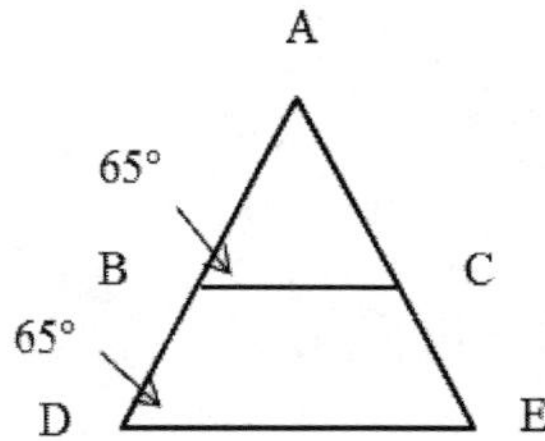

a. ASA
b. AA
c. SAS
d. SSS

99. Which of the following transformations has been applied to ΔABC?

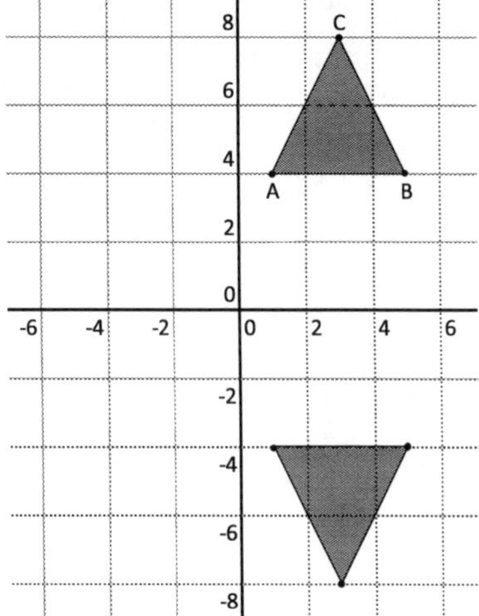

a. translation
b. rotation of 90 degrees
c. reflection
d. dilation

100. Which of the following steps were applied to ΔABC?

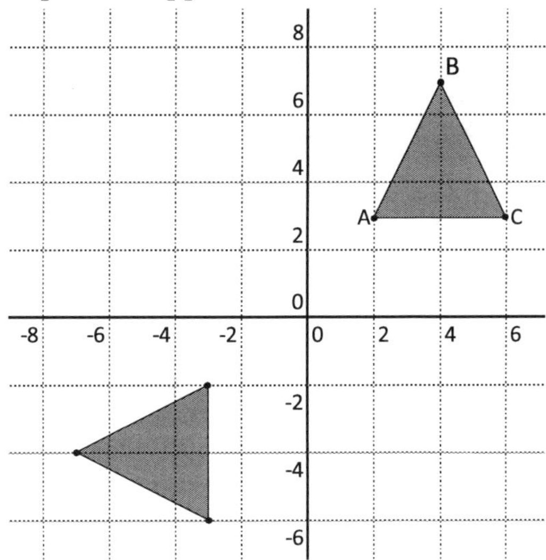

a. reflection across the x-axis and rotation of 90 degrees
b. reflection across the x-axis and rotation of 180 degrees
c. reflection across the x-axis and rotation of 270 degrees
d. reflection across the y-axis and rotation of 180 degrees

101. What is the midpoint of the line segment below?

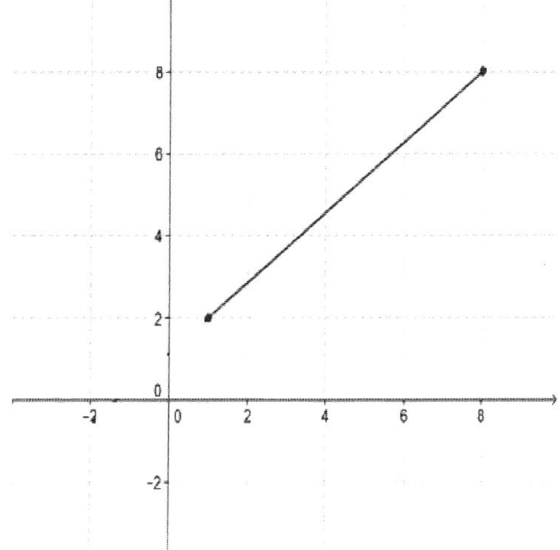

a. (3.5, 4)
b. (4, 4)
c. (4.5, 5)
d. (5, 5)

102. What is the distance on a coordinate plane from (−8, 6) to (4, 3)?

a. $\sqrt{139}$
b. $\sqrt{147}$
c. $\sqrt{153}$
d. $\sqrt{161}$

103. What is the perimeter of the trapezoid graphed below?

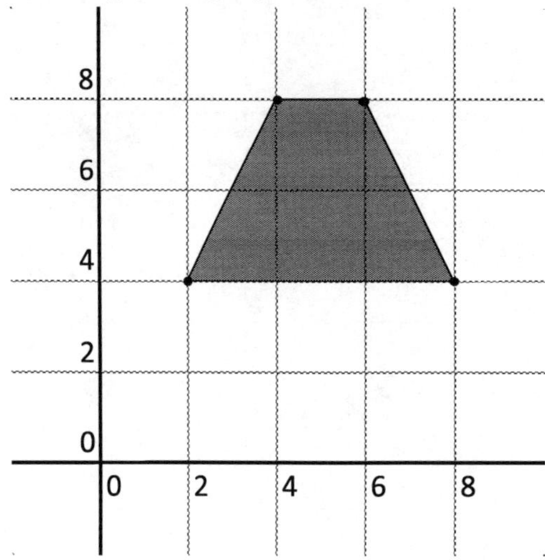

a. $4 + \sqrt{10}$
b. $8 + 4\sqrt{5}$
c. $4 + 2\sqrt{5}$
d. $8 + 2\sqrt{22}$

104. What is the area of the figure graphed below?

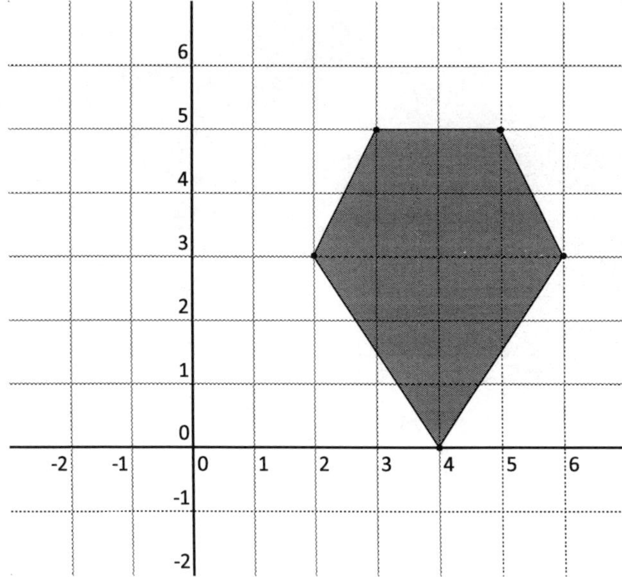

a. 11 $units^2$
b. 11.5 $units^2$
c. 12 $units^2$
d. 12.5 $units^2$

105. What scale factor was applied to the larger triangle to obtain the smaller triangle below?

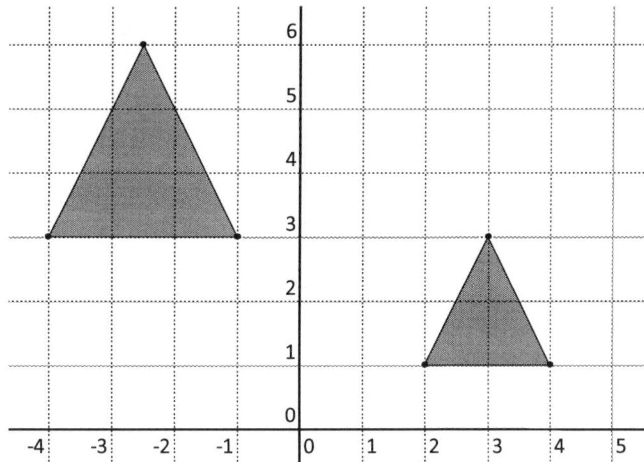

a. $\frac{1}{4}$
b. $\frac{1}{3}$
c. $\frac{1}{2}$
d. $\frac{2}{3}$

106. Which of the following pairs of equations represents the lines of symmetry in the figure below?

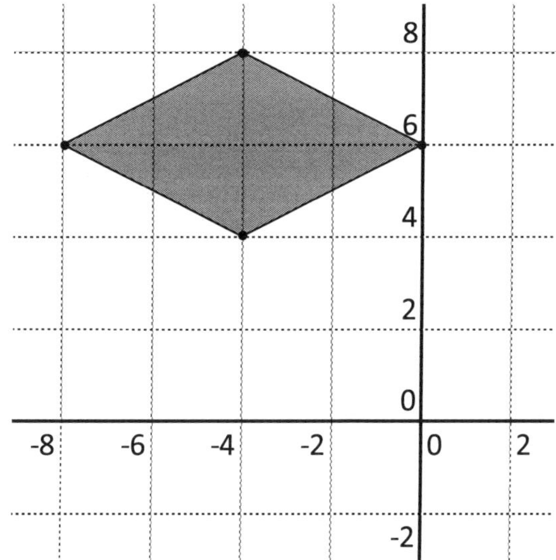

a. $x = -4, y = 6$
b. $x = 4, y = 6$
c. $y = -4, x = 6$
d. $y = 4, x = -6$

107. Which of the following pairs of shapes may tessellate a plane?

a. regular pentagons and squares
b. regular pentagons and equilateral triangles
c. equilateral triangles and regular hexagons
d. regular octagons and equilateral triangles

108. Andrea must administer $\frac{1}{12}$ of a medicine bottle to a patient. If the bottle contains $3\frac{4}{10}$ fluid ounces of medicine, how much medicine should be administered?

a. $\frac{17}{60}$ fluid ounces
b. $\frac{15}{62}$ fluid ounces
c. $\frac{3}{19}$ fluid ounces
d. $\frac{17}{67}$ fluid ounces

109. What is the slope of the leg marked x in the triangle graphed below?

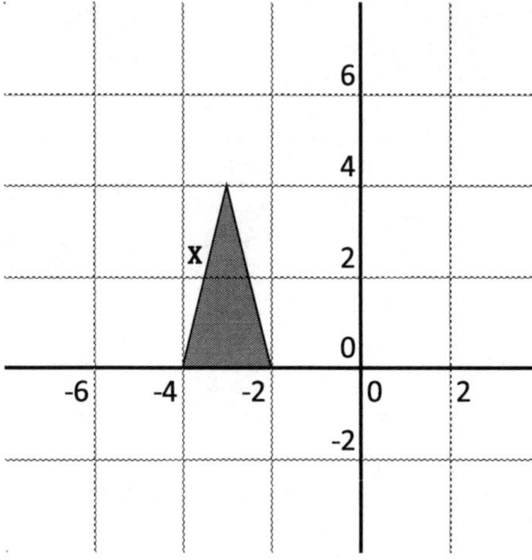

a. 2
b. 3.5
c. 4
d. 4.5

110. Ann must walk from Point A to Point B and then to Point C. Finally, she will walk back to Point A. If each unit represents 5 miles, which of the following best represents the total distance she will have walked?

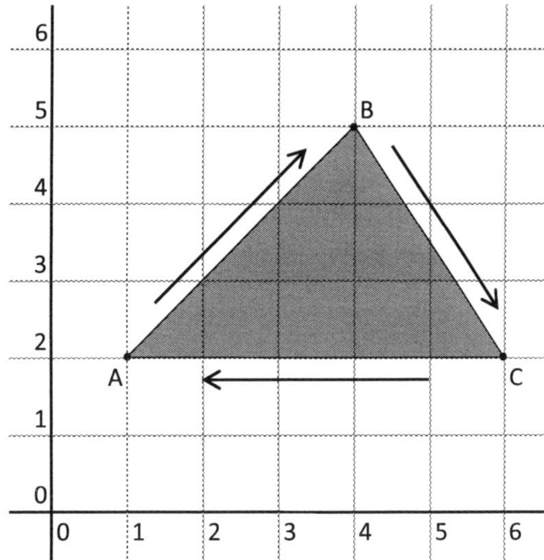

a. 42 miles
b. 48 miles
c. 56 miles
d. 64 miles

111. Which of the following measurements is the best approximation of 2,012 square inches?

a. 11.85 ft^2
b. 12.28 ft^2
c. 13.97 ft^2
d. 15.29 ft^2

112. What is the length of the hypotenuse in the triangle shown below?

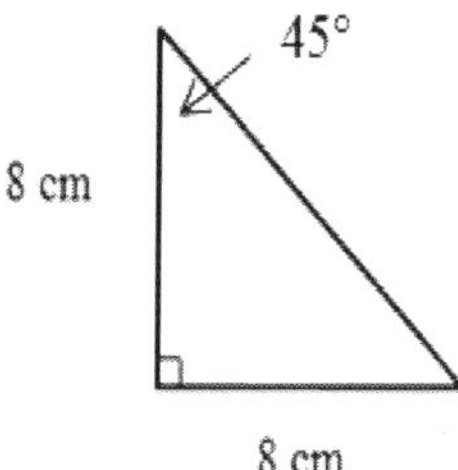

a. 4 cm
b. $8\sqrt{3}$ cm
c. 16 cm
d. $8\sqrt{2}$ cm

Statistics, Probability, and Discrete Mathematics

113. For which of the following data sets would the mean be an appropriate measure of center to use?

a. 7, 15, 20, 24, 27, 28, 31, 36, 41, 50
b. 6, 7, 8, 8, 9, 9, 10, 20, 34, 50
c. 5, 18, 30, 42, 43, 44, 46, 48, 49, 50
d. 8, 10, 12, 13, 14, 16, 20, 22, 24, 2200

114. A student scores 82 on a final exam. The class average is 87, with a standard deviation of 2 points. How many standard deviations below the class average is the student's score?

a. 1.5
b. 2
c. 2.5
d. 3

115. A student scores 61 on a test. The class average is 81, with a standard deviation of 10 points. What percentage of the class scored below this student?

a. 1.26%
b. 1.43%
c. 1.96%
d. 2.28%

116. A student scores 96 on a test. The class average is 84, with a standard deviation of 4 points. What percentage of the class scored below this student?

a. 78.89%
b. 82.77%
c. 92.67%
d. 99.87%

117. A student scores 68 on a final exam. Another student scores 84 on the exam. The class average is 80, with a standard deviation of 8 points. What percentage of the class scored within the range of these two students' scores?

a. 44.32%
b. 48.54%
c. 58.39%
d. 62.47%

118. Class A, with a total of 28 students, had a final exam average of 85 and a standard deviation of 4.5 points. Class B, with a total of 30 students, had a final exam average of 88, with a standard deviation of 4 points. Which of the following statements is true?

a. There is no significant difference between the classes, as evidenced by a p-value greater than 0.05.
b. There is no significant difference between the classes, as evidenced by a p-value less than 0.05.
c. There is a significant difference between the classes, as evidenced by a p-value greater than 0.05.
d. There is a significant difference between the classes, as evidenced by a p-value less than 0.05.

119. A beverage manufacturer claims to include 20 ounces in each bottle. A random sample of 30 bottles shows a mean of 19.8 ounces, with a standard deviation of 0.2 ounces. Which of the following statements is correct?

a. The manufacturer's claim is likely true, as evidenced by a p-value less than 0.01.
b. The manufacturer's claim is likely true, as evidenced by a p-value greater than 0.01.
c. The manufacturer's claim is likely false, as evidenced by a p-value less than 0.01.
d. The manufacturer's claim is likely false, as evidenced by a p-value greater than 0.01.

120. An oatmeal manufacturer claims to include 18 ounces in each container, with a standard deviation of 0.3 ounces. A random sample of 25 containers shows a mean of 17.9 ounces. Which of the following statements is true?

a. The manufacturer's claim is likely true, as evidenced by a p-value less than 0.05.
b. The manufacturer's claim is likely true, as evidenced by a p-value greater than 0.05.
c. The manufacturer's claim is likely false, as evidenced by a p-value less than 0.05.
d. The manufacturer's claim is likely false, as evidenced by a p-value greater than 0.05.

121. A professor claims that the average on his final exam is 82. A random sample of 30 students shows an exam mean of 83 and a standard deviation of 2 points. Which of the following statements is true?

a. The professor's claim is likely true, as evidenced by a p-value less than 0.05.
b. The professor's claim is likely false, as evidenced by a p-value less than 0.05.
c. The professor's claim is likely true, as evidenced by a p-value greater than 0.05.
d. The professor's claim is likely false, as evidenced by a p-value greater than 0.05.

122. Which of the following describes a sampling technique that will likely increase the sampling error?

a. choosing every 5th person from a list
b. grouping a sample according to gender and then choosing every 10th person from a list
c. using an intact group
d. assigning numbers to a sample and then using a random number generator to choose numbers

123. What is the area under the normal curve between ±2 standard deviations?

a. approximately 68%
b. approximately 90%
c. approximately 95%
d. approximately 99%

124. Which of the following best represents the standard deviation of the data below?

3, 4, 4, 5, 6, 12, 12, 15

a. 2.9
b. 3.4
c. 4.1
d. 4.6

125. Given the boxplots below, which of the following statements is correct?

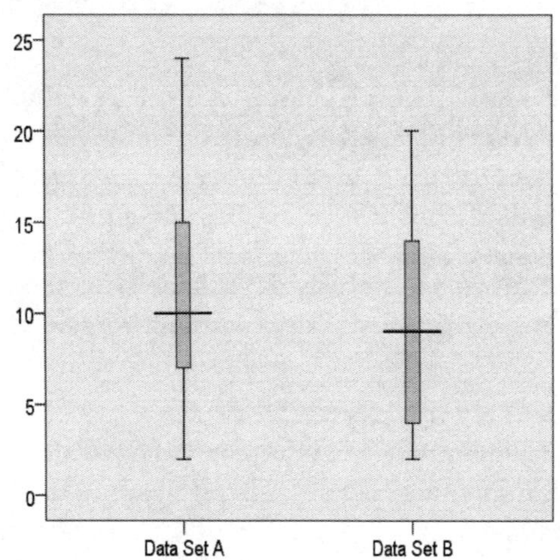

a. Data Set A has a larger range and a larger median.
b. Data Set A has a smaller range and a larger median.
c. Data Set A has a larger range and a smaller median.
d. Data Set A has a smaller range and a smaller median.

126. What is the interquartile range of the data below?

2, 4, 6, 8, 10, 12, 14, 16, 18, 20

a. 10
b. 11
c. 12
d. 13

127. According to the scatter plot below, which of the following is the *best* estimate for the earnings received for 20 hours of work?

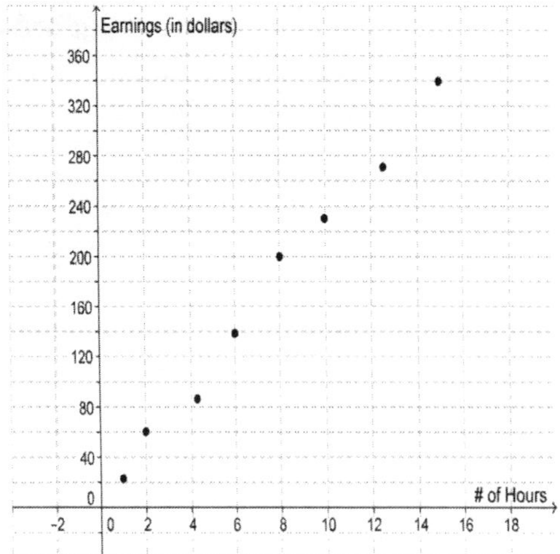

a. $342
b. $446
c. $528
d. $602

128. Which of the following statements is *not* true?

a. In a skewed distribution, the mean is pulled towards the tail.
b. In a skewed distribution, the mean is pulled towards the area with a higher frequency of scores.
c. In a normal distribution, the mean, median, and mode are the same value.
d. The area under a normal curve is 1.

129. Given the two-way frequency table below, which of the following *best* represents *P*(male or graduate)?

	Undergraduate	Graduate	Total
Male	2940	2045	4985
Female	3026	2068	5094
Total	5966	4113	10,079

a. 55%
b. 60%
c. 70%
d. 75%

130. Adam rolls a standard six-sided die. What is the probability he rolls a number greater than or equal to 5?

a. $\frac{1}{6}$
b. $\frac{1}{5}$
c. $\frac{1}{4}$
d. $\frac{1}{3}$

131. Kayla rolls a die and tosses a coin. What is the probability she gets an even number and heads?

a. $\frac{1}{6}$
b. $\frac{1}{4}$
c. $\frac{1}{3}$
d. 1

132. Eli rolls a die and tosses a coin. What is the probability he gets a prime number or tails?

a. $\frac{1}{2}$
b. $\frac{2}{3}$
c. $\frac{3}{4}$
d. $\frac{5}{6}$

133. Andrew rolls a die. What is the probability he gets a 4 or an even number?

a. $\frac{1}{4}$
b. $\frac{1}{2}$
c. $\frac{2}{3}$
d. $\frac{3}{4}$

134. The simulation of a coin toss is completed 300 times. Which of the following best represents the number of tosses you can expect to show heads?

a. 50
b. 100
c. 150
d. 200

135. How many ways can you arrange the letters below, if order does not matter?

HANNAH

a. 30
b. 60
c. 90
d. 120

136. How many ways can 1st – 3rd place winners be chosen from 6 people?

a. 120
b. 60
c. 30
d. 20

137. How many ways can the numerals 0 – 9 be arranged?

a. 36,045
b. 182,492
c. 1,048,644
d. 3,628,800

138. What is the limit of the series below?

$$1+\frac{1}{2}+\frac{1}{4}+\frac{1}{8}+\frac{1}{16}+\cdots$$

a. 2
b. $2\frac{1}{4}$
c. $2\frac{3}{4}$
d. 3

139. What is the size of the sample space for tossing four coins?

a. 8
b. 12
c. 16
d. 20

140. 320 students are surveyed. 120 of the students like only Dallas. 150 of the students like only Houston. 48 of the students like neither city. How many students like Dallas *and* Houston?

a. 2
b. 3
c. 4
d. 5

141. $A = \{5, 9, 2, 3, -1, 8\}$ **and** $B = \{2, 0, 4, 5, 6, 8\}$**. What is** $A \cap B$**?**

a. $\{5, 2, 8\}$
b. $\{-1, 0, 2, 3, 4, 5, 6, 8, 9\}$
c. $\emptyset$
d. $\{5, 8\}$

142. $A = \{9, 4, -3, 8, 6, 0\}$ **and** $B = \{-4, 2, 8, 9, 0\}$**. What is** $A \cup B$**?**

a. $\{9, 8, 0\}$
b. $\{9, 4, -3, 8, 6, 0, -4, 2\}$
c. $\emptyset$
d. $\{9, 8, 0, 2, 4\}$

143. $A = \{3, -4, 1\}$ **and** $B = \{0, 5, 9, 2\}$**. What is** $A \cap B$**?**

a. $\{3, -4, 1, 0, 5, 9, 2\}$
b. $\{-4, 2, 3\}$
c. $\{0, 1, 2, 3, 5, 9\}$
d. $\emptyset$

144. What is the contrapositive of the statement below?

If I get paid, then I go to the beach.

a. If I get paid, then I do not go to the beach.
b. If I go to the beach, then I get paid.
c. If I do not get paid, then I go to the beach.
d. If I do not go to the beach, then I do not get paid.

145. What is the converse of the statement below?

If I go skiing, then it is winter.

a. If it is not winter, then I do not go skiing.
b. If it is winter, then I go skiing.
c. If it is not winter, then I go skiing.
d. If I go skiing, then it is not winter.

146. Using logic, when is $p \lor q$ **false?**

a. When p is true and q is true.
b. When p is true and q is false.
c. When p is false and q is true.
d. When p is false and q is false.

147. Using logic, when is $p \land q$ **true?**

a. When p is true and q is true.
b. When p is true and q is false.
c. When p is false and q is true.
d. When p is false and q is false.

148. Which of the following is logically equivalent to $p \rightarrow q$**?**

a. $q \rightarrow p$
b. $\neg p \rightarrow \neg q$
c. $\neg q \rightarrow \neg p$
d. $p \land q$

149. Eric's dietary plan consists of 4 different entrées, 5 different appetizers, and 3 different desserts. How many possible meals may he create containing one entrée, one appetizer, and one dessert?

a. 12
b. 24
c. 60
d. 120

150. Which of the following represents a tautology?

a. $p \wedge \neg p$
b. $p \vee \neg p$
c. $p \vee \neg q$
d. $p \vee q$

Constructed Response

1. A family bought a new car for a purchase price of $32,000. The car will lose 15% of its value the day it is purchased and the car will depreciate at a constant rate following that. The value of the car as a function of time can be modeled by $y = c - 0.09cx$, where y is the value of the car x years after the car was purchased and c is the value of the car after the initial 15% depreciation.

a. What is the value of the car 2 years after its purchase date? Show your work.
b. On an xy-grid, graph the value, y, of the car, as a function of x, where x represents the number of years after the purchase date, for $0 \leq x \leq 7$ years. Label the axes and show the scales used for the graph.
c. Use your graph to estimate the number of years, x, after the purchase date that the value of the car is $15,000. Label this point on your graph and indicate the approximate coordinates of the point.
d. Algebraically find the number of years, x, after the purchase date that the value of the car is exactly $15,000. Round your solution to the nearest tenth of a year. Show your work.

2. The diagram below shows the plan Berenice has for a triangular splash pad in a local city park. There will be three circles, each with a diameter of 6 feet, and the circles will be enclosed by an equilateral triangle with a side length of 30 feet. Berenice plans to have splash areas/fountains within the circles and walkways in the shaded areas of the triangle.

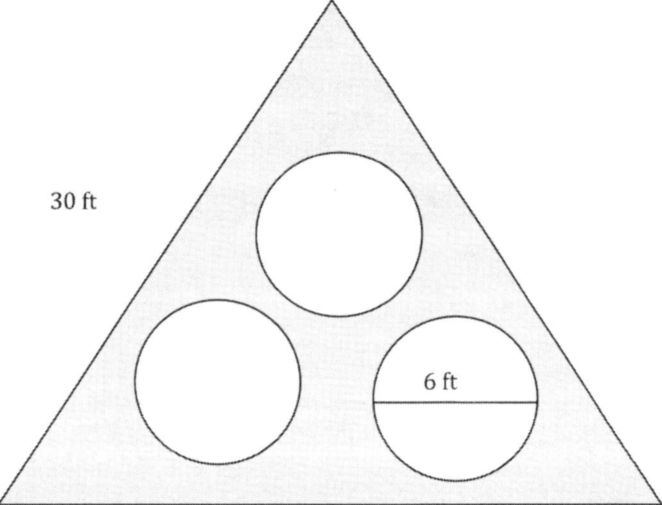

a. According to the diagram, what is the maximum area, in square feet, available for Berenice to have for splash/fountain areas in the triangle? Show your work.

b. According to the diagram, what percentage of the triangle will be set aside for walkways? Show your work.

c. If a ball were to fall on a random point within the triangular splash pad, what is the probability that the ball would fall where Berenice plans to have splash areas? Show your work or explain your reasoning.

3. Below are listed the heights in centimeters of the 19 students in a class.

48, 53, 53, 54, 55, 56, 59, 60, 60, 63, 63, 63, 64, 65, 66, 67, 69, 71, 73

a. For the numbers above, define and identify the median and the range.

b. Define and calculate the mean for the list of numbers above.

c. Draw a stem and leaf plot of the data using the tens digits as the stems and the units digits as the leaves.

Answer Key and Explanations

Number Sense and Operations

1. C: The sum is written as:

$$\begin{array}{r} 2222 \\ +\ 303 \\ \hline 3030 \end{array}$$

The sum of 2 and 3 equals 5, which must be represented as a 10. In the base-5 number system, a number cannot contain any 5's. The 1 of each 10 is carried to the next column to the left.

2. D: The percent increase is represented as $\frac{1100-800}{800}$, which equals 0.375 or 37.5%.

3. C: The set of integers is contained within the set of rational numbers, and is hence, a subset. A rational number may be written as the ratio, $\frac{a}{b}$, where a and b are integers and $b \neq 0$.

4. D: You first divide 2 into 55, recording the remainder. You then divide 2 into each resulting quotient, until the quotient is smaller than 2. Next, you put the final quotient as the first digit. You then go backwards and write the remainders and place them as digits, in order from left to right.

5. D: The original cost may be represented by the equation $45 = x - 0.25x$ or $45 = 0.75x$. Dividing both sides of the equation by 0.75 gives $x = 60$.

6. A: If a number is divisible by 2 and 3, it is also divisible by the lowest common multiple of these two factors. The lowest common multiple of 2 and 3 is their product, 6.

7. B: The decimal expansion of an irrational number does not terminate or repeat. The decimal expansion of $\sqrt{2}$ does not terminate or repeat.

8. C: The original price may be represented by the equation $24{,}210 = x - 0.10x$ or $24{,}210 = 0.9x$. Dividing both sides of the equation by 0.9 gives $x = 26{,}900$.

9. C: His monthly salary may be modeled as $\frac{1}{8}x = 320$. Multiplying both sides of the equation by 8 gives $x = 2{,}560$.

10. C: Division of a nonzero rational number by another nonzero rational number will always result in a nonzero rational number.

11. D: The set of integers is represented as {..., −3, −2, −1, 0, 1, 2, 3, ...}. The numbers 1, 2, 3, ..., are counting numbers, or natural numbers. Thus, the set contains the counting numbers, zero, and the negations of the counting numbers.

12. C: The set of irrational numbers is separate from the set of rational numbers. A rational number cannot be irrational, and an irrational number cannot be rational.

13. B: The multiplicative inverse property states: the product of a number and its reciprocal is 1.

14. A: If $a|b$ and $a|c$, it does not necessary follow that $b|c$. One counterexample is $3|6$ and $3|15$, but 6 does not divide 15.

15. A: The repeating decimal may be converted to a fraction by writing:

$$\begin{array}{r} 10x = 4.\overline{4} \\ -\quad x = 0.\overline{4} \\ \hline \end{array}$$

which simplifies as $10x - x = 4.\overline{4} - 0.\overline{4}$.

16. C: The amount he donates is equal to 0.01(45,000). Thus, he donates $450.

17. B: The amount she spends on rent and utilities is equal to 0.38(40,000), or $15,200, which is approximately $15,000.

18. D: The 8 is in the tenths place, the 6 in the hundredths place, and the 7 in the thousandths place. Thus, 0.867 is equal to the sum of the product of 8 and $\frac{1}{10}$, the product of 6 and $\frac{1}{100}$, and the product of 7 and $\frac{1}{1000}$.

19. D: The rectangular array represents the product of the side lengths of 7 and $(4 + 2)$.

20. A: $b|a$ means that a is divisible by b: that is, that a is equal to the product of b and some quotient, q.

21. C: Subtraction of a natural number from another natural number may result in an integer that is not a natural number. For example, $1 - 2 = -1$, which is not a natural number.

22. C: The original price may be modeled by the equation, $(x - 0.45x) + 0.0875(x - 0.45x) = 39.95$, which simplifies to $0.598125x = 39.95$. Dividing each side of the equation by the coefficient of $\boldsymbol{x}$ gives $x \approx 66.79$.

23. C: There are 36 months in 3 years. The following proportion may be written: $\frac{450}{3} = \frac{x}{36}$. The equation $3x = 16{,}200$, may be solved for x. Dividing both sides of the equation by 3 gives $x = 5{,}400$.

24. D: The total rainfall is 25.38 inches. Thus, the ratio $\frac{4.5}{25.38}$, represents the percentage of rainfall received during October. $\frac{4.5}{25.38} \approx 0.177$ or 17.7%.

25. D: The decimal point is 4 places to the right of the first digit, 3. Thus, $30{,}490 = 3.049 \times 10^4$.

Algebra and Functions

26. C: The ratio between successive terms is constant (2), so this is a geometric series. A geometric sequence is represented by an exponential function.

27. A: The sum of 3 and the product of each term number and 5 equals the term value. For example, for term number 4, the value is equal to $5(4) + 3$, or 23.

28. B: A vertical line will cross the graph at more than one point. Thus, it is not a function.

29. C: The graph is a straight line that passes through the origin, or point (0, 0).

30. C: This graph is shifted 4 units to the right and 3 units up from that of the parent function, $y = x^2$.

31. D: The product of $(x - 5)(2x + 6)$ equals $2x^2 + 6x - 10x - 30$, which simplifies to $2x^2 - 4x - 30$.

32. D: The constant of proportionality is equal to the slope. Using the points, (2, –8) and (5, –20), the slope may be written as $\frac{-20-(-8)}{5-2}$, which equals –4.

33. C: An inverse proportional relationship is written in the form $y = \frac{k}{x}$, thus the equation $y = \frac{3}{x}$ shows that y is inversely proportional to x.

34. D: The expression $(x-2)^2$ may be expanded as $x^2 - 4x + 4$. Multiplication of $-3x$ by this expression gives $-3x^3 + 12x^2 - 12x$.

35. A: This graph shows a slope of 3, a y-intercept of –6, and the correct shading above the line. Using the test point (0, 0), the equation $0 \geq 0 - 6$ may be written. Since $0 \geq -6$, the solution is the shaded area above the line, which contains the point (0, 0).

36. C: Substituting 2 for each x-value gives $f(2) = \frac{2^3-2(2)+1}{3(2)}$, which simplifies to $f(2) = \frac{5}{6}$.

37. D: The table shows the y-intercept to be –5. The slope is equal to the ratio of change in y-values to change in corresponding x-values. As each x-value increases by 1, each y-value increases by 3. Thus, the slope is $\frac{3}{1}$, or 3. This graph represents the equation $y = 3x - 5$.

38. C: Each of the graphs shows the correct y-intercept of –6, but only graph C shows the correct slope. Using the points (0, –6) and (–2, 2), the slope of graph C may be written as $m = \frac{2-(-6)}{-2-0}$, which simplifies to $m = -4$.

39. B: The graph shows $f(2) = 10$. Since the y-intercept of the parabola is 2, the following equation may be written: $10 = a(2)^2 + 2$, which simplifies to $10 = 4a + 2$. Subtracting 2 from both sides gives $8 = 4a$. Dividing both sides of the equation by 4 gives $a = 2$. Thus, the graph represents the function, $f(x) = 2x^2 + 2$. Evaluating this function for an x-value of 5 gives $f(5) = 2(5)^2 + 2$ or $f(5) = 52$. The average rate of change may be written as $A(x) = \frac{52-10}{5-2}$, which simplifies to $A(x) = 14$.

40. C: The slope is equal to 4, since each ticket costs $4. The y-intercept is represented by the constant fee of $30. Substituting 4 for m and 30 for b into the equation $y = mx + b$ gives $y = 4x + 30$.

41. D: The lines cross at the point with an x-value of –3 and a y-value of 2. Thus, the solution is (–3, 2).

42. A: On a graph, the lines intersect at the point, (–5, 9). Thus, (–5, 9) is the solution to the system of linear equations.

43. A: The test point of (0, 0) indicates that shading should occur below the line with the steeper slope. The same test point indicates that shading should occur above the other line. The overlapped shading occurs between these two lines, in the upper right.

44. D: A graph of the function shows the positive x-intercept to occur at approximately (2.6, 0). Thus, the ball will reach the ground after approximately 2.6 seconds.

45. D: The table represents a geometric sequence, with a common ratio of 2. Geometric sequences are modeled by exponential functions.

46. C: Using the points (–3, 1) and (1, –11), the slope may be written as $m = \frac{-11-1}{1-(-3)}$ or $m = -3$. Substituting the slope of –3 and the x- and y-values from the point (–3, 1), into the slope-intercept form of an equation gives $1 = -3(-3) + b$, which simplifies to $1 = 9 + b$. Subtracting 9 from both sides of the equation gives $b = -8$. Thus, the linear equation that includes the data in the table is $y = -3x - 8$.

47. B: The slope of the graphed line is −2. A line perpendicular to this one will have a slope of $\frac{1}{2}$. Substituting the slope and the x- and y-values from the point (3, 2), into the slope-intercept form of an equation gives: $2 = \frac{1}{2}(3) + b$, which simplifies to $2 = \frac{3}{2} + b$. Subtracting $\frac{3}{2}$ from each side of the equation gives $b = \frac{1}{2}$. So the equation of a line perpendicular to this one and passing through the point (3, 2) is $y = \frac{1}{2}x + \frac{1}{2}$.

48. D: The slope of the graphed line is 2. A line parallel to this one will also have a slope of 2. Substituting the slope and the x- and y-values from the point (−1, 4), into the slope-intercept form of an equation gives: $4 = 2(-1) + b$, which simplifies to $4 = -2 + b$. Adding 2 to both sides of the equation gives $b = 6$. So the equation of a line parallel to this one and passing through the point (−1, 4) is $y = 2x + 6$.

49. B: The graph is a straight line that passes through the origin, or (0, 0). Thus, it is linear and proportional.

50. A: This situation may be modeled by a geometric sequence, with a common ratio of 2 and initial value of 0.02. Substituting the common ratio and initial value into the formula $a_n = a_1 \times r^{n-1}$, gives $a_n = 0.02 \times 2^{n-1}$.

51. D: This situation may be modeled by an arithmetic sequence, with a common difference of 4 and initial value of 3. Substituting the common difference and initial value into the formula, $a_n = a_1 + (n-1)d$, gives $a_n = 3 + (n-1)4$, which simplifies to $a_n = 4n - 1$.

52. D: If we divide both terms in the numerator by n, the expression reduces to $n + \frac{1}{n}$. Although $\frac{1}{n}$ converges to 0, n increases without bound. The expression therefore has no limit.

53. C: The limit is simply the quotient of $5n$ divided by n, or 5.

54. B: The sum of an infinite geometric series may be modeled by the formula $S = \frac{a}{1-r}$, where a represents the initial value and r represents the common ratio. Substituting the initial value of 3 and common ratio of $\frac{2}{3}$ into the formula, gives $= \frac{3}{1-\frac{2}{3}}$, which simplifies to $S = \frac{3}{\frac{1}{3}}$ or 9.

55. C: The situation may be modeled by the system $\begin{matrix} 4x + 3y = 9.55 \\ 2x + 2y = 5.90 \end{matrix}$. Multiplying the bottom equation by -2 gives $\begin{matrix} 4x + 3y = 9.55 \\ -4x - 4y = -11.80 \end{matrix}$. Addition of the two equations gives $-y = -2.25$ or $y = 2.25$. Thus, one box of crackers costs $2.25.

56. C: The derivative of an equation of the form $y = ax^n$ is equal to $(n \times a)x^{n-1}$. So the derivative of $y = 9x^2$ is equal to $(2 \times 9)x^{2-1}$ or $18x$.

57. C: The limit of the expression $\frac{4x}{x}$, is 4, so the limit of the entire function is 1,004. The function converges.

58. B: The sequence $\frac{1}{5}, \frac{1}{25}, \frac{1}{125}, \frac{1}{625}, \ldots$, may be used to represent the situation. Substituting the initial value of $\frac{1}{5}$ and common ratio of $\frac{1}{5}$ into the formula $S = \frac{a}{1-r}$ gives $= \frac{\frac{1}{5}}{1-\frac{1}{5}}$, which simplifies to $S = \frac{\frac{1}{5}}{\frac{4}{5}}$ or $S = \frac{1}{4}$.

59. B: As the denominator approaches infinity, the value of the function will get smaller and smaller and converge to 0.

60. B: The derivative of an equation of the form $y = x^n$ is equal to $n \times x^{n-1}$. So the derivative of $g(x) = x^{ab}$ is equal to $ab \times x^{ab-1}$.

61. A: An inverse proportional relationship is represented by an equation in the form $y = \frac{k}{x}$, where k represents some constant of proportionality. The graph of this equation is a hyperbola with diagonal axes, symmetric about the lines $y = x$ and $y = -x$.

62. C: The value of the 50th term may be found using the formula $a_n = a_1 + (n - 1)d$. Substituting the number of terms for n, the initial value of 2 for a, and the common difference of 2 for d gives: $a_{50} = 2 + (50 - 1)(2)$, which simplifies to $a_{50} = 100$. Now, the value of the 50th term may be substituted into the formula, $S_n = \frac{n(a_1+a_n)}{2}$, which gives: $S_{50} = \frac{50(2+100)}{2}$, which simplifies to $S_{50} = 2{,}550$.

63. B: The sign of the constant, inside the squared term, is positive for a shift to the left and negative for a shift to the right. Thus, a movement of 5 units left is indicated by the expression $y = (x + 5)^2$. A shift of 4 units down is indicated by subtraction of 4 units from the squared term.

64. B: Relation B is the only one in which there is not any x-value that is mapped to more than one y-value. Thus, this relation represents a function.

65. C: The position of an accelerating car is changing according to a non-constant speed. Thus, the graph will show a curve with an increasing slope. The slope is increasing since it represents the velocity, and the velocity is increasing.

66. A: The inequality will be less than or equal to, since he may spend $100 or less on his purchase.

67. D: Since she spends at least $16, the relation of the number of packages of coffee to the minimum cost may be written as $4p \geq 16$. Alternatively, the inequality may be written as $16 \leq 4p$.

68. B: The horizontal asymptote is equal to the ratio of the coefficient of x to the coefficient of $2x$, or $\frac{1}{2}$.

69. C: The horizontal asymptote is equal to the ratio of the two coefficients of x, or $\frac{1}{1}$, which equals 1.

70. D: As x goes to positive or negative infinity, only the leading term of a polynomial function of x matters. Therefore, we can ignore the "+2" in the denominator; $\lim_{x\to-\infty} \frac{4x^2}{x+2} = \lim_{x\to-\infty} \frac{4x^2}{x} = \lim_{x\to-\infty} 4x$. As x goes to negative infinity, $4x$ decreases without bound. The expression therefore has no limit.

71. A: Evaluation of the expression for an x-value of -2 gives: $(3(-2)^3 - 6(-2)^2 + 4)$, which equals -44.

72. B: The situation may be modeled with the equation $\frac{1}{3} + \frac{1}{2} = \frac{1}{t}$, which simplifies to $\frac{5}{6} = \frac{1}{t}$. Thus, $t = \frac{6}{5}$. If working together, it will take them 1.2 hours to decorate the cake.

73. A: The situation may be modeled by the inequality $3x + 2y \geq 20$. Isolating the y-term gives $2y \geq -3x + 20$. Solving for y gives $y \geq -\frac{3}{2}x + 10$. Thus, the y-intercept will be 10, the line will be solid, and a test point of (0, 0) indicates the shading should occur above the line.

74. C: The situation may be modeled by the following system of inequalities: $\begin{matrix} 6x + 3y \leq 75 \\ x + y \leq 30 \end{matrix}$. A test point of (0, 0) indicates shading should occur below the blue line and below the red line. The overlapped shading occurs below the blue line. Thus, graph C represents the correct combinations of items that she may buy, given her budget.

75. D: The table represents part of a geometric sequence, with a common ratio of 2, so it also represents points of an exponential function.

Measurement and Geometry

76. B: The following proportion may be written and solved for x: $\frac{5,280}{1} = \frac{6,700}{x}$. Thus, $x \approx 1.27$.

77. C: The volume of a cylinder may be calculated using the formula $V = \pi r^2 h$, where r represents the radius and h represents the height. Substituting 1.5 for r and 3 for h gives $V = \pi(1.5)^2(3)$, which simplifies to $V \approx 21.2$.

78. B: The volume of a sphere may be calculated using the formula $V = \frac{4}{3}\pi r^3$, where r represents the radius. Substituting 3.5 for r gives $V = \frac{4}{3}\pi(3.5)^3$, which simplifies to $V \approx 179.6$.

79. C: The surface area of a rectangular prism may be calculated using the formula $SA = 2lw + 2wh + 2hl$. Substituting the dimensions of 14 inches, 6 inches, and 8 inches gives $SA = 2(14)(6) + 2(6)(8) + 2(8)(14)$. Thus, the surface area is 488 square inches.

80. C: The volume of a pyramid may be calculated using the formula $V = \frac{1}{3}Bh$, where B represents the area of the base and h represents the height. Since the base is a square, the area of the base is equal to 6^2, or 36 square inches. Substituting 36 for B and 9 for h gives $V = \frac{1}{3}(36)(9)$, which simplifies to $V = 108$.

81. C: The surface area of a sphere may be calculated using the formula $SA = 4\pi r^2$. Substituting 9 for r gives $SA = 4\pi(9)^2$, which simplifies to $SA \approx 1017.36$. So the surface area of the ball is approximately 1017.36 square inches. There are twelve inches in a foot, so there are $12^2 = 144$ square inches in a square foot. In order to convert this measurement to square feet, then, the following proportion may be written and solved for x: $\frac{1}{144} = \frac{x}{1017.36}$. So $x \approx 7.07$. He needs approximately 7.07 square feet of wrapping paper.

82. D: The volume of a prism may be calculated using the formula $V = Bh$, where B represents the area of the base and h represents the height of the prism. The area of each triangular base is represented by $A = \frac{1}{2}(9)(12)$. So the area of each base is equal to 54 square centimeters. Substituting 54 for the area of the base and 15 for the height of the prism gives $V = (54)(15)$ or $V = 810$. The volume of the prism is 810 cm^3.

83. B: Since the figures are similar, the following proportion may be written and solved for x: $\frac{6}{4} = \frac{8}{x}$. Thus, $x = \frac{32}{6}$ or $5\frac{1}{3}$.

84. C: $\angle g$ and $\angle c$ are alternate exterior angles. Thus, they are congruent.

85. D: The corresponding angles have congruent angle measures, each measuring 44°. According to the Corresponding Angles Converse Theorem, two lines are parallel if a transversal, intersecting the lines, forms congruent corresponding angles.

86. C: The measure of the inscribed angle is half of the measure of the intercepted arc. Since the intercepted arc measures 110°, the inscribed angle is equal to $\frac{110°}{2}$ or 55°.

87. B: The following proportion may be written and solved for x: $\frac{15}{5} = \frac{6}{x}$. Solving for x gives $x = 2$. Thus, the shadow cast by the man is 2 feet in length.

88. C: The following equation may be written and solved for x: $\sin 40° = \frac{x}{6}$. Multiplying both sides of the equation by 6 gives: $6 \times \sin 40° = x$, or $x \approx 3.9$.

89. D: The area of the square is equal to $(30)^2$, or 900 square centimeters. The area of the circle is equal to $\pi(15)^2$, or approximately 707 square centimeters. The area of the shaded region is equal to the difference of the area of the square and the area of the circle, or $900 \text{ cm}^2 - 707 \text{ cm}^2$, which equals 193 cm^2. So the area of the shaded region is about 193 cm^2.

90. B: Two of the angles, plus one side, not included between the angles, are congruent to the corresponding angles and side of the other triangle. Thus, the AAS (Angle-Angle-Side) Theorem may be used to prove the congruence of the triangles.

91. D: The Pythagorean Theorem may be used to find the diagonal distance from the top of his head to the base of the shadow. The following equation may be written and solved for c: $5.8^2 + 6.2^2 = c^2$. Thus, $c \approx 8.5$. The distance is approximately 8.5 ft.

92. D: The cross-section of a cylinder will never be a triangle.

93. D: The measure of an angle formed by intersecting chords inside a circle is equal to one-half of the sum of the measures of the intercepted arcs. Thus, $x = \frac{1}{2}(48° + 62°)$, or 55°.

94. D: The measure of the angle formed by the chord and the tangent is equal to one-half of the measure of the intercepted arc. Since the measure of the angle is 68°, the measure of the intercepted arc may be found by writing $68° = \frac{1}{2}x$. Dividing both sides of the equation by $\frac{1}{2}$ gives $x = 136°$. The measure of the intercepted arc may also be found by multiplying 68° by 2. Thus, the value of x is 136°.

95. A: The net of a triangular prism has three rectangular faces and two triangular faces. This is true of both A and C, but net C cannot be folded into a triangular prism, because the two rectangular faces on the end cannot be made to join each other. So only A can be folded into a triangular prism.

96. B: The relationship between number of faces, edges, and vertices is represented by Euler's Formula, $E = F + V - 2$. Substituting 9 for E and 6 for V gives: $9 = F + 6 - 2$, which simplifies to $9 = F + 4$. Thus, $F = 5$.

97. C: When two parallel lines are cut by a transversal, the consecutive angles formed inside the lines are supplementary.

98. B: The two triangles are similar because they each have an angle measuring 65°, and the measurement of ∠A is the same for both triangles, due to the Reflexive Property. So the two triangles are similar according to the AA (Angle-Angle) Similarity Postulate.

99. C: The triangle was reflected across the x-axis. When reflecting across the x-axis, the x-values of each point remain the same, but the y-values of the points will be opposites:

$$(1,4) \rightarrow (1,-4), \qquad (5,4) \rightarrow (5,-4), \qquad (3,8) \rightarrow (3,-8)$$

100. A: A reflection across the x-axis results in a triangle with vertices at (2, −3), (4, −7), and (6, −3). A rotation of 270 degrees is denoted by the following: $(a, b) \rightarrow (b, -a)$. Thus, rotating the reflected triangle by 270 degrees will result in a figure with vertices at (−3, −2), (−7, −4), and (−3, −6). The transformed triangle indeed has these coordinates as its vertices.

101. C: The midpoint may be calculated by using the formula $m = \left(\frac{x_1+x_2}{2}, \frac{y_1+y_2}{2}\right)$. Thus, the midpoint of the line segment shown may be written as $m = \left(\frac{1+8}{2}, \frac{2+8}{2}\right)$, which simplifies to $m = (4.5, 5)$.

102. C: The distance may be calculated using the distance formula, $d = \sqrt{(x_2 - x_1)^2 + (y_2 - y_1)^2}$. Substituting the given coordinates, the following equation may be written:

$$d = \sqrt{(4 - (-8))^2 + (3 - 6)^2}$$
$$d = \sqrt{153}$$

103. B: The perimeter is equal to the sum of the lengths of the two bases, 2 and 6 units, and the diagonal distances of the other two sides. Using the distance formula, each side length may be represented as $d = \sqrt{20} = 2\sqrt{5}$. Thus, the sum of the two sides is equal to $2\sqrt{20}$, or $4\sqrt{5}$. The whole perimeter is equal to $8 + 4\sqrt{5}$.

104. C: The area of a trapezoid may be calculated using the formula, $A = \frac{1}{2}(b_1 + b_2)h$. Thus, the area of the trapezoid is represented as $A = \frac{1}{2}(4 + 2)(2)$, which simplifies to $A = 6$. The area of the triangle is represented as $A = \frac{1}{2}(4)(3)$, which also simplifies to $A = 6$. Thus, the total area is 12 square units.

105. D: The larger triangle has a base length of 3 units and a height of 3 units. The smaller triangle has a base length of 2 units and a height of 2 units. Thus, the dimensions of the larger triangle were multiplied by a scale factor of $\frac{2}{3}$. Note that $3 \times \left(\frac{2}{3}\right) = 2$.

106. A: The vertical line of symmetry is represented by an equation of the form $x = a$. The horizontal line of symmetry is represented by an equation of the form $y = a$. One line of symmetry occurs at $x = -4$. The other line of symmetry occurs at $y = 6$.

107. C: Equilateral triangles and regular hexagons may tessellate a plane. Each triangle may be attached to each side of a hexagon, leaving no gaps in the plane.

108. A: The amount to be administered may be written as $\frac{1}{12} \times \frac{34}{10}$, which equals $\frac{17}{60}$. Thus, she should administer $\frac{17}{60}$ fluid ounces of medicine.

109. C: The slope may be written as $m = \frac{4-0}{-3-(-4)}$, which simplifies to $m = 4$.

110. D: The perimeter of the triangle is equal to the sum of the side lengths. The length of the longer diagonal side may be represented as $d = \sqrt{(4-1)^2 + (5-2)^2}$, which simplifies to $d = \sqrt{18}$. The length of the shorter diagonal side may be represented as $d = \sqrt{(6-4)^2 + (2-5)^2}$, which simplifies to $d = \sqrt{13}$. The base length is 5 units. Thus, the perimeter is equal to $5 + \sqrt{18} + \sqrt{13}$, which is approximately 12.85 units. Since each unit represents 5 miles, the total distance she will have walked is equal to the product of 12.85 and 5, or approximately 64 miles.

111. C: The following proportion may be written and solved for x: $\frac{144}{1} = \frac{2012}{x}$. $144x = 2012$. Dividing both sides of the equation by 144 gives $x \approx 13.97$. Thus, 2,012 square inches is approximately equal to 13.97 square feet.

112. D: The triangle is a 45-45-90 right triangle. Thus, if each leg is represented by x, the hypotenuse is represented by $x\sqrt{2}$. Thus, the hypotenuse is equal to $8\sqrt{2}$ cm.

Statistics, Probability, and Discrete Mathematics

113. A: Data sets B and C are asymmetrical: data set B is skewed toward lower values, and data set C is skewed toward higher values. This makes the mean a poor measure of center. Data set D is mostly symmetrical, but has a large outlier. The mean is very sensitive to outliers, and is not an appropriate measure of center for data sets that include them. Data set A is roughly symmetrical and has no outliers; the mean would be an appropriate measure of center here.

114. C: A z-score may be calculated using the formula $z = \frac{X-\mu}{\sigma}$. Substituting the score of 82, class average of 87, and class standard deviation of 2 into the formula gives: $z = \frac{82-87}{2}$, which simplifies to $z = -2.5$. Thus, the student's score is 2.5 standard deviations below the mean.

115. D: The z-score is written as $z = \frac{61-81}{10}$, which simplifies to $z = -2$. A z-score with an absolute value of 2 shows a mean to z area of 0.4772. Subtracting this area from 0.5 gives 0.0228, or 2.28%.

116. D: The z-score is written as $z = \frac{96-84}{4}$, which simplifies to $z = 3$. A z-score of 3 shows a mean to z area of 0.4987. Adding 0.5 to this area gives 0.9987, or 99.87%.

117. D: Two z-scores should be calculated, one for each student's score. The first z-score may be written as $z = \frac{68-80}{8}$, which simplifies to $z = -1.5$. The second z-score may be written as $z = \frac{84-80}{8}$, which simplifies to $z = 0.5$. The percentage of students scoring between these two scores is equal to the sum of the two mean to z areas. A z-score with an absolute value of 1.5 shows a mean to z area of 0.4332. A z-score of 0.5 shows a mean to z area of 0.1915. The sum of these two areas is 0.6247, or 62.47%.

118. D: A two-sample t-test should be used. Entering the sample mean, sample standard deviation, and sample size of each group into a graphing calculator reveals a p-value that is less than 0.05, so a significant difference between the groups may be declared.

119. C: A t-test should be used. A t-score may be calculated using the formula $t = \frac{\bar{X}-\mu}{\frac{s}{\sqrt{n}}}$. Substituting the sample mean, population mean, sample standard deviation, and sample size into the formula gives $t = \frac{19.8-20}{\frac{0.2}{\sqrt{30}}}$, which simplifies to $t \approx -5.48$. For degrees of freedom of 29, any t-value greater than 3.659 will have a p-value less than 0.001. Thus, there is a significant difference between what the manufacturer claims and the actual amount included in each bottle. The claim is likely false, due to a p-value less than 0.01.

120. B: A z-test may be used, since the population standard deviation is known. A z-score may be calculated using the formula $z = \frac{\bar{X}-\mu}{\frac{\sigma}{\sqrt{n}}}$. Substituting the sample mean, population mean, population standard deviation, and sample size into the formula gives $z = \frac{17.9-18}{\frac{0.3}{\sqrt{25}}}$, which simplifies to $z \approx -1.67$. The p-value is approximately 0.1, which is greater than 0.05. Thus, there does not appear to be a significant difference between what the manufacturer claims and the actual number of ounces found in each container. The claim is likely true, due to a p-value greater than 0.05.

121. B: A t-test should be used. A t-score may be calculated using the formula $t = \frac{\bar{X}-\mu}{\frac{s}{\sqrt{n}}}$. Substituting the sample mean, population mean, sample standard deviation, and sample size into the formula gives $t = \frac{83-82}{\frac{2}{\sqrt{30}}}$, which simplifies to $t \approx 2.74$. For degrees of freedom of 29, the p-value is approximately 0.01. Thus, there is a significant difference between what the professor claimed to be the final exam average and what the actual sample average showed. His claim is likely false, as evidenced by a p-value less than 0.05.

122. C: Use of an intact group is called a convenience sample. Such a sample increases sampling error, since randomization was not employed. The other described techniques utilize random sampling.

123. C: A z-score of 2 has a mean to z area of 0.4772, or 47.72%. Twice this percentage is about 95%.

124. D: The standard deviation is equal to the square root of the ratio of the sum of the squares of the deviation of each score from the mean to the square root of the difference of n and 1. The mean of the data set is 7.625. The deviations are −4.625, −3.625, −3.625, −2.625, −1.625, 4.375, 4.375, and 7.375. The sum of the squares of the deviations may be written as:

$$21.39 + 13.14 + 13.14 + 6.89 + 2.64 + 19.14 + 19.14 + 54.39 = 149.87$$

Division of this sum by $n - 1 = 7$ gives 21.41. The square root of this quotient is approximately 4.6.

125. A: The ends of Data Set A are farther apart, indicating a larger range. The horizontal line in the middle of a boxplot represents the median, so Data Set A also has a larger median.

126. A: The median of the lower half of the scores is 6. The median of the upper half of the scores is 16. The interquartile range is equal to the difference in the first and third quartiles. Thus, the interquartile range is 10.

127. B: The points may be entered into a graphing calculator or Excel spreadsheet to find the least-squares regression line. This line is approximately $y = 22x + 6$. Substituting 20 for x gives $y = 22(20) + 6$, or $y = 446$. Thus, $446 is a good estimate for the earnings received after 20 hours of work. If a line of best fit is predicted visually, the slope between points near that line is around 20, and the line passes near the origin. Thus, another good estimate would be $400. The estimate of $446 is closer to $400 than any of the other choices.

128. B: The mean is pulled towards the tail of a skewed distribution. It is not pulled towards the area with the larger frequency of scores. Outliers pull the mean towards those outliers.

129. C: The probability may be written as $P(M \text{ or } G) = P(M) + P(G) - P(M \text{ and } G)$. Substituting the probabilities, the following may be written: $P(M \text{ or } G) = \frac{4985}{10{,}079} + \frac{4113}{10{,}079} - \frac{2045}{10{,}079}$, which simplifies to $P(M \text{ or } G) = \frac{7053}{10{,}079}$ or approximately 70%.

130. D: The number of outcomes in the event is 2 (rolling a 5 or 6), and the sample space is 6 (numbers 1 – 6). Thus, the probability may be written as $\frac{2}{6}$, which simplifies to $\frac{1}{3}$.

131. B: The probability may be written as $P(E \text{ and } H) = P(E) \times P(H)$. Substituting the probability of each event gives $(E \text{ and } H) = \frac{1}{2} \times \frac{1}{2}$, which simplifies to $\frac{1}{4}$.

132. D: Since they are not mutually exclusive events, the probability may be written as $P(P \text{ or } T) = P(P) + P(T) - P(P \text{ and } T)$. Because the events are independent, $P(P \text{ and } T) = P(P) \times P(T)$. Substituting the probability of each event gives $(P \text{ or } T) = \frac{1}{2} + \frac{1}{2} - \left(\frac{1}{2} \times \frac{1}{2}\right)$, or 3/4.

133. B: Since they are not mutually exclusive events, the probability may be written as $P(4 \text{ or } E) = P(4) + P(E) - P(4 \text{ and } E)$. Substituting the probability of each event gives $(4\ or\ E) = \frac{1}{6} + \frac{1}{2} - \frac{1}{6}$, or $\frac{1}{2}$.

134. C: The theoretical probability is $\frac{1}{2}$, and $\frac{1}{2}(300) = 150$.

135. C: The number of ways the letters can be arranged may be represented as $\frac{6!}{2!2!2!}$, which equals 90.

136. A: This situation describes a permutation, since order matters. The formula for calculating a combination is $P(n, r) = \frac{n!}{(n-r)!}$. This situation may be represented as $P(6,3) = \frac{6!}{(6-3)!}$, which equals 120.

137. D: Since there are 10 numerals, the answer is equal to 10!, or 3,628,800.

138. A: The series is an infinite geometric series. The sum may be calculated using the formula $S = \frac{a}{1-r}$, where a represents the value of the first term and r represents the common ratio. Substituting 1 for a and $\frac{1}{2}$ for r gives $S = \frac{1}{1-\frac{1}{2}}$ or 2.

139. C: The number in the sample space is equal to the number of possible outcomes for one coin toss, 2, raised to the power of the number of coin tosses, or 4. $2^4 = 16$.

140. A: A Venn diagram such as the one shown below may be drawn to assist in finding the answer.

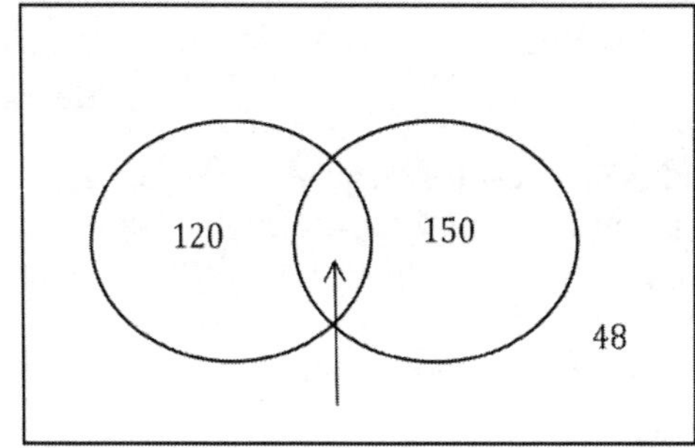

Since the set contains 320 total people, the solution is equal to $320 - (120 + 150 + 48)$ or 2 people.

141. A:$A \cap B$ means "A intersect B," or the elements that are common to both sets. "A intersect B" represents "A and B," that is, an element is in the intersection of A and B if it is in A *and* it is in B. The elements 2, 5, and 8 are common to both sets.

142. B:$A \cup B$ means "A union B," or all of the elements in either of the two sets. "A union B" represents "A or B," that is, an element is in the union of A and B if it is in A *or* it is in B. The elements in sets A and B are 9, 4, −3, 8, 6, 0, −4, and 2.

143. D: The intersection of the two sets is empty, denoted by the symbol, $\emptyset$. There are not any elements common to both sets.

144. D: If the statement is written in the form $p \rightarrow q$, then the contrapositive is represented as $\neg q \rightarrow \neg p$. Thus, the contrapositive should read, "If I do not go to the beach, then I do not get paid."

145. B: If the statement is written in the form $p \rightarrow q$, then the converse is represented as $q \rightarrow p$. Thus, the converse should read, "If it is winter, then I go skiing."

146. D: Only when both p and q are false is the union of p and q false.

147. A: Both p and q must be true in order for the intersection to be true.

148. C: A conditional statement $p \rightarrow q$ and its contrapositive $\neg q \rightarrow \neg p$ are logically equivalent because of the identical values in a truth table. See below.

p	q	$\neg p$	$\neg q$	$p \rightarrow q$	$\neg q \rightarrow \neg p$
T	T	F	F	T	T
T	F	F	T	F	F
F	T	T	F	T	T
F	F	T	T	T	T

149. C: This is a counting problem. The possible number of meals is equal to the product of the possibilities for each category. The product of 4, 5, and 3 is 60. Thus, there are 60 meals that he may create.

150. B: A tautology will show all true values in a truth table column. Look at the table below:

p	q	$\neg p$	$\neg q$	$p \vee \neg p$	$p \wedge \neg p$	$p \vee \neg q$	$p \vee q$
T	T	F	F	T	F	T	T
T	F	F	T	T	F	T	T
F	T	T	F	T	F	F	T
F	F	T	T	T	F	T	F

Only the statement $p \vee \neg p$ shows all T's in the column.

Constructed Response

1A. First, according to the problem, c is the value of the vehicle after its initial depreciation. The vehicle's value drops by 15%, so:

$$c = \$32{,}000 - (0.15) \times (\$32{,}000) = \$27{,}200$$

Using this value for c and substituting it in, the value formula then becomes:

$$y = \$27{,}200 - (0.09) \times (\$27{,}200) \times (x)$$

Finally, solve for y when $x = 2$:

$$y = \$27{,}200 - (0.09) \times (\$27{,}200) \times (2)$$

$$y = \$27{,}200 - \$4896$$

$$\boldsymbol{y = \$22{,}304}$$

1B. The graph of y will be linear since x is raised to the first power. Reordering the function to the $y = mx + b$ format, the y-intercept and slope are readily identifiable:

$$y = \$27{,}200 - \left(\frac{\$2{,}448}{year}\right) \times (x)$$

$$y = -\left(\frac{\$2{,}448}{year}\right) \times (x) + \$27{,}200$$

Thus, the slope is $-\$2448$ per year and the y-intercept is \$27,200. Plotting this function looks like the following.

1C. Using the axis values, it is readily apparent that the value function approaches \$15,000 when x is around **5 years**.

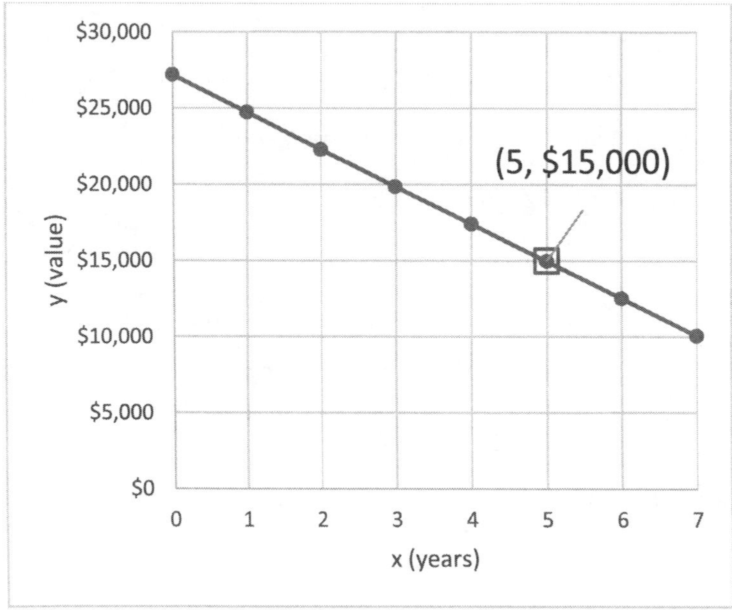

1D. The way to use the function to find when the value is \$15,000 is to substitute it in for y and solve for x:

$$\$15{,}000 = \$27{,}200 - \left(\frac{\$2{,}448}{year}\right) \times (x)$$

$$-\$12{,}200 = -\left(\frac{\$2{,}448}{year}\right) \times (x)$$

$$\frac{-\$12{,}200}{-\left(\frac{\$2{,}448}{year}\right)} = x$$

$$x = 4.984\ years$$

After rounding to the tenths place: $\boldsymbol{x = 5.0\ years}$

2A. The splash/fountain area is in the 3 circles only. To find the area, first find the radius of the circles: $r = \frac{d}{2} = \frac{6ft}{2} = 3ft$. Thus, the area for the splash/fountains is given by:

$$A_{splash} = 3 \times \pi \times r^2$$

Using $\pi \cong 3.14$:

$$A_{splash} \cong 3 \times 3.14 \times (3ft)^2$$

$$\boldsymbol{A_{splash} \cong 84.78ft^2}$$

2B. The first step in finding the percent walkway area is to find the height of the triangle, since the area is known to be $\frac{1}{2}base \times height$. An equilateral triangle has equal side lengths and equal angles of 60°. Thus, we know that the base is 30ft and the height can be found by $h = 30ft \times \sin(60°)$.

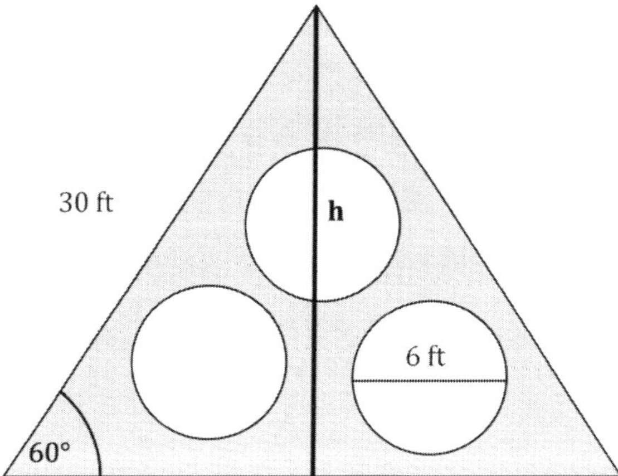

$h = 30ft \times \sin(60°) = 30ft \times \frac{\sqrt{3}}{2}$, so $h \cong 30ft \times \frac{1.73}{2}$. Thus, $height \cong 25.95ft$. Using this to find the area of the triangle minus the area of the circular splash/fountain sections will give us the total walking area:

$$A_{triangle} = \frac{1}{2}base \times height$$

$$A_{triangle} \cong \frac{1}{2}(30ft) \times (25.95ft) \cong 389.25ft^2$$

$$A_{walkway} = A_{triangle} - A_{splash}$$

$$A_{walkway} \cong (389.25ft^2) - (84.78ft^2)$$

$$A_{walkway} \cong 304.47ft^2$$

The percent walkway area is found by:

$$walkway\% = \frac{A_{walkway}}{A_{triangle}} \times 100\%$$

$$walkway\% \cong \frac{304.47ft^2}{389.25ft^2} \times 100\%$$

$$\boldsymbol{walkway\% \cong 78.2\%}$$

2C. It can be assumed that a ball would have an equal chance of landing anywhere in the area of the triangle. Thus, the probability it will land in a splash/fountain area is given by:

$P_{splash} = \frac{A_{splash}}{A_{triangle}}$, so $\boldsymbol{P_{splash}} \cong \frac{84.78ft^2}{389.25ft^2} \cong \boldsymbol{0.218}$

3A. The median of a list of values is the centermost value of an ordered list. If the ordered list has an even number of members, then the median is the average of the two centermost values. The range of a list is the difference of the highest value and the lowest value. Thus, for this problem, the **median is 63cm and the range is 73cm − 48cm = 25cm.**

3B. The mean of a list of values is the sum of all the members of the list divided by the number of members in the list: mean =

$$\frac{48+53+53+54+55+56+59+60+60+63+63+63+64+65+66+67+69+71+73}{19}$$

Thus, $\mathbf{mean = 61.2\ cm}$

3C. The stem and leaf plot would look like this:

Stem	Leaf
4	8
5	3 3 4 5 6 9
6	0 0 3 3 3 4 5 6 7 9
7	1 3

Thank You

We at Mometrix would like to extend our heartfelt thanks to you, our friend and patron, for allowing us to play a part in your journey. It is a privilege to serve people from all walks of life who are unified in their commitment to building the best future they can for themselves.

The preparation you devote to these important testing milestones may be the most valuable educational opportunity you have for making a real difference in your life. We encourage you to put your heart into it—that feeling of succeeding, overcoming, and yes, conquering will be well worth the hours you've invested.

We want to hear your story, your struggles and your successes, and if you see any opportunities for us to improve our materials so we can help others even more effectively in the future, please share that with us as well. **The team at Mometrix would be absolutely thrilled to hear from you!** So please, send us an email (support@mometrix.com) and let's stay in touch.

If you'd like some additional help, check out these other resources we offer for your exam: http://MometrixFlashcards.com/NESINC

Additional Bonus Material

Due to our efforts to try to keep this book to a manageable length, we've created a link that will give you access to all of your additional bonus material.

Please visit http://www.mometrix.com/bonus948/nesincmgmath to access the information.